Monstrous Anger of the Guns

Monstrous Anger of the Guns

How the Global Arms Trade is Ruining the World and What We Can Do About It

Edited by Rhona Michie,
Andrew Feinstein and Paul Rogers

With Jeremy Corbyn

PLUTO PRESS

First published 2024 by Pluto Press
New Wing, Somerset House, Strand, London WC2R 1LA
and Pluto Press, Inc.
1930 Village Center Circle, 3-834, Las Vegas, NV 89134

www.plutobooks.com

Sponsored by the Peace and Justice Project

Copyright © Peace and Justice Project 2024

British Library Cataloguing in Publication Data
A catalogue record for this book is available from the British Library

ISBN   978 0 7453 5036 3   Paperback
ISBN   978 0 7453 5038 7   PDF
ISBN   978 0 7453 5037 0   EPUB

This book is printed on paper suitable for recycling and made from fully
managed and sustained forest sources. Logging, pulping and manufacturing
processes are expected to conform to the environmental standards of the
country of origin.

Typeset by Stanford DTP Services, Northampton, England

Simultaneously printed in the United Kingdom and United States of
America

What passing-bells for these who die as cattle?
– Only the monstrous anger of the guns.

Wilfred Owen, 'Anthem for Doomed Youth'

This book is dedicated to all those across the globe who are committed to building a more just and peaceful world.

Contents

Preface

Jeremy Corbyn

We live in an age of rapid armament and rising geopolitical tensions amid growing division between the super-rich and the more than a billion people who suffer poverty, hunger and reduced life prospects. It is in this context that the Peace & Justice Project has produced the book you are holding in your hands. *Monstrous Anger of the Guns* offers a broad perspective to the public debate that is usually obscured by well-funded ideas of security based on the capacity to kill others, and not the security of being able to lead a peaceful and productive life. So many times in my political life journalists from corporate media have asked me if, as prime minister, I would 'push the nuclear button', but I can count on the fingers of one hand the number of times I have been asked how we can reduce the threat of nuclear conflict and build a world of peace.

This book exposes the market of death, known in polite society as the arms trade. It is a product of the work of many brilliant and well-informed people, who have spent much of their lives documenting how weapons companies, with the support of governments, enrich themselves and cause sorrow around the world. They tell the story, chapter by chapter, of how lobbying, corruption and networks of power prop up this deadly system.

In addition to providing expert and fine-grained analysis, the book tells the stories of a diverse range of inspiring campaigns from around the world opposing militarism and the arms trade that feeds it.

Weapons and their ability to kill are not new. Slings, axes, swords, bows and arrows, guns, cannon balls, explosives, rifles, machine guns, air war, naval powers and nuclear weapons all illustrate the development of different forms of weaponry, each more destructive and more lethal than the last. There have been many turning points that have shifted the global arms industry from 'defence' to the ability to fight wars of aggression and conquest.

The basic tool of European expansion and colonialism from the fifteenth century onwards was the technical advantage of guns and explosives, originally invented in China, that were able to destroy the defences and the peoples of Africa, the Americas and Asia. Colonial expansion into the Americas inflicted numerous genocides, as much by diseases to which there was no immunity as by guns and explosives. Scholarly estimates for the collapse in the indigenous population range from 80 per cent to 95 per cent.

The four-year Civil War in the United States of America, which ended in 1865, resulted in a massive surplus of arms, as well as a massive and innovative armaments industry. These arms contributed to the conquest of the indigenous American people west of the Mississippi River, the war with Mexico, and then further conflicts for trading advantage in the Pacific and the rest of the Americas. The Monroe Doctrine, a now 200-year-old US foreign policy position, held the entire Western Hemisphere as its exclusive backyard. European powers were warned to stay out of the politics of the Americas. Massive and superior arms underwrote this demand.

While European colonial control of North America ended and was replaced by the domination of the white settler class, this historic position enabled the European powers to rapidly occupy almost all of Africa using their superior weapons to kill, maim and exploit. The slave trade was founded on the guns and ships used to destroy the hopes and lives of millions as they were taken in vile conditions across the Atlantic to the Caribbean and North America.

The Boer wars in South Africa were a significant turning point where one European power was more than challenged by a settler class fighting back. The effectiveness of the Boer guerrilla tactics shocked Britain's military top brass, and caused significant change in British military structures.

At the same time, the rapid development of technology and shipping was fuelling an era of rapid globalisation, but also intense competition between European powers for colonial expansion and control. An arms race ensued.

As the First World War loomed, the arms industries – many wholly or partly state owned – grew and became major employers, emerging as a significant feature of industrial life in all major European countries. Technology, profits and innovation grew rapidly after 1914. The First World War was an industrial war: competition over the production of air and sea power, as well as chemical weapons and massive explosives, were at its core. This industrial competition, along with the deaths of millions of young conscripts and colonial subjects, who were taken thousands of miles across the oceans to fight a European war, were its defining, horrific features.

The drive to war always creates a peace movement to oppose it, and efforts to prevent and limit conflict arose through international agreements. The Hague Conventions of 1899, initiated by Tsarist Russia, attempted both to regularise war and prevent fighting, as well as to establish a system of international arbitration. That system collapsed before the outbreak of the First World War, but its principles survived in the mentality the big powers used for the Treaty of Versailles after the end of the war. Versailles, which spawned the League of Nations, was also a vehicle for European colonialism, with the victorious powers dividing up non-European lands among themselves, including by drawing straight lines on maps of

West Asia. The same crude system was used forty years earlier in the Congress of Berlin, when Africa was divided into neat colonial lines, ignoring language, community, trade arrangements and people's lives.

The establishment of the League of Nations was also accompanied by the Geneva Protocol of 1925, a serious attempt to ban the use of asphyxiating gas and biological weapons. All parties had used gases in the First World War, and also in quashing anti-colonial uprisings, such as the Kurdish revolt in 1919.

Weaponry, especially military aircraft and navigation systems, developed rapidly after the First World War, as competing companies vied for government contracts. The new weapons were tested in real-time in colonial wars and, memorably, in the oppression of the Palestinian uprising of 1936 and the fascist bombing of Guernica in 1937 during the Spanish Civil War.

The Second World War brought massive new weapons and industrial advances used for mass killing. These included radar and mass surveillance techniques, but also new technologies of destruction at a scale humanity had never known. First, the Nazi gas chambers created the ultimate horror of the Shoah, as European Jewry suffered industrialised genocide, exterminating 6 million Jews. Then came nuclear weapons, first used in tests in New Mexico in 1945 and then deployed in Japan. Their destructive power, killing hundreds of thousands at once and creating a firestorm in their wake, made them the new terror weapon.

As with the First World War, the end of hostilities produced a new architecture for international relations in the form of the United Nations (UN). With all its limitations, strange power structure and chronic underfunding, it has survived and, for many, is often the credible voice for peace.

The relief that accompanied the end of the Second World War also brought the possibility of converting the industrial production that had been used for conflict towards production that would secure life: health, housing, transport, education.

This opportunity did not last long. The Cold War became the new reason to keep a large part of our collective efforts and resources trained on creating the means of death, rather than the means of life. Much of the world was divided into competing blocs. First, NATO, the North Atlantic Treaty Organization, was formed in 1949. Then, in 1955, the Warsaw Pact. Massive rearmament followed.

The wars in Korea, from 1950 to 1953, and Vietnam, from 1955 to 1975, were testing grounds for new weapons. Arms manufacturers in the global North opened up – often by staggeringly corrupt means – export markets in the South.

As the spectre of nuclear Armageddon stalked the planet, the peace movement grew. In Britain, the Campaign for Nuclear Disarmament was formed in 1957, which continues to struggle for a peaceful world to this day.

Intermittent negotiations between the USSR and the US, while never leading to peace, did yield the Nuclear Non-Proliferation Treaty (NPT) in 1968 and the Anti-Ballistic Missile Treaty in 1972. The NPT, at least, achieved nuclear-weapon-free zones in Africa, South America and parts of Asia.

Despite the best efforts of the peace movement, spending on weapons increased. The great winners were the arms companies. They were on to a good thing, with research costs met by defence ministries and profit wired into the system. Exports boomed around the world, alongside the corruption that was endemic in the trade.

But these vast profits and bulging defence budgets came under threat when the Soviet Union's collapse ended the Cold War: another historic opportunity to end the competing military alliances that had so scarred the twentieth century.

In 1991, the Warsaw Pact dissolved. This should have been the signal for the end of NATO too, and the construction of a new peace and security framework. Instead, the weapons company-funded Western think tanks spent their time casting around for a role for NATO, while paying lip service to disarmament and arms conversion. Instead of rolling up NATO, Western leaders first expanded it eastwards and then sought a global role for it.

An opportunity arrived in 2001. In the wake of the attack on the World Trade Center, President George W. Bush and Prime Minister Tony Blair led the chorus in favour of military intervention in Afghanistan.

Eighteen months later, as confronting Bush's 'Axis of Evil' became a foreign policy strategic goal, the war against Iraq was launched. New fortunes were made by companies winning vast no-tender contracts for the destruction, then reconstruction – with a handy side of resource extraction – of Iraq. Millions poured onto the streets around the world to voice their fierce opposition to the illegal invasion of Iraq. The invasion and its disastrous consequences for the people of Iraq and the wider West Asian region spawned a new wave of peace movements.

Wars in Libya, Syria and Yemen followed. Each was either directly promoted by Western countries or backed by them in the form of a reliable supply of arms. The 'success' of the weapons was then shown on videos at glitzy arms fairs. The war zones had become film studios for the arms suppliers to encourage governments to buy their weapons.

Profits and share prices of weapons companies are once more through the roof. The war in Ukraine, already in its third year with no ceasefire in sight, has already resulted in billions being spent by Russia, Ukraine and its Western allies on weapons. Since October 2023, the world has watched as all aspects of life in Gaza are destroyed in retribution for the killing of 1,200 people in Israel by Hamas; this has only resulted in increased arms sales to Israel. While the big wars are closely followed by global media, other conflicts, equally deadly and vicious, but with lower calibre weapons, rage on. The Democratic Republic of the Congo has been a killing field for decades, driven by conflict over minerals, while the conflict in West Papua is driven by mining interests, with Indonesia using Western arms to oppose Papuan independence. Conflicts like these remain a significant source of profits for the global market in small arms.

The lobbying power of defence interests – what President Eisenhower termed the 'the military-industrial complex' over sixty years ago – exerts huge pressure on governments. In the UK, defence spending is rising towards 2.5 per cent of GDP; a rise to 3.0 per cent is on the cards. All at a time of falling living standards and trashed public services.

As debates about 'security' are conducted over business breakfasts, expensive dinners and at arms fairs, notions of peace processes and diplomatic solutions are ignored. We must ask: does security come from spending vast amounts of time and the energy and skills of brilliant people on producing ever more sophisticated weapons, or is real security the ability to live happy, fulfilled and healthy lives?

This book is a contribution to the effort to move towards the latter. We want to develop our real collective security, not the fake security of the bomb and the bullet. We must expose the cynical and corrupt lobbying that presents ever more sophisticated weaponry as somehow bringing peace. All those who have marched for a ceasefire in Gaza, been appalled by the images of Ukraine, distressed by the human devastation of Yemen, shocked by the conflict in the Democratic Republic of Congo, and who yearn for a world of peace will find this book useful.

Twenty years of war and over $2 trillion spent by the US alone have left Afghanistan poor, hungry and socially oppressed. Many of its people are forced to try to survive as refugees in a heartless world. That is the true price paid to add to the profit of weapons producers.

Those companies that make the weapons have done very well for themselves. It is for those of us committed to peace and justice across the globe to put an end to this war profiteering. By dismantling the war machine, we can create a more peaceful, sustainable and just world.

Introduction

Rhona Michie, Andrew Feinstein
and Paul Rogers

Why the Arms Trade Matters

On 22 April 2018, in Al-Raqa village in Bani Qais District of the Hajjah Governorate in Yemen, 20-year-old Yahya and Fatma Al-Musabi were celebrating their wedding day. Hundreds of guests had been at the festivities since the morning. One of them, 55-year-old farmer Fadhl Al-Musabi, recalls: 'We were dancing happily like any other people who had weddings. It was a happy time and people were happy.... I could hear the jets hovering overhead, and I was praying that things would go well that day.' Suddenly, a Saudi/United Arab Emirates (UAE)-led coalition bomb soared through the air. 'I saw a bomb and heard it whistle. I saw the bomb in the sky with a flame emerging from it. I could not move ...' The bomb struck the groom's wedding tent. Fadhl described the aftermath of the deadly attack: 'The situation was tragic. Body parts were everywhere. It was like the Day of Judgment.'[1]

A few minutes later, the aeroplanes returned and people ran, terrified of further strikes. Fadhl began assisting the wounded. 'It was a horrifying scene. It was hard to know who was dead and who was injured. The blood was everywhere. The body parts were mixed with each other – we buried the dead and we did not know which body parts belonged to whom. The drummers and dancers were killed, and the happiness turned into grief and sorrow.'

Twenty-one innocent civilians were killed, including eleven children. Ninety-seven more were injured, including 48 children. This happened 25 kilometres away from the nearest military checkpoint. The intentional targeting of civilians is a flagrant violation of international humanitarian law.

In this instance, the monstrous anger of the guns emanated from US-made GBU-12 Paveway II laser-guided bombs. The GBU-12 bomb is equipped with a 227-kilogram Mk-82 warhead. The Mk-82 contains 87 kilograms of Composition H6, a highly explosive substance also used in the US Air Force's so-called 'Mother of all Bombs'. The Mk-80 series of low-drag, general-purpose bombs are typically used to inflict maximal blast and explosive damage. Less than two years earlier, US defence contractor General Dynamics was awarded a multi-million dollar contract to supply Saudi Arabia and the UAE with Mk-82 bomb casings. In 2017, the sale of Paveway Weapons Systems worth $298 million[2] to the Saudi/UAE-led coalition was authorised by the US government . The bombs could just as easily have been made in the UK, Italy, France or Germany, all of which supply ordinance to the coalition.

Since March 2015, the world's largest weapons makers have enabled the Saudi/UAE-led coalition in Yemen to commit repeated and systemic violations of international humanitarian law and war crimes with impunity. Arms export control laws, multilateral agreements and international treaties have been ignored. With over $2.2 trillion spent on defence in 2022, the global arms trade has never been more lawless, more deadly, more corrupt – or more profitable. Accounting for, on average, half a million deaths a year, and responsible for around 40 per cent of corruption in all world trade, the weapons business counts its profits in billions and its cost in human lives.[3]

This cost is further exacerbated by socioeconomic factors, as all over the world healthcare, education, nutrition, shelter, welfare support and other basic needs are ignored in favour of more arms and bigger bribes. In addition, the military is one of the largest contributors to climate change, with the Pentagon widely recognised as the largest institutional polluter on the planet.

Just five years after its first democratic election, South Africa took the decision to spend around $10 billion on weapons that it had no use for. In order to get the deal through, at least $350 million of bribes were paid to senior politicians, officials, defence company executives and intermediaries.[4] At the same time, then-President Thabo Mbeki announced that the state could not afford to provide life-saving anti-retroviral medication to the 6 million South Africans living with HIV and AIDS. During the following five years this policy choice resulted in the avoidable deaths of over 360,000 people and the birth of over 30,000 HIV positive babies every year. South Africa could not afford mother-to-child-transmission treatment but could afford to spend $10 billion on weapons, some of which have gone completely untouched.

In addition to the human cost, the arms trade makes a mockery of foreign policy. In the most corrupt commercial transaction in history, the Al Yamamah arms deal, £6 billion of bribes were paid to senior members of the Saudi royal family, senior executives of BAE Systems, Mark Thatcher (the son of the British prime minister at the time) and a number of insalubrious intermediaries. The son of the Saudi defence minister at the time, who was the country's ambassador to the US, not only received over a billion pounds but also a birthday gift from BAE Systems of a 707 jet, painted in the colours of his favourite American football team. Some of the money, paid into his account in Riggs Bank in Washington, DC, made its way via his wife's account into the accounts of two of the 9/11 hijackers.

The Military-Industrial Complex

This deadly and corrupt trade is allowed to operate with virtual impunity due to its inclusion in a much larger system of states organising for war. This system is often termed the military-industrial complex but is better described as the military-industrial-academic-bureaucratic complex. All states with substantial armed forces have such complexes with considerable power, regardless of how democratic or otherwise they may be. They are not confined within state borders; they extend across the globe, especially through military alliances such as NATO, which cement their influence.

Some of these complexes, such as those in the United States, UK and France, have long histories of manufacturing and exporting armaments. A few, such as in Sweden and Switzerland, remain primarily defensive in their own security policy, while fuelling foreign wars with their substantial arms export industries. China has considerably increased its military spending in the past two decades, leading to much larger corporations with heavy state involvement. China has so far focused on their domestic military but that is expected to change as they look to develop export markets. Russia has a long history of arms exports, boosted by desperate need in the early 1990s when the economy went into free fall with the transition to turbo-capitalism, and today maintains an export market and the use of private military companies. However, the arms trade in the rest of the world still pales into insignificance compared with that of the United States.

The UK, as a middle power with pretensions to greatness, has a security complex showing most of the features exhibited elsewhere. At its centre are the military, the civil service and the corporations working hand in hand, with most of the latter being arms manufacturers but also including private military companies and intelligence outfits. While the military

4

describe their role as 'defenders of the realm', for individuals working in this area, career prospects will loom large, as they will in the civil service and corporations.

In the business sector and especially at the senior corporate level, profitability is the overarching concern within a mainly shareholder capitalist system. Corporate leaders have the added attraction of a generous bonus culture so often linked to profitability. And the icing on the cake: these profits are practically guaranteed in an industry that is frequently propped up by states themselves and where monopolies of production prevail, with states favouring single sources for submarines, tanks, aircraft or other major items.

Beyond this core of armed forces, civil service and arms companies, the arms industry is propped up by the intelligence agencies, consultancies, think tanks and universities which buy into and support the prevailing military posture. Even some trade unions, concerned with the interests of their members in the employ of weapons manufacturers, demonstrate uncritical support for the industry, although there is increasing interest in a process of converting high-skilled jobs from the manufacture of arms into different fields, such as renewable energy. In the UK there has long been a cross-party political assumption of the need for a strong military capability that includes nuclear weapons. Over the last twenty years, Britain has also put more resources into being able to deploy force as far as the Pacific, part of a near-desperate and expansive effort to be a major power on the world stage. Since the Russian invasion of Ukraine, the UK has been one of many countries that plan to increase its military budget towards 2.5 per cent of GNP (gross national product) and quite possibly higher.

Within the complex, senior military officers and civil servants get seconded to corporations on a rolling basis, movement which flows both ways. Universities and think tanks take on military and corporate staff, with corporations particularly keen to integrate if those individuals are concerned with weapons research and development or procurement. When such people are heading for retirement, their knowledge and experience will be attractive to the corporate sector, and they will look towards well-paid advisory posts, consultancies, and directorships. This system creates the perfect environment for corruption, as 'incentivisation' through financial and career opportunities becomes the business norm. This revolving door system is not restricted to the military and civil service – former and even serving politicians will regularly find lucrative posts to supplement their income. At the end of the day, high-level strategic decisions are influenced, or even made, by those who stand to make vast profits from their outcomes – at the expense of human lives.

While the structure of the complex – military, civil service, corporations and all the other groups – is helpful in understanding it, just as important is the culture that permeates the entire system. In the UK, the Rethinking Security Group identifies this as a thoroughly outmoded (if deeply embedded) narrative about what security means. That narrative:

> privileges UK national security as always coming first and to which other needs are readily subordinated, rather than recognising security as a common value to which all people have equal claim;

> aims to advance 'national interests' defined by the political establishment, including corporate business interests and UK 'world power' status, and therefore dissociates the definition of security from the needs of people in their communities;

> assumes a short-term outlook and presents military threats as the main risks, largely overlooking the long-term drivers of insecurity such as climate breakdown; and

responds by exerting control over the strategic environment, concentrating on offensive military capabilities, transnational alliances and restrictions on civil liberties.[5]

This narrative around security is pushed by a small group of the social elite, involving a disproportionate influence of business interests (especially the arms industry). It is therefore difficult for alternative concepts of security to be recognised. The presiding culture holds a bias towards values associated with hegemonic masculinity, which reduces thinking to a calculus of threats and coercive responses, with little or no concern for social and ecological elements of security.

In the past quarter of a century, the UK's involvement in major wars has been an experience of grievous failure that is readily brushed under the rug in the current culture. The 20-year war in Afghanistan ended with the Taliban gaining control of the country and imposing its rigid rule. In the process, the economy was wrecked, health conditions worsened and women's rights were repeatedly torn down. The 2003–11 war in Iraq had immense human costs, was a primary factor in the rise of ISIS (Islamic State of Iraq and Syria) and led directly to the intense 2014–18 air war that killed at least 60,000 people. At its end ISIS still survives and thrives across much of the Sahel region of the Sahara, and parts of Eastern Africa and South Asia.

The 2011 war against the Gaddafi regime in Libya left the country deeply insecure, a condition from which it has not escaped more than a decade later. The clear winner of the conflict, however, was the arms corporations, which made a killing by selling to both sides. Prior to the start of the war in March 2011, French and Italian corporations were working to upgrade the Gaddafi regime's military equipment, but in a matter of days the NATO-led aerial assault looked to destroy the same equipment.

After the war, arms companies sold France, Britain and other NATO partners replacements for the bombs and missiles used. They might also have been expecting a post-conflict oil-rich and stable Libyan government to invest heavily in new armaments, but that hope was dashed. Instead, Libya deteriorated into a deeply unstable state that served as a conduit for arms and Islamist paramilitary militias operating across the Sahel region of the Sahara and south-east to Eastern Africa. Furthermore, in Derna in 2023, political instability, poor infrastructure and a deterioration of social services all contributed to the magnitude of the tragic climate disaster that claimed, by some estimates, up to 20,000 lives.

The extent of these failures has since been largely ignored and the complex carries on with scarcely a pause, even if those failures help explain why opinion across much of the global South is far less sympathetic to the West over the Russian violence in Ukraine. The Western media has rightly reported on the appalling destruction of Ukrainian cities and the killing of thousands of civilians by Russian forces; but what is not recognised is the impact of similarly intense attacks on cities in Iraq and Syria, especially in the latter stages of the 2014–18 air war. The destruction in Raqqa, Fallujah, Ramadi and especially the old city of Mosul go largely forgotten in the West, but not across the Middle East.

The appalling and indefensible assault on Gaza by Israel, which has cost over 32,000 lives at the time of writing – 40 per cent of whom are children – has been the latest and most despicable of the military-industrial complex's killing fields. The probable genocide committed by Israel has been enabled and facilitated by an almost continuous flow of weapons from the US, UK, Germany and other European countries. This wanton slaughter of so many, the immiseration of even more, and the almost total destruction of the infrastructure of the Gaza Strip has also utterly obliterated the entire architecture of the international rules-based order, created in the wake of the Holocaust. But senior executives at the world's largest arms companies regularly inform their shareholders how good it all is for business. And, to their delight, Israel's killing spree is threatening to envelop the region, with the US and Britain bombing Yemen in an attempt to secure safe passage for ships through the Red Sea, thus threatening the fragile decline in hostilities in that war-torn country.

In summary, when assessing the importance of military-industrial complexes to the arms trade, four elements should be recognised. First, an embedded culture sees military force as the primary response to perceived security threats; second, the arms trade tends to be highly profitable, with plenty of scope for bribery, usually termed 'commission'; third, opposition is easily dismissed as defeatist, unpatriotic or even a potential security threat; and, finally, the system positively needs wars to thrive. Better still is a war in which it is possible to arm both sides, which lasts a long time and which does not directly involve the militaries of the country providing the armaments. A long-lasting violent stalemate makes for a highly profitable environment.

The Global National Security Elite Making a Killing

As a system of collusion between senior politicians, government officials, military and intelligence leaders, and senior executives of the world's leading arms makers, the trade in weapons circulates some of its profits through our political systems as donations to political parties, straight bribes and/ or lucrative jobs after leaving office for the global national security elite.

The militarist distortion of the political process is heightened by the concentration of weapons manufacturing in a small number of gargantuan companies. Giants that dominate the trade include Lockheed Martin, BAE Systems, Boeing, Northrop Grumman and Raytheon. They produce most large conventional weapons systems, nuclear weapons, many homeland security products, including those used for surveillance, and are at the forefront of the development of AI (artificial intelligence) weapons. This consolidation occurred in phases: post-Second World War and at the onset of the Cold War, as part of the privatisations that swept the world with the advent of neoliberal capitalism, and as the Cold War was replaced by the catch-all 'War on Terror'. It has not only concentrated power in the national security elite but has also reduced competition and meaningful oversight.

This, in turn, has created an absurd national security environment in which the world's most expensive weapons system, the F-35 fighter jet, is severely deficient in performance, and an arms maker can charge the US government over $50,000 for a refuse bin that costs a couple of hundred dollars to produce.[6] The collusion between these companies and their well-paid allies in government and the military also ensures that defence budgets remain stratospherically high, resulting in record annual global defence spending in excess of $2 trillion since 2021.[7]

This level of spending, which has such lucrative consequences for the national security elite, also requires the maintenance of a constant climate of fear, with Manichean enemies a prerequisite. The goading of Russia with the continual eastward expansion of NATO despite assurances to the contrary – although in no way justifying Russia's invasion of Ukraine – has certainly contributed to tensions in the region; the re-emergence and intensification of anti-China rhetoric by the mainstream Western media, much of which is owned by corporate and private interests with large stakes in the defence sector, has seen defence company share prices reach record levels; while Hamas (and ridiculously all residents of Gaza) are presented a threat to not just Israel but Western democracy.

NATO's eastward expansion was a welcome financial opportunity for the defence behemoths, especially Lockheed Martin, the world's biggest weapons maker: Bruce Jackson, Lockheed's vice president for international operations, chaired the US Committee to Expand NATO. Jackson promised eastern European governments that he would ensure US support for their accession to NATO if they undertook the mandatory modernisation of their military arsenals by purchasing Lockheed weapons.[8] The company then spent furiously to influence votes in favour of the expansion of NATO in the Senate – in the 1995–96 election cycle alone, the company and its executives distributed $2.3 million in political donations. This all paid off when, for example, in late 2003 Lockheed Martin sold $3.8 billion worth of F-16s to Poland. The planes were dogged with problems, but the company was laughing all the way to the bank.[9]

However, no-one encapsulates the corrupt intertwining of politics and arms quite like Dick Cheney. As Defense Secretary under George W.H. Bush, Cheney requested defence contractor Haliburton to recommend aspects of the Pentagon that could be privatised. After leaving government with Bush's election defeat, Cheney became CEO of the self-same Haliburton. In this capacity he advised the Pentagon that all aspects of war making should be privatised. Back in office as George W. Bush's vice president, Cheney was the most vocal champion for the invasion of Iraq. The illegal and disastrous invasion netted Haliburton almost $40 billion in contracts, increasing Cheney's personal wealth by tens of millions of dollars.[10] In every conflict there are multiple Dick Cheneys pulling the levers of power, ensuring the descent into ever bloodier wars, and banking the proceeds of the carnage.

The relationship between making war and making money was inadvertently vocalised shortly before the Russian invasion of Ukraine: the CEO of Raytheon hailed the tense situation in the region, as well as deteriorating relations with China, as good for the company's business. He claimed: 'We are seeing, I would say, opportunities for international sales. And of course, the tensions in eastern Europe, the tensions in the South China Sea, all of those things are putting pressure on some of the defence spending over there. So I fully expect we're going to see benefit from it.'

The aggressive rhetoric towards China occurs in the context of the United States spending more on defence than the five next biggest spending countries combined. It also occurs as China is becoming a more active diplomatic player than ever before: a Chinese-brokered rapprochement between Saudi Arabia and Iran has done more to create hope for a cessation of hostilities in Yemen than anything the US or its allies have half-heartedly attempted since 2015. But a focus on conflict rather than diplomacy is unsurprising if key political and military decision makers benefit materially from that conflict. It is, therefore, unsurprising that the United States government employs more people to maintain a single aircraft carrier than it has diplomats across the entire world – and the US has twelve aircraft carriers.

As a cost-of-living crisis engulfs much of the world, and as the climate crisis intensifies, the tiny ruling political and economic elite seem willing, like never before, to deploy force abroad and against their own people to maintain the status quo. This enhances the profits of the arms makers, which in turn feeds our sclerotic, corrupted political systems. It has never been more urgent to break this cycle of 'profitable militarism': for the sake of democracy, accountability, justice, equality and a safer, more peaceful world.

The Book

The Monstrous Anger of the Guns hopes to provide a window into this shadowy world of the arms trade that is so often obscured from view. Many excellent and varied resources have been produced on the arms trade and the action that is being taken to challenge it; this book combines these approaches, drawing from a range of experiences in order to expose and undermine the narrow national security paradigm and the militarism that underpins it. Sponsored by the Peace & Justice Project, it has brought together a global range of perspectives, from activists and campaigners to journalists and academics across five continents – in Latin America, sub-Saharan Africa, the Middle East, western Europe, and India and the Pacific.

Throughout this unusually wide coverage the book demonstrates the many different ways in which individuals and groups persistently question the power and influence of the military-industrial system and its lack of accountability. There is really no better way into such a topic than starting with the first-hand expertise of the people who live with, and fight against, the realities of the global arms trade every day. The book shows the wealth of experience and determination of people across the world to oppose the trade in death.

In Part I, Anna Stavrianakis' opening chapter gives an overview of the international arms trade and the context in which it operates, the patterns and dynamics entrenched in it, and what measures have (and could further) be taken to control it. Vijay Prashad follows with a section on how the trade in weapons defines international relations, and the impact that has on diplomacy and the so-called rules-based international order. Antony Loewenstein then offers a case study, demonstrating how Israel uses its occupation of Palestine to test the development of weapons and surveillance technology, which it can then market and sell to the rest of the world as battle-tested.

Part II brings together contributions on the climate and humanitarian crises caused by the trade. Stuart Parkinson writes about militarism and the climate emergency: the carbon 'bootprint' of the military itself and the ways it is concealed; further environmental damage caused by war, exposing the myth of the green military; and the increasingly militarised perception of human security despite far more pressing needs.

The five other chapters focus on the realities of the global arms trade and the humanitarian impact that it has across the globe. Ahmed Alnaouq tells the story of his family and their experiences in Gaza, and how the Israeli occupation is supported by the global arms trade. The organisation Mwatana for Human Rights has written about the war in Yemen and the role of the West in enabling violations of international humanitarian and human rights laws. Tabitha Agaba and Ian Katusiime examine the Lord's Resistance Army War and its impact on Uganda and the surrounding region, the Nairobi Protocol, and the devastating impact of the arms trade on women and children. Binalakshmi Nepram discusses the impact of weapons on India and the mobilisation of Indigenous women in advocating for peace and disarmament. Finally, Ana Penido talks about the disproportionate impact of small arms and light weapons (weapons that are designed for individual use, such as guns) on Latin America, as well as the global political context behind the arms trade and its impact on the politico-economic climates of countries historically exploited by colonialism.

The simple fact is that we can't tackle these global catastrophes without going to the root of the trade and re-examining the special relationships that arms companies enjoy with national and international power, their relative legal impunity, as well as the individuals who enable and benefit from the trade every day. A wealth of people from all around the world are taking steps towards challenging this embedded culture of militarism and its devastating effects. Part III of this book is written by a selection of these people, to demonstrate the variety of ways we can work to undermine the pervasive influence of the arms trade and fight for a better future.

Lindsey German has written about the response to the War on Terror in the UK, how to mobilise a nation, and the successes and failures of mass campaigns against the arms trade. The Palestine Action organisation demonstrates the vital role of direct action in how it is taking on Israeli arms giant Elbit Systems – and winning. Lorenzo Buzzoni gives an overview of industrial action being taken by workers in Europe to prevent the shipments of weapons into conflict zones, and why the workers in question feel it is their responsibility to prevent those weapons from reaching their goal. Carmen Wilson explains how a community of modern-day peacemakers work to untangle, expose and end university ties to the global arms trade, and the global significance of student activism. Valentina Azarova summarises the fight for legal accountability for the perpetrators and enablers of human rights violations – including what national and international legal frameworks exist, what their limitations are, and how lawyers and campaigners are working together to take governments to court for approving illegal arms sales. Finally, Kawena'ulaokalā Kapahua tells the story of the military occupation of Hawai'i, the damage it has done to the Hawaiian people, and the ways they are fighting back.

This book has brought together a variety of chapters by different authors, united by a common understanding that the consequences of the global trade in weapons are indefensible, and that to end them we must expose the political and economic roots of war. As such, it also represents a diversity of experiences and perspectives; ultimately, the issues we are challenging are broad, and the voices speaking out need to be led by individuals and organisations from impacted communities.

These snapshots showing some of the many ways that people are struggling against the arms trade and the pervasive culture of militarism can show us how and where to focus our efforts, and give us hope for the future of the struggle.

Overall, what clearly emerges from this book is a need to rethink what we mean by security, especially in a future of increasing insecurity. The highly militarised focus on 'national security' ignores the real threats to our society, threats that cannot be contained by borders. War, health crises, inequality and the climate emergency are all real, prevailing threats to humanity. The disproportionate focus on national security and the framing of arms as a means to achieve foreign policy goals is a direct result of the unique relationship – set out in this book – that the defence sector enjoys with the state. The lessons we can learn from the people who brought this book together will ultimately divert our understanding of security away from the interests of the few, and back towards the long-term health and stability of humanity.

PART I

The Global Arms Trade

1

The Global Arms Trade: How it Works, and How We Might Control It

Anna Stavrianakis

Anna Stavrianakis is a Professor of International Relations at the University of Sussex and Director of Research and Strategy at Shadow World Investigations, where she researches the international arms trade, UK arms export policy and international arms transfer controls. Her chapter gives an overview of the main trends in the global arms trade and sets them in the context of the operation of economic, military and political power in world politics. It argues, first, that the global order is militarised, in the sense that military and security interests play an outsized role in the allocation of resources and in decision making about the public good. Second, that the disproportionate power the United States continues to wield in global politics is reflected in its overwhelming dominance of global expenditure on, and trade in, the means of armed violence. Third, that a focus on the US state alone is not adequate. Stavrianakis contends that we need to think transnationally about the arms trade to understand how power works in the global system.

Introduction

In 2021, global military expenditure passed the $2 trillion mark for first time.[1] Despite a financial crisis, a global Covid pandemic and the climate emergency, governments continued to devote massive amounts of their resources to preparing for war and armed violence. However, the distribution of this spending was wildly uneven. The $800 billion spent by the United States alone accounted for over one third of the global total, dwarfing even its closest geopolitical competitors, China and Russia, who spent $293 billion (estimated) and $77 billion respectively. Meanwhile, the entire regions of Africa and Latin America combined account for less than 5 per cent of world military spending.

In the last decade, the volume of international arms transfers has been higher than at any point since the 1990s, although it remains lower than at the height of the Cold War in the early 1980s. While the arms trade is global – in that most countries produce, import or export weapons to some extent – participation in it is very uneven. The USA alone accounts for over one third of global arms transfers and the top ten exporters account for 80 per cent of global exports. This unevenness and concentration tells us something about the operation of power in international politics.

The United States spends more, produces more, and sells more weapons than any other country in the world. The US also exercises oversight of a system of alliances and networks through institutions such as NATO, overseas bases and military coalitions, which incorporate Western states and many in the global South into its aegis. It uses foreign military sales as a direct expression of state policy that simultaneously allows a handful of companies to make vast profits, with state and corporate power acting hand in glove. No other state plays such a role in the global system. But this role is subject to competition, tension and friction – not only from the USA's traditional antagonist, Russia, and contemporary competitor China, but also from states within and outside its orbit. One of the under-appreciated elements of the arms trade is the way in which arms recipients try to play sellers off against each other in an effort to create room for manoeuvre in the international system and the global economy.

The operation of the arms trade gives us a glimpse into global economic, political and military relationships. But it is only a glimpse: the trade is marked by secrecy and obfuscation, veiled behind a toxic combination of national security, commercial confidentiality and masculinist assumptions about what it means to be powerful and strong. And the trade in weaponry is never just about the hardware. Arms sales are accompanied by engineering and logistics support, military training, diplomatic support and wider economic projects, often corrupt. Indeed, the arms trade has been described by economist Joe Roeber as being hard-wired for corruption.[2] But something else it often also hardwires is the military and therefore the strategic relationship between exporter and importer states.

The first part of the chapter lays out who makes, sells and buys weapons, before going on to make the case for a more transnational understanding of the dynamics of the arms trade. The latter part of the chapter explores international arms transfer controls, setting out the main tenets of the Arms Trade Treaty that entered into force in 2014. It examines the treaty's effectiveness in relation to the war in Yemen and closes with an assessment of future developments.

Who Makes and Sells Weapons?

The USA alone accounts for over one third of global arms transfers, selling or giving weapons to over a hundred countries, far more than any other exporter.[3] Forty-one of the top one hundred arms-producing companies are headquartered in the USA, accounting for just over half of the combined arms sales by that group.[4] The USA – its companies and its government acting together – thus dominates the global market for weapons, with the widest reach and the biggest share. This includes many ongoing large export orders, which will be delivered over the coming years. Most US arms sales are made through the government's Foreign Military Sales programme, in which the US government uses the Department of Defense acquisition system to procure weapons from US companies for foreign countries. So while US-based arms companies are officially private, they are thoroughly enmeshed with state power.

The next biggest arms exporter is Russia, accounting for about one fifth of the world's arms exports (although only about 3 per cent of world military spending). Russia's share of the arms trade has declined since the end of the Cold War. Most Soviet military production was centred in Russia. The dissolution of the USSR into independent states meant that Russia inherited the vast majority of the Soviet defence industrial base, which remains state owned. Military production and transfers became slightly more dispersed in the 1990s as states like Ukraine and Belarus inherited some of the Soviet defence industrial base. In more recent times, Russia's share of the global arms trade has been declining and has shrunk significantly since 2020. Its major weapons exports are also more concentrated among a smaller set of recipients than those of the USA. While Washington transfers weapons to over 100 countries across the globe, Moscow transfers weapons to around half that number. Just four states – India, China, Egypt and Algeria – account for three quarters of Russian arms exports. Of the top 100 arms-producing companies, 9 are headquartered in Russia, compared to 41 in the USA.

West European states are the next biggest exporters, each with under one tenth of the global share. Alongside the USA and USSR/Russia, they have been the world's major arms exporters in the post-Second World War period. European states' share of arms exports fluctuate according to the shifting patterns of war and consequent opportunities for arms sales. And the nature of the relationship between the state and the arms industry varies from one European power to another. The French arms industry is state owned or state controlled to a greater degree than many other European arms producers, for example. It has seen a recent increase in its share of the global arms trade due to growing exports to India, Qatar and Egypt. In the UK, the arms industry is officially private, but the government holds what is known as a 'golden share' in the largest companies such as BAE Systems and Rolls Royce. This allows it to block changes in ownership or control that it deems not to be in the national interest. While the British arms industry is not subject to official state direction, in practice it operates together with the state as an integrated whole, sharing assumptions about the economic, political and military benefits of arms exports., For example, government and industry – and a significant proportion of the British trade union movement – share the assumptions that arms exports are good for the economy and an effective way of promoting national and global security, both of which are contested claims. UK arms exports have become increasingly concentrated on sales to a single country, Saudi Arabia, due to its increased demand because of the war in Yemen. But deliveries related to a major deal for combat aircraft ended in 2017, which led to a fall of 41 per cent in British arms exports to Saudi Arabia between the periods 2012–16 and 2017–21.

At the supranational level in Europe, the European Union's (EU's) European Peace Facility supports the export of weapons by Member States to third countries, signalling the EU's growing preference for military responses to peace, security and development challenges. While the initiative is ostensibly aimed at supporting peace and any arms exports facilitated by it are supposed to respect European and international arms transfer control rules, this will be a challenge because many recipients are likely to already be affected by conflict.[5] China is both a significant arms exporter and importer, and distinct from other major exporters because of its history as a developing country. Just over 80 per cent of its arms imports come from Russia and almost half of its exports are to a single recipient, Pakistan. China is the world's second largest military spender after the USA. Its military expenditure has increased for 27 consecutive years and is currently estimated by the Stockholm International Peace Research Institute (SIPRI) to stand at 14 per cent of the global total. This is all part of an ongoing military modernisation programme that started in the 1960s, aimed at making China self-reliant in advanced weapons. Its arms industry is state owned and, while Beijing is a major importer of arms, it is steadily becoming less dependent on foreign technology. Its industry has now developed to the point where there is increasing demand for its weapons overseas.

Most international debate about Chinese involvement in the arms trade is framed in terms of US-led geopolitical concerns and fear of Chinese regional influence in the Pacific. Yet China exercises its global influence primarily in economic and political terms through trade, infrastructure loans and development aid, rather than the development of military relations through arms exports. SIPRI describes Chinese levels of military aid to other states as trivial in volume and substance in comparison to Australian or US military aid. So talk about the 'rise' or 'influence' of China is not neutral. Beijing's exertions in the South China Sea do raise concerns among its neighbours. Yet talk of the rising threat of China is both West-centric and disproportionate, based on the assumption that the US-led order should remain unchallenged.

Transfers of major conventional weapons systems: things like aircraft, ships, armoured vehicles, artillery and missiles are a good indicator of state policy and the ways in which economic, military and political power go together in shaping global order. But there is also a vibrant international trade in small arms and light weapons (SALW), which are cheaper, easier to produce and transfer, and manufactured in a larger and wider number of countries around the world.

The Small Arms Survey estimated that there were 1 billion firearms in circulation around the world in 2017.[6] The effects of small arms can go beyond those of major weapons. While they are crucial military instruments, they are also central to policing, crime, domestic violence and other practices that are all too often placed in a separate category from war in the conventional sense. But if we think of armed violence as a continuum that goes from major inter-state war at one end to intimate partner violence at the other, then we can think about small arms on the same spectrum as major weapons. We can then think about how economic, military, political and gendered power combine through the exercise of armed violence.

Mirroring patterns in the trade in major weapons, the USA is the world's largest producer and exporter of small arms, and it is also the largest importer.[7] The USA is the largest market for firearms among civilians. European states, Russia and China are among the other major exporters. But countries like Brazil and Japan are also major exporters of small arms, even though they are not significant producers or exporters of major weapons systems.

Small arms producers in the global South often produce weapons under licence from North American and western European companies, or Russian ones. Supplier states are less protective of small arms technologies than they are of the more advanced technologies involved in the production of major weapons systems. This has allowed a greater number of countries to produce small arms without having to spend the money on developing research and development programmes. Some states, such as India, Pakistan and Iran, produce small arms for national purposes such as arming the police and military and do not export them in large quantities.

The USA is far and away the world's largest producer and exporter, followed by Russia, western European states and China. Patterns of SALW production and trade show many similarities but are less concentrated. Let us turn to look now at who buys weapons. While it is mainly states in the global North that are the main producers and exporters, it is states in the global South who are the main importers.

Who Buys Weapons?

The world's largest importers of major conventional weapons systems in the period 2017–21 were India, Saudi Arabia, Egypt, Australia and China. Of these, Saudi Arabia and Australia are dependent on the USA and its allies for its arms imports, while Russia is the main supplier to India, Egypt and China. More generally, the Middle East and Asia/Oceania have been the main importing regions in the post-Second World War period.

The USA dominates the Middle Eastern regional arms market. Over half of all arms imports to the Middle East are from USA, in comparison to 12 per cent from France and 11 per cent from Russia. As a region, Asia and Oceania shows perhaps the most diverse set of supply relationships: the major importers in the region buy variously from the USA, Russia, France and China, depending largely on how friendly or otherwise their relations are with Beijing.

South America and sub-Saharan Africa are not major importing regions of major conventional weapons. The former accounts for around 2.5 per cent of global arms imports and the latter 2 per cent. Russia is the main supplier to Africa as a region, but individual states have a more diverse supplier base. The largest importers in South America – Brazil and Chile – buy weapons mainly from the USA and European states; while the region has never been dominated by a single supplier, the USA is the largest supplier to the region.

Broadly speaking, the USA and European states tend to sell higher technology, and more expensive weapons to richer states in the Middle East and Asia, along with associated components and engineering and logistical support services, as well as training. Russia and China, in contrast, sell lower cost and lower tech weapons to middle-income and poorer countries, and those that are politically barred from receiving Western weapons. So when we talk about arms imports, we tend to talk about states in the global South. Southern or developing states often do not have the defence industrial base required to manufacture the full range of military equipment, itself a legacy of the colonial era and the orientation of colonial economies to the needs of the metropole. Since independence, ongoing enmeshment in relationships of political, economic and military patronage with arms suppliers, including corruption, combined with the desire for military strength as a symbol of statehood, has contributed to ongoing arms imports.

Many southern states are in relationships of defence dependency with the USA and its allies. Saudi Arabia, for example, has long been reliant on the USA and UK as its main weapons suppliers. Historically, it has been reliant on foreigners to serve as soldiers, engineers, technicians and trainers for its varied coercive agencies. To minimise and offset this dependency, Saudi Arabia often threatens its regular suppliers that it will turn to other major suppliers such as France. Indeed, it increasingly does just that. Such manoeuvrings afford importers a degree of leverage with their key suppliers. There is thus a situation of mutual interdependence in which leverage is exercised both ways.

Many importing states will try to play suppliers off against each other in order to increase their room for manoeuvre and reduce dependency. India, for example, has historically bought most of its weapons from the USSR/Russia, but has also bought from the USA and from European states, while increasing its military spending and prioritising its efforts at self-reliance in arms production as well, albeit not very successfully. So the arms trade is marked both by some long-standing relationships and also competition and friction within and beyond those relationships, which mirror and shape wider geopolitical contestation.

It is important to remember, however, that no country, not even the USA, is entirely self-reliant in arms production, and that it is not just states in the global South that import weapons. In the last five-year period measured by SIPRI, the USA was the world's thirteenth largest arms importer; its top three suppliers were the UK, the Netherlands and France. The UK, in turn, was the twelfth largest importer, with its top suppliers being the USA, South Korea and Germany. The USA is the dominant supplier to the EU regional market, accounting for over half of all European imports of major weapons. Beyond Europe and NATO, states like South Korea, Japan and Israel are integrated into an arms production and transfer system under the aegis of the US.

This internationalisation of arms production and trade is one of the things that complicates our usual story about the arms trade. We tend to talk in national and state-centric terms. Indeed, this chapter has so far primarily talked in terms of major suppliers such as 'the USA' and 'Russia', and major importers like 'Saudi Arabia' and 'India'. However, a more complicated story needs to be untangled.

Thinking Transnationally about the Arms Trade

The arms trade is marked by enduring patterns: the USA, USSR/Russia and European states are the main producers and exporters; states in the Middle East, Asia and Oceania are the main importers. For most of the period known in the West as the Cold War, the USSR and USA, as the world's two main superpowers, dominated the arms markets of their respective alliances and networks. The end of the Cold War led to (temporary) reductions in military spending and a concentration of arms supply. US dominance of the global arms market became more pronounced, and Russia's share of the arms market fell. The contraction of military spending in Europe and North America post-Cold War led companies to internationalise through things like mergers and acquisitions, joint ventures and subcontracting.

In the early 2000s, due to the impact of the so-called War on Terror, global military spending, arms production and exports increased again. The arms market became less concentrated as so-called emerging suppliers – states such as Brazil, Turkey, South Korea – became more involved in the arms market, and technology transfer agreements increased. So over time, there are fluctuations and changes in arms production and supply even if some of the overall patterns look the same.

Much of what passes for debate about the arms trade assumes the legitimacy of the US-led international order and internalises its geopolitical and security concerns, specifically the rise of China and the aggression and revanchism of Russia. But the US-centric nature of this debate does not mean that there is not objectively something to be worried about, for anyone concerned about peace and justice. Chinese military spending and involvement in the arms trade is growing and it is engaged in a long-term military modernisation programme. It supplies weapons to states involved in conflict and repression such as Myanmar, Sri Lanka and Sudan. The war that Russia unleashed on Ukraine in February 2022 has shocked western Europe and the USA – but perhaps less so the eastern European states that used to be part of the USSR or ruled by client regimes of Moscow. Russia has participated directly in the war in Syria in support of the Assad regime, as well as being the latter's main arms supplier. It is also currently the largest supplier of weapons to Africa as a whole, including to states involved in conflict.

The response from critics of US foreign policy is often to draw attention to the US's own crimes: its invasions of Iraq and Afghanistan, its war on Libya, its support for Israeli apartheid and its history of invasions and occupations around the world, not least its involvement in and support for Latin American dictatorships in the 1970s and 1980s. This is an important corrective. But it also obscures the ways in which states in the global South – and other smaller states with ties to one or another of the major powers – themselves participate in global war making and war preparation, and how most if not all national states are enmeshed in transnational relationships of coercion and predation.

States of the Middle East, in particular the Gulf, are major military spenders and growing arms producers. They are also increasingly belligerent as military actors, as seen in the war in Yemen, and involvement in the war in Libya. Israel's occupation and now genocidal destruction of Palestine is both reliant on its military and diplomatic relationship with the USA and a key node through which knowledge, equipment and practices of counter-insurgency circulate globally and are applied from Palestine to Iraq and elsewhere. The volume and financial value of the arms trade in Africa and Central and South America is significantly lower than in other parts of the world but practices of war, counterterrorism and counter-insurgency across countries as different as Nigeria, Kenya, Uganda, Mexico and Colombia have all demanded increases in military spending and the acquisition of weapons. States in the global South are more dependent on arms imports as they cannot make their own weapons, and so our attention is often directed to their import practices. But even Western states are involved to a considerable degree in the transnational production and circulation of weapons.

When we think about the operation of power in international politics, we need to think transnationally as well as geopolitically. Many of the transnational relationships in play have their roots in colonialism and informal empire. It is no coincidence that the world's largest arms exporters are to be found in the European world. The USA, Russia and the major states of western Europe all derive their power in the world system from an imperial or colonial past to some degree, and those roots continue to entangle them with states in the periphery that are now themselves independent.

If we understand the post-Second World War era as one of informal US empire, then the envelopment of European states into NATO, US dominance of the Middle East arms market, and the legacy of its support for Latin American dictatorships can all be seen as part of the same overarching project. And the spread of weapons to Third World states and liberation movements via military assistance from the USSR, Warsaw Pact states and China was the flip side of the coin. The patterns of exports from European states often reflect both their colonial lineages and their enmeshment in the US-led empire of the present day. It is no surprise that the UK is a major exporter to both Saudi Arabia and the USA, for example. And within this historical legacy, states in the global South try to generate room for manoeuvre in ways that are themselves often militarising. India, for example, has a history of non-alignment that today is expressed by being a strategic partner of both the USA and Russia, as well as being the world's largest arms importer.

The internationalisation of arms production is growing but uneven.[8] Internationalisation means that companies have a geographical spread beyond the country in which they are headquartered. This internationalisation tends to map on to existing geopolitical networks and alliances. For example, US companies have a strong presence in Australia and Canada, and also Israel, Japan, South Korea and Taiwan. BAE Systems was formerly known as British Aerospace but changed its name to appear more international, even though all its advertising in the UK takes place against the backdrop of the Union Jack flag. BAE now sells more to the US Department of Defense than it does to the UK Ministry of Defence. And to meet the demands of the USA's Buy America Act – a national protectionist mechanism that requires the US government to preferentially buy from American companies – BAE Systems set up a US subsidiary to qualify as an American company.

Russian and Chinese companies have a much more limited international presence. No North American or western European companies have foreign entities in Russia or China, although some Chinese companies have foreign subsidiaries in the West. China maintains long-standing military cooperation with Pakistan and Cambodia. The Russian arms industry has foreign subsidiaries in India, Kazakhstan and Vietnam, which are all major importers of Russian weapons. Both Russia and China are more focused on domestic development of weapons than Western countries are, and the sanctions on Russia that followed its 2014 annexation of Crimea have further limited its scope for international cooperation.

Some southern states are growing as military producers and exporters, for example Brazil, Turkey, South Korea and the UAE (United Arab Emirates). These states are reliant on foreign technology, which can be restricted by the supplier. They therefore use offsets to try to develop their domestic arms industrial base, in which foreign firms have to contribute to co-production facilities, transfer technology, and invest in national arms firms. Through these means, they are able to establish themselves in niche sectors. For example, the UAE makes light armoured vehicles and Brazil makes trainer and light combat aircraft. Their exports tend to go to low- and middle-income countries in Africa, Asia, Middle East and Latin America. These mid-tier importer/exporter states often host subsidiaries of major Western arms companies, in line with their geopolitical alliances, networks and ties. For example, Turkey, a NATO member, hosts foreign entities of North American and European companies, and Saudi Arabia and the UAE host foreign entities of US and UK companies. Indeed, the UAE is now the world's 18th largest arms producer and has a company in the top 100 largest arms companies.

Another way in which the arms trade is internationalised is through the wide network of banks, law firms, brokers, dealers and other intermediaries that facilitate weapons transfers. They do much of the crucial behind-the-scenes work that allows the flow of weapons around the world, whether legally, illicitly or illegally. While some of these actors work very much in the shadows, using covert means and multiple identities, others have the imprimatur of official state policy or institutional backing to legitimise them. This allows them to exploit loopholes in legal, economic and accounting systems.

Two examples are instructive: the network of air cargo companies operated by Viktor Bout to transfer weapons into conflict zones; and the global money-laundering network institutionalised by BAE Systems to facilitate corrupt payments to agents in arms-buying countries. While ostensibly quite different, both examples share the common feature of access to state power and military material, and an ability to navigate the loopholes of economic, legal and political accountability.[9]

Viktor Bout – widely nicknamed as 'the merchant of death' – is the sort of character we might commonly think of when we hear the term 'arms dealer' or 'arms broker'. Born in Dushanbe in what was then the Tajik Soviet Socialist Republic, he served in the Soviet armed forces in the late 1980s. With the dissolution of the Soviet army in 1991, he started an air cargo business, taking advantage of the break-up of the USSR and the privatisation of resources to source and transport weapons on the illicit market, making use of his access to state power and military materiel.

Bout supplied weapons in contravention of UN arms embargoes to conflicts in Angola, Liberia, Sierra Leone and the Democratic Republic of Congo (DRC). To do this, he used a fleet of Soviet Antonov planes based in the UAE and deployed a plethora of corrupt means and practices. He faked end-use certificates, exploited loopholes in aircraft registration rules, and sourced weapons from former Soviet states such as Ukraine. But he was also contracted by the USA and UK to fly equipment into Iraq during the US-led occupation, as well as by the UN to transfer peacekeepers into Somalia and East Timor. His expertise in challenging environments outweighed his record of breaking international law. Bout was imprisoned in Illinois, USA, in 2010, having been found guilty of providing material support to a foreign terrorist organisation and conspiring to kill US citizens. He was released in December 2022 in exchange for US basketball player Brittney Griner, who had been imprisoned in Russia for ten months on drugs charges.

Contrast Bout's type of arms trade facilitation to that of the banks, law firms and brokers involved in Western states' projects, such as arms deals with Saudi Arabia. Major arms deals like the Al Yamamah deal between the UK and Saudi Arabia – the biggest arms deal in British history – simply could not have happened without the bribery that facilitated it, as authors such as Andrew Feinstein and Nicholas Gilby have laid out in painstaking detail.[10] Yet the corruption could be hidden as the deal was an official government-to-government deal, in which BAE Systems was contracted by the UK Ministry of Defence.

Through revelations from whistleblowers, journalists and anti-bribery officials it slowly emerged that BAE had established a global money-laundering network centred on two companies registered in the British Virgin Islands, Poseidon Trading Investments Ltd and Red Diamond Trading Ltd. They used accounts with major banks in major financial cities such as London, New York and Geneva to make payments to agents in arms-purchasing countries, including Saudi Arabia, but also countries as diverse as Tanzania, Romania, Chile and others. The executives of BAE Systems retain unfettered access to state leaders and policymakers, having so far swerved accountability measures for corruption in a number of cases – not to mention for their role in facilitating likely war crimes in Yemen by selling arms to the Saudi-led coalition involved in the conflict there. While BAE Systems has faced little to no accountability in the UK, in 2010 it pleaded guilty in the US District Court in Washington DC to conspiring to defraud the USA and paid a $400 million fine. Court documents indicated there had been substantial payments to shell companies and intermediaries, false statements had knowingly been made, and there had been a failure to ensure compliance with anti-bribery laws.

Thinking transnationally about the arms trade means foregrounding the ways in which states are enmeshed in transnational relationships that have their roots in colonialism and informal empire. It means thinking about the uneven internationalisation of the arms industry and its relationships to states. And it means thinking about the legal and illegal activities of banks, law firms, brokers, dealers and other intermediaries as points on a spectrum of facilitation, rather than discrete or distinct activities. In these ways, the global trade in weapons is facilitated. So what are the prospects for controlling the trade?

Prospects for Controlling the Arms Trade

Since 2014, there has been an international set of rules in place to control the arms trade. The Arms Trade Treaty (ATT) requires the countries which have signed up to the treaty (the 'States Parties') to prohibit arms transfers that would violate an arms embargo, contribute to illicit trafficking, or be used in genocide, crimes against humanity or war crimes. Then they are required to conduct a risk assessment to check whether transfers would contribute to or undermine peace and security. They must refuse to authorise exports where there is an over-riding risk that they could be used to commit or facilitate a serious violation of international humanitarian law (IHL), international human rights law (IHRL), terrorism, transna-tional crime or gender-based violence.

Of the major arms suppliers, all European states, includ-ing the UK, are States Parties to the ATT. EU member states are also already bound by the EU Common Position, which shares some of the same criteria as the ATT. The USA is a sig-natory but not a State Party, meaning it is bound by the spirit but not the letter of the treaty. (President Trump un-signed the treaty while in office, which was a largely symbolic move.) The US has what is commonly lauded as the gold standard of national arms export control systems, at least on paper. Its export control system is considered to be highly transparent and includes reference to restraining arms supplies to regions of conflict and instability, alongside supporting US economic and national security needs. So when US arms exports become controversial, it is generally not because of lax policy imple-mentation or mistakes: they are an expression of state policy. Russia is neither a signatory nor a State Party to the ATT, while China acceded to the treaty in 2020. Both states have national arms export control systems but they do not refer-ence conflict prevention, human rights or humanitarian law. It remains to be seen how China will incorporate the ATT into its national control system, given the treaty's reference to IHL and IHRL.

Most of the world's largest arms importers – states in the Middle East and Asia such as India, Saudi Arabia, Egypt, Qatar, Pakistan and the UAE – are neither signatories nor States Parties to the ATT. But many if not most of the states in South America and sub-Saharan Africa are States Parties. These are states that, as we saw earlier, are not major arms importers but may be conflict-affected and thus have an interest in regulating the flow of weapons. As of December 2022, there are 113 States Parties to the treaty.

A contrast is often drawn between states that have export control regimes that mention human rights, humanitarian law and conflict prevention, and those that do not. Of the major exporters, this translates into a distinction between the USA and European states on the one hand, and Russia and China on the other. This reflects the wider basic contours of mainstream Western security discourse that assumes the idea of Western benevolence and non-Western malfeasance. It also reflects the fact that, as democracies, Western states are exposed to more domestic scrutiny and critique, which forces them to pay lip service to international law to a greater degree. But there are two factors that complicate this mainstream narrative.

First is the political economy of the global arms market. As we saw earlier, China and Russia tend to sell lower tech, cheaper weapons to countries that cannot afford expensive weapons or are barred from receiving Western arms supplies. China sells more weapons to conflict-affected African states than the USA and Europe do, for example. The wars in Sri Lanka and Sudan were both facilitated by Russian and Chinese arms sales rather than Western ones. And Russia is the major international military patron and diplomatic supporter of the Assad regime in Syria. But this does not mean that these states are necessarily worse than Western ones in terms of their arms export records.

This takes us to the second complicating factor: the fact that all major suppliers – regardless of whether they have control regimes that reference conflict prevention, human rights and humanitarian law – have supplied substantial volumes of arms to at least some of the wars of the current century. A report from the World Peace Foundation found there to be very little evidence that war or armed conflict leads to restraint in arms transfers by major exporters, whether they have policies referencing conflict prevention or not.[11] Overall, the difference in arms export practices between exporters such as Russia – which do not reference conflict, human rights or humanitarian law in their policies – and the US and western European suppliers, who do, is relatively minor.

This takes us neatly to thinking about the actual practice of export controls. There are plenty of examples of arms exports and military aid from across the range of major exporters that have contributed to war and armed violence around the world. But it is worth paying attention to examples where – on paper at least – one would expect existing controls to kick in. There is no clearer example of this than arms supplies to the Saudi- and UAE-led coalition involved in the war in Yemen (for an account of the impacts of the war in Yemen, see Chapter 6).

The Saudi/UAE-led coalition has been credibly accused of violations of the laws of war, including war crimes. Allegations of violations of IHL include the targeting of entire towns; attacks on hospitals, schools, markets, weddings and other civilian objects; and the bombing of a funeral in Sanaa, including double-tap strikes (where a second strike follows on quickly from a first, in order to also hit those who rush to the scene to help the wounded). The coalition's aerial and naval blockade has contributed to politically induced famine and the spread of disease.

The Houthis and Saleh-aligned forces – against whom the coalition intervention was launched – have also been credibly accused of violations of the laws of war, including war crimes. Arms transfers to these groups have been prohibited since a 2015 UN arms embargo, alongside a travel ban and an asset freeze against those declared to be threatening peace in the country. The Houthis have continued to be able to obtain weapons from Yemeni military stockpiles and through the illicit trade, including small arms and light weapons smuggled via Somalia and increasingly sophisticated missile technologies supplied by Iran, often via Oman, according to the UN Panel of Experts on Yemen.

So all parties to the war are credibly accused of violating international law. And states with arms export control regimes that commit them to the prevention of conflict and respect for international humanitarian and human rights law are supplying the Saudi- and UAE-led coalition. In 2019, the UN Group of Independent Eminent International and Regional Experts on Yemen reported that the practices of the Saudi-led coalition and its allies in the government of Yemen may amount to war crimes and that arms-supplying states could be held responsible for providing aid or assistance for international law violations, if the conditions for complicity are fulfilled.

The UK and European states are States Parties to the ATT, so the emergence of wide-ranging, credible allegations of violation of the laws of war committed by the Saudi-led coalition since the earliest days of the war in March 2015 should have triggered the restriction of their arms exports. Under the ATT, states are required to prohibit arms transfers if there is an 'overriding risk' they 'might' contribute to or facilitate a serious violation of human rights or IHL. The US, even though it is not a State Party to the ATT, has laws and rules that reference the outbreak or escalation of conflict, and claims that its national control regime is stronger than the ATT.

Nonetheless, despite extensive evidence of serious viola-tions on the part of the Saudi-led coalition, and despite the stated goal of the ATT being to 'reduce human suffering', Western arms exports to the coalition have continued – and in some cases, such as the USA and UK, increased significantly. This is in line with historic Western support for Saudi Arabia and the UAE. Both states are dependent on their Western patrons for weapons, military training and diplomatic support.

It was not until the murder of Jamal Khashoggi in 2018 that some arms suppliers took steps to restrain their exports. Some European suppliers, such as Austria, Denmark, Finland, the Netherlands and the Belgian region of Wallonia, suspended exports to the coalition. And the European Parliament passed a resolution urging Member States to ban weapons sales to the kingdom. But some of these national responses had caveats and loopholes. For example, the German government announced the suspension of exports to Saudi Arabia but has continued to participate in international weapons production projects destined for the kingdom, granting licences for com-ponents and ammunition for export to the UK where they will be incorporated into Tornados and Eurofighters for export to Saudi Arabia.

Germany is also a good example of what is called offshor-ing: the process in which multinational companies seek to take advantage of the most lax regulatory regimes available to them. The South African non-governmental organisation (NGO) Open Secrets has documented the way German mul-tinational arms company Rheinmetall has continued to sell weapons to Saudi Arabia via its subsidiaries overseas, despite Germany's suspension of exports to the kingdom because of concerns over the conduct of the war. Weapons fragments made by Rheinmetall subsidiaries in Italy (RWM Italia) and South Africa (Rheinmetall Denel Munition) – including weapons made in a Rheinmetall Denel Munition production facility in Saudi Arabia – have been found at the site of attacks on civilians in Yemen. German researchers have expressed the concern that German companies have been setting up production facilities overseas while German law and policy creates loopholes that allows them to avoid domestic controls. National policy may look progressive on paper, but the internationalisation of the arms industry means that, increasingly, global companies seek to take advantage of loopholes where they can find them.

Another way to hold states accountable when they fail to implement their legal obligations under the ATT is the use of strategic litigation. A group of non-governmental experts called the ATT Expert Group has documented legal proceedings in nine countries – Belgium, Canada, France, Italy, the Netherlands, South Africa, Spain, the UK and USA – against governments which have permitted arms exports to the Saudi-UAE-led coalition in apparent violation of their own arms export policies. There has also been a complaint lodged with the Office of the Prosecutor of the International Criminal Court (ICC) against corporate managers of several EU and UK arms companies, as well as senior government officials, on grounds of aiding and abetting war crimes. States, operating in tandem with arms capital, have a vested interest in the ongoing supply of weapons, but they also have an interest in a positive international reputation as being seen to be committed to human rights and international law. It is the space between these two commitments that activists try to leverage by using the law to hold states to account and to hold them to their commitments.

While the legal process can take many years, a different and more immediate type of intervention to try to stop weapons reaching the Saudi-led coalition has been undertaken by dock workers.[12] Weapons made in the USA and Canada are shipped to Saudi Arabia via European ports, where additional weapons are loaded, by the Bahri shipping company. Bahri is a Saudi government-controlled shipping and logistics company; of its 90 ships, 6 are used to transport weapons. In Canada, activists held protests at the port of Saint John, New Brunswick, where armoured vehicles were being loaded on to the *Bahri Yanbu* for delivery to Saudi Arabia and lobbied the longshoremen to refuse to move the cargo. The longshoremen in turn refused to cross the protest line, forfeiting their wages as a consequence.

In Europe, the first protests against Bahri ships were in Bilbao, Spain, in March 2017, when a firefighter responsible for supervising the loading operations refused to carry out his duties on grounds of conscientious objection (for more on European industrial action against the arms trade, see Chapter 12). Investigate Europe, a network of European journalists, has documented the way workers and activists realised that shipments were passing through Bilbao every month and sometimes every two weeks. Within two years, coordinated activism had started across European ports. Protests at the French port of Le Havre were combined with legal action, when a French NGO, ACAT, lodged a court appeal to stop the Bahri ship *Yanbu* docking on the grounds this would contravene France's obligations under the ATT. The ship did not dock in Le Havre, and activists shared information of the ship's progress so that when it arrived in Genoa, Italy, it was met with a banner proclaiming 'ports closed to weapons, ports open to migrants' – in reference to Italian state pressure against migrant arrivals.

Conclusion

The contemporary moment is one of a crisis – if not the death throes – of the so-called liberal international order led and dominated by the USA since the end of the Second World

War. Thinking about the arms trade provides some useful insights that can enrich our understanding of the military, political and economic dimensions of this international order. From the wars in Syria and Yemen, to the war in Ukraine, to the less internationally visible wars in places like Tigray, gun violence in the Americas, and the occupations of Kashmir and Palestine, the arms trade plays a significant role in providing the means of violence and facilitating both coercion and also resistance to domination.

What future developments might there be in the arms trade, and what would be their significance for global order? One key trend that is likely to continue apace is the internationalisation of the arms industry. Arms-producing companies will continue to seek to open up new markets and capture increased market share, taking advantage of state security practices that emphasise the use of force to resolve conflict and difference. BAE Systems, for example, calls itself a global business organised around five home markets – Australia, India, Saudi Arabia, the UK and the USA – and yet emphasises its claim to being a British company in public debate in the UK. It has production facilities in India and Saudi Arabia, contributing to government attempts at defence indigenisation there, while also potentially opening up new export markets for the company.

This internationalisation brings further challenges for control of the arms trade. The example, given earlier, of exports from a South African subsidiary of a major German company to the Saudi-led coalition fighting in Yemen indicates the gaps in control through which exports can pass. If an Indian or a Saudi subsidiary of a US- or UK-headquartered company exports weapons to a conflict zone, who is responsible? Arms trade regulation remains premised on national state controls, so the future of arms control will need to grapple with trying to hold company executives and state officials accountable while also extra-territorialising these controls, such that multinational companies can no longer play states' regulations off against each other.

Despite these challenges, it is also clear that where power is exercised, resistance is generated. While the rich and powerful devote their energy, resources and connections to the production of mass violence, civil society activists devote theirs to resisting it. Whether in the form of direct action against weapons producers, community disarmament campaigns, or strategic litigation, ordinary people are confronting the forces of violence on a daily basis and reshaping global order as they do so.

Further Reading

Feinstein, Andrew, *The Shadow World: Inside the Global Arms Trade* (London: Penguin, 2011).

Gilby, Nicholas, *Deception in High Places: A History of Bribery in Britain's Arms Trade* (London: Pluto Press, 2014).

Perlo-Freeman, Sam, *Business as Usual: How Major Weapons Exporters Arm the World's Conflicts*. World Peace Foundation, 2021, https://sites.tufts.edu/wpf/business-as-usual/.

SIPRI (2022) 'The top 100 arms-producing and military services companies, 2021'.

SIPRI (2022) 'Trends in international arms transfers, 2021'.

SIPRI (2022) 'Trends in world military expenditure, 2021'.

All from https://www.sipri.org/publications.

2

If You Have a Hammer, Everything Looks Like a Nail: How Guns Define International Relations

Vijay Prashad

Vijay Prashad is an Indian historian, author, journalist, political commentator, and Marxist intellectual. His chapter shows how the militarised state of the world directly affects international relations and US foreign policy decisions, as shown by the imbalance between funds earmarked for diplomacy and those earmarked for war. It exposes how US diplomats and government officials act as agents, not only for the military but also for the private arms industry, undermining any push for long-term peace and security.

Charles 'Chuck' Cogan is sitting with his overcoat on in Henrietta's Table, a lovely, airy café in the Charles Hotel in Cambridge, Massachusetts. From 1954 to 1991, Chuck worked for the Central Intelligence Agency (CIA), including as Chief of the Near East (South Asia Division) in the Directorate of Operations from 1979 to 1984. We met to talk about the assassination of the US Ambassador Adolph 'Spike' Dubs in Kabul in 1979, just before Chuck took charge of the overall operations in that region.[1] Dubs, a Kremlinologist, had been

45

dispatched to Kabul to find out about the Afghan communists and the Democratic Republic of Afghanistan that had
been established after the August 1978 *coup d'état*. The White
House had been eager to arm a group of hard-core conserva-
tives, who had begun small insurgencies in the southern part
of Afghanistan. Dubs cautioned against getting involved in
that resistance – not because the men held grotesque views
on social rights – but because the Afghan communists were
not puppets of Moscow and might in fact drive a social justice
agenda (tens of thousands of communists and leftists went
into the countryside in this period as part of a nationwide
literacy campaign, which was being targeted with violence
by these small insurgencies). The mysterious assassination of
Dubs opened the floodgates for US-Saudi money to build up
this minuscule right-wing resistance into the mujahideen. I
had been interviewing a range of people – including veterans
from AGSA (Afghanistan's intelligence agency) – about who
killed Dubs, when I got a call from Cogan to come meet him.

A dapper man with an expensive overcoat sat across from me
and spoke over many hours about his time in the CIA. Chuck
had several stories to recount, including about the situation in
Afghanistan, Iran and Pakistan during his tenure as head of
CIA operations in that region.[2] While he would demur when
the details became necessary, he did tell me what he needed
to: 'stay away from the Dubs story'. That was that. When I
pressed him, he said that there was nothing to the story, that
in fact Dubs had been killed in a botched rescue operation
at Kabul Serena Hotel after he had been kidnapped by some
Shia-Maoists (or *Settam-e-Melli*, a Tajik-Uzbek left organisation). There has been no clarification in either the documents
released by the US government or by the Soviet Union.
Assadullah Sarwani, who headed AGSA at that time, was in
jail from 1992 till 2016 and is not in the mood to talk about the
killing. One theory, told to me by a senior communist, Ana-

hita Ratebzad, who was then an ambassador to Belgrade, was that Dubs had become an inconvenience for the United States since he was against the arming of the mujahideen. This left the question hanging in the air: who killed Dubs?

'There's an old adage in the CIA', Cogan was telling me when we talked about the use of armed force by the United States to get its way when confronted with political disobedience. 'If you have a hammer, everything looks like a nail.' In other words, the approach taken by a complex system – like the US government – can be defined by logic or humanism in the best-case scenario but is more often defined by the tools available to the system. Why continue long-drawn out diplomatic conversations that will either result in a compromise or a loss when you can easily use threats of force or force itself to get your way? Weakened by the Saur Revolution in August 1978 (Afghanistan), the Iranian Revolution (which started in January 1978) and the emergence of the Islamic Republic (which was declared in December 1979), the United States moved hastily from the possibility of negotiation with these two governments to a posture of belligerence: funding the mujahideen in Afghanistan and refusing to hand over the Shah of Iran (the head of the previous regime) to the new government, leading to the confrontation with Iran that continues till this day. Since the use of covert and overt hostile tactics – including assassinations and war – are available to the United States government, and since they are sometimes effective in extending US power, these become the weapons of choice. The hammer defines the politics: the world looks like a set of nails.

* * *

When WikiLeaks released the tranche of US State Department cables in 2010, the dispatches from the US embassies around the world revealed the character of US power. In early

2009, US Ambassador to Egypt, Margaret Scobey, wrote to US Secretary of State Hillary Clinton to prepare for Clinton's visit with Egyptian foreign minister Aboul Gheit. The cable provides a character sketch of Gheit ('smart, urbane with a tendency to lecture') and offers a series of possible requests that Gheit might make (such as an invitation to the Gaza Donors' Conference to be held in Cairo). Scobey, a career foreign service officer, tells Clinton that Gheit 'may not raise human rights (specifically Ayman Nour), political reform or democratisation; but you should'. Ayman Nour is the leader of the El Ghad liberal party, who had been in Cairo's prisons since 2005 (he was released shortly after Clinton's meeting with Gheit).[3]

The issue here is not whether Clinton raised the issue of human rights with Gheit or what Scobey thought of these matters. Because, while Scobey drafted this cable, in other – more shadowy rooms – the officials of the US military, of US military intelligence, and of the CIA carried a more powerful brief. Since 1995, the US government had provided the Egyptian secret service (the Mukhabarat) with various prisoners through the extraordinary rendition programme. These prisoners, accused of being members of al-Qaeda, had been tortured in the very prisons that Scobey criticised. What such cables demonstrate is the cynical idealism of the US State Department, which had been marginalised by the diplomacy of the shadows, conducted by the US government's arms of war.

In cable after cable, we read of the visits of the US military officers and their conversations with heads of state and intelligence chiefs of various countries. The US ambassadors act as fixers or go-betweens for their military counterparts. For instance, Ambassador Stephen Seche, another career diplomat, filed a cable from Sana'a, Yemen, in January 2010 about General David Petraeus's meeting with Yemen's president Ali

Abdullah Saleh. Seche sat by as the stenographer as Petraeus and Saleh colluded against Yemeni sovereignty. The United States had an active military presence in Yemen, including attacking various political forces from the air. When the issue of these military attacks was raised in Yemen's parliament, the US military and President Saleh agreed that he would lie about them. 'We'll continue saying that the bombs are ours, not yours', Saleh told Petraeus.[4] Saleh's deputy, Rashad al-Alimi, had just told the Yemeni parliament that the US was not involved in these attacks, but that the Yemeni military had – without the necessary means – conducted these strikes.[5]

The experience of these ambassadors – reduced to note-takers for the US military – is represented in the US budget. Calculating the US military budget is always a chore, largely because considerable sections of the overall military architecture of the United States – such as its nuclear budget – is buried in other departments – in the case of the nuclear budget, in the Department of Energy; and large parts of the intelligence budget is classified. While most of this book uses SIPRI data for military expenditure, the figures in this chapter are taken from more accurate accounting done in *Hyper-imperialism: A Dangerous Decadent New Stage*.[6] These figures demonstrate that while the US government apportions $84 billion to the US State Department, close to $1 trillion goes to the US military each year; that is to say, diplomacy in the United States is worth 0.084 of the value of the US military. No wonder that the US diplomatic corps has become a secretarial service for the US armed forces.

A glance at the international level is even more dispiriting. The total military expenditure in the world is now more than $2 trillion per year, while the total UN budget (including peacekeeping) is merely $3 billion, which makes the UN budget less than 0.002 of the global military budget.

It is difficult to look at these numbers and these percentages and not feel the futility of moving an agenda for peace diplomacy. Half of the world's arms budget is expended by one country, the United States, which dominates the world through its hard and soft power, its use of 902 overseas military bases and of the calcified Wall Street-Dollar-IMF (International Monetary Fund) complex. Ever since the UN peacekeeping mission was founded in 1945, it has run on a minuscule budget and, through political manoeuvring, has been kept away from missions that would interfere with the operations of the great powers, notably in the wars conducted by the United States (which funds 28 per cent of the UN peacekeeping budget, and so holds it in check, and has even used the UN forces in its war in Afghanistan).[7]

Due to the overwhelming power of the US military in its statecraft, new concepts have been developed to justify its occlusion of traditional diplomacy: military diplomacy and defence diplomacy. The term 'defence diplomacy' first makes its appearance in the UK Ministry of Defence's *Strategic Defence Review* from 1998.[8] The US strategic community uses an acronym – DIME – to reflect on the sources of national power, namely diplomatic, informational, military, and economic. In these circles, while the military is supposedly only one aspect of national power, it is indeed the one that leads. A 2019 assessment by the liberal Brookings Institute's Colonel Amy Ebitz suggests that the United States needs to develop a comprehensive plan of action for international diplomacy that foregrounds the role of the military, since – as she put it – 'the US military helps to carry out the diplomatic mission of the United States'.[9] US military ties through the United Nations, NATO, Theatre Security Cooperation (between the US and allied countries), US military bases, and so on, provide the basis for the use of the military to project

US power in hard and soft terms.[10] This is the best evidence of the clearcut militarisation of diplomacy.[11]

Even more egregious is the role of the US embassy as the promoter of the US arms industry. The State Department cables reveal several instances where the US ambassador offered his services to work for private companies, using the full power of the United States over the life and debt of these countries to insist that contracts be signed with US arms dealers.[12] There's the US ambassador in Bangkok trying to convince Lockheed Martin to sell Thailand F-16 jets so that these are not procured from Russia's Sukhoi. The catch: the Thai government wanted to pay for them with 80,000 tons of frozen chickens. When Lockheed expressed interest, a coup put paid to the deal. There's a US ambassador trying to get the government of Chad to buy Lockheed Martin C-130 transport planes from 2007 to 2009.

Furthermore, in the 1990s when, with the USSR gone, there seemed little reason to maintain NATO, Lockheed Martin and other arms manufacturers formed the 'Committee to Expand NATO', which lobbied the US Congress to extend the borders of the security alliance into eastern Europe simply because they wanted to sell Poland, Hungary, and the Czech Republic weapons.[13] The deliberate march of NATO toward the Russian border is partly explained by the extravagant interest taken by the arms merchants in the market for their weapons in the new states in eastern Europe, a march that led inexorably to the war in Ukraine. In each of these cases, and many more, the US embassy operates as a lobbying firm for the private arms industry, putting the full weight of US power behind the negotiation.

* * *

In his 1992 book *Arms and the State*, Keith Krause suggests three different reasons for states to develop a robust arms industry: the pursuit of power, the pursuit of victory in war, and the pursuit of wealth. Krause's argument rests on the assumption that states are driven by a logic of contest and conflict, by a dog-eat-dog environment where there is a compulsion to prevail over competitors. Nonetheless, his analysis does capture the actual situation in the world today, where many states – notably great powers – maintain massive militaries and arms industries to facilitate these three motivations.

A country such as the United States uses its military capacity and weapons sales to extend its power beyond its borders, fulfilling each of the three motivations. No other power on the planet currently has the same capacity to use weapons systems to pursue power, pursue victory in war, and pursue wealth. Not only does the United States have the world's largest military (outspending all nations in the world), but it is the largest exporter of weapons (40 per cent of global arms exports are from the US). To compare the US military establishment and the US military industry with other countries, or to speak in general about the global arms trade without being specific about the role of the United States, obfuscates the actual source of global problems.

In the case of China and the United States, there is simply no comparison between the US military capacity and its power project as compared to that of China (Table 2.1). There are US military bases that encircle China from Diego Garcia (in the Indian Ocean) to Okinawa (in Japan), while the only Chinese overseas military base in Djibouti was established for China to assist in a UN mission against piracy. US navy vessels constantly enter or come near Chinese territorial waters, conducting 'freedom of navigation' missions based on the UN Convention on the Law of the Sea (1994). No Chinese war ship comes near US territorial waters. This is an interesting issue, since China is legally authorised to conduct 'freedom of navigation' missions since it signed and ratified the UN Convention, while the US has no legal authority to conduct them since it has not ratified the Convention.

Table 2.1   US and China military expenditure, 2022[14]

	United States	China
Military spending:	$1.537 trillion	$292 billion
Military spending per capita	12.6%	0.6%
Military exports (market share)	39%	4.6%
Number of overseas military bases	902	1

The Third Great Depression that began in 2007–8, spurred on by the collapse of the US housing market and several key US financial institutions, signalled to the rest of the world that the US-centred financial system was untrustworthy.[15] The US could not remain the market of last resort for the world's commodities. The G7 countries – which saw themselves as the guardians of the global capitalist system – begged states outside their orbit, such as China and India, to put their surpluses into the Western financial system to prevent its total meltdown. In return for this service, countries outside the G7 were told that, henceforth, the G20 would be the executive body of the world system and the G7 gradually disbanded.[16] Yet almost twenty years later, the G7 remains in place, and it has arrogated to itself the role of world leader, with NATO, the Trojan horse of the US, now positioning itself as the world's policeman. The US-led military bloc, which includes NATO, accounts for nearly three quarters of all of the world's military spending.

NATO's Secretary-General Jens Stoltenberg has said that NATO will undergo the 'biggest overhaul of our collective deterrence and defence since the Cold War'.[17] The NATO member states, now with the addition of Finland and Sweden, will expand their 'high readiness forces' from 40,000 troops to 300,000, who, equipped with a range of lethal weaponry, will 'be ready to deploy to specific territories on the alliance's eastern flank', namely the Russian border. The UK's chief of the general staff, General Sir Patrick Sanders, said that these armed forces should prepare to 'fight and win' a war against Russia. Fears that the US would place 'battlefield nuclear weapons' in Ukraine rose.

In 2019, the United States unilaterally withdrew from the Intermediate Nuclear Forces (INF) Treaty, which upset the apple cart of nuclear arms control (already damaged by the US government's 2002 unilateral withdrawal from the Anti-Ballistic Missile treaty and the Open Skies treaty). Such withdrawals meant that the US contemplated the use of these nuclear weapons against both Russia and China. These statements came long before Russian president Vladimir Putin said – disturbingly – that Russia would consider the use of nuclear weapons to attain its aims in Ukraine.[18]

With the conflict in Ukraine ongoing, it was obvious that NATO would foreground Russia at its 2022 Madrid Summit. But the materials produced by NATO made it clear that this was not merely about Ukraine or Russia, but about preventing Eurasian integration. China was mentioned for the first time in a NATO document at the 2019 London meeting and it was said that the country presented 'both opportunities and challenges'.[19] By 2021, the tune had changed: NATO's Brussels Summit communiqué accused China of 'systemic challenges to the rules-based international order'.[20] The revised 2022 Strategic Concept accelerates this threatening rhetoric, with accusations that China 'challenge[s] our interests, security, and values', and that China seeks to 'subvert the rules-based international order'.[21]

Four non-NATO countries, Australia, Japan, New Zealand and South Korea (the Asia-Pacific Four) attended the 2022 NATO summit for the first time, which drew them closer to the US and NATO's agenda to put pressure on China. Australia and Japan, along with India and the US, are part of the Quadrilateral Security Dialogue (Quad), often called the 'Asian NATO', whose clear mandate is to constrain China's partnerships in the Pacific Rim area. The Asia-Pacific Four held a meeting during the summit to discuss military cooperation against China, erasing any doubt about the intentions of NATO and its allies.

What nails in Eurasia have provoked the United States to wield its hammer at both ends, in Ukraine and in Taiwan?

In the wake of the revelations of the Third Great Depression and broken promises of the G7, the Chinese adopted two pathways to gain more independence from the US consumer market. First, they improved the domestic Chinese market, through increased social wages, integration of China's western provinces into the economy, and the abolition of absolute poverty. Second, they built trade, development, and financial systems that were not centred around the US. The Chinese participated actively with Brazil, India, Russia, and South Africa to set in motion the BRICS process (2009) and put considerable resources into the Belt and Road Initiative or BRI (2013), the former an economic and political grouping and the latter an investment structure for infrastructure and trade. China and Russia settled a long-standing border dispute, enhanced their cross-border trade, and developed a strategic collaboration (but, unlike the West, did not formulate a military treaty).

During this period, Russian energy sales to both China and Europe grew and several European countries joined the BRI, which increased mutual investments between Europe and China. Earlier forms of globalisation in Eurasia were limited by colonialism and the Cold War; this marked the first time in two hundred years that integration began to take place on an equitable foundation across the region. Europe's trade and investment choices were utterly rational, with piped natural gas through Nord Stream 2 being far cheaper and less dangerous than Liquefied Natural Gas from the Persian Gulf and the Gulf of Mexico. Considering the chaotic Brexit situation and difficulties in getting the Transatlantic Trade and Investment Partnership off the ground, much of Europe saw Chinese investment opportunities as far more generous and dependable than other alternatives. In contrast, risk-averse and rent-seeking private equity from Wall Street became less attractive to the European financial sector.

Europe was drifting inexorably towards Asia, which threatened the basis of the US-dominated economic and political system (also known as the 'rules-based international order'). In 2018, US President Donald Trump publicly chastised NATO's Stoltenberg, telling him: 'So, we're protecting Germany. We're protecting France. We're protecting all of these countries. And then numerous [sic] of these countries go out and make a pipeline deal with Russia, where they're paying billions of dollars into the coffers of Russia.... Germany is captive to Russia.... I think it's very inappropriate.' While NATO's language turned to threats of war against China and Russia, the G7 pledged to challenge China-led initiatives through the development of a new project, the Partnership for Global Infrastructure and Investment (PGII), a $200 billion fund to invest in the global South. In fact, the European Union does not object to Eurasian integration per se. In 2021, the European Parliament shared a briefing in which it called for this integration, but now defined by the Europeans rather than China.[22] Control over integration was far more important than the integration itself. China, which has been characterised as a military threat in these NATO discussions, accounts for merely 12 per cent of global military spending. As noted in our study *Hyper-imperialism*, 'The United States spends 21 times more on its military per person than China does.'[23]

Meanwhile at the BRICS summit, held at the same time, the leaders offered a sober appraisal of the times, calling for negotiations to end the Ukraine War and for measures to be taken to stem the cascading crises experienced by the world's poor. There was no talk of war from this body, which represents 40 per cent of the world's population and BRICS' strength may well grow as Argentina and Iran have applied to join the bloc.

The US and its allies seek either to remain hegemonic and weaken China and Russia or to erect a new iron curtain around these two countries. Both approaches could lead to a suicidal military conflict. The mood across the global South is for a more measured acceptance of the reality of Eurasian integration and for the emergence of a world order based on national and regional sovereignty and the dignity of all human beings. None of these can be realised through war and division.

* * *

In 2020, the Stockholm International Peace Research Institute (SIPRI) studied the correlation in low-income states between inflow of Overseas Development Assistance (ODA) and the outflow of money to buy arms. It is important to note that the largest military spenders are not the poorer nations, but the largest economies of the world. However, SIPRI found, 'it is often the poorest states that allocate the largest proportion of their government expenditure to the military'.[24] The countries that are the largest recipients of ODA are also large spenders on arms, although this should not surprise anyone. Poverty and despair – among the main drivers of conflict – are both the reason for ODA (to try to ameliorate the poverty) and for the arms (to quell insurgencies driven by despair). But here is the diabolical circularity of our problem: the root cause of so many insurgencies in the global South – poverty and despair – can only be uprooted in time, through a massive infusion of resources and ingenuity, whereas the insurgencies themselves must be dealt with immediately, so the arms sales become pressing. The numbers can be startling.

Nigeria's National Bureau of Statistics says that 133 million out of its population of 211 million live in poverty, roughly 63 per cent of the population. In 2002, the International Monetary Fund published a paper with a revealing title: 'Poverty in a wealthy economy: The case of Nigeria'. Nigeria's oil wealth, discovered in 1956, is leached by multinational corporations, and what little is invested goes into the capital-intensive urban areas of the south and not the labour-intensive rural areas of the rest of the country. This draining of wealth by the Western-based oil companies directly exacerbates existing regional and class imbalances. The immense poverty and despair in Nigeria, despite the outflow of oil, led Nigeria to the IMF's structural adjustment system in 1986. During the decades before and after the adjustment era, Nigeria lurched from insurgency (Biafra War, 1967–70) to insurgency (Boko Haram, started in 2009). Despite other options for the governments of Nigeria – if they had listened to the popular movements – they have decided not to challenge the plunder-austerity model of maldevelopment and to expand their military to fight the insurgency with force. In 2021, Nigeria increased its military budget by 56 per cent, to reach $4.5 billion. Just as the oil money was drained away by Western oil companies, the weapons money was leached by foreign arms dealers.[25]

The main victors in this diabolical circularity are the arms dealers, whose profits have been increasing steadily each year for the past decade.[26] Neither inflation nor supply chain issues dampen the enthusiasm for the new weapons systems, their feasibility less important than their delivery. Arms companies located in the five countries that hold permanent seats in the UN Security Council (P-5), and who therefore have a veto vote over UN actions, account for almost all of the arms sales in the world. Private companies, with billions of dollars in profits, dominate foreign policy decision making in these states, which then undermine any attempt to push forward a peace agenda at the UN. In other words, arms companies in the P-5 countries dominate the world system, not only in terms of the extraction of precious surplus wealth but through their commanding role over international institutions.

A clear example of how guns overwhelm International relations can be extracted from what happened at the December 1997 COP-3 meeting on climate change held in Kyoto, Japan. In October 1997, US government officials began to circulate a draft text that sought to exempt the US military – and potentially other military forces – from any and all carbon accounting. US Deputy Undersecretary of Defence for Environmental Security Sherri W. Goodman argued that the Kyoto Protocol would harm 'military readiness'. US Secretary of State Madeleine Albright argued, in a cable to Ambassador Mark Hambley, 'We believe energy use patterns may be similar in most NATO countries. Moreover, given the active involvement of many NATO countries in UN peacekeeping operations and NATO operations, such as for IFOR and SFOR (Implementation and Stabilisation Forces) in Bosnia, it would make sense to make sure operations were not compromised by greenhouse gas emissions limitations.'

Months later, Goodman wrote a letter to the *Washington Times*, in which she argued that the Kyoto Protocol would not hamper the US 'ability to conduct military operations' because it allows exemptions for 'multilateral' peacekeeping work, and since 'virtually all current military operations are multilateral in nature', these exemptions have great width.[27]

The Pentagon, which nonetheless worries about the national security risk of climate change, is the largest institutional polluter in the world.[28] Arms companies are two steps ahead of the Pentagon, eagerly trying to market their eco-weapons systems, attempting to greenwash war. Raytheon, for example, told the Carbon Disclosure Project in 2019 that it plans to invest in technologies that could be 'low carbon or do not require much fossil fuel'. Weapons based on laser technology, for instance, are to be part of this arsenal.

* * *

The trade in weapons and the reliance upon weapons to project power poisons the world, enabling the powerful to use force to get their way against those whom they deem to be adversaries. If you have a hammer that is big enough, why negotiate when you can just clobber your adversaries into submission? That's the situation of diplomacy in our world, where reason is set aside in favour of muscle. There are limits to the success of this strategy, since war and intimidation create new adversaries or deepen the frustration of those who are on the receiving end of the bombs.

Sitting with an arms dealer in Beirut (Lebanon), two of his six phones receiving texts in tandem on the table, I began to understand slowly how ugly the world has become. The war in Syria, just 100 kilometres away, shook Beirut each day, with refugees crossing the border and armed bands threatening to bring the war to the Mediterranean coastline. The arms dealer, a charming young man, told me that there are hundreds of men like him, people who sell small weapons to equally young men, who go about shooting people just like them. The documentaries and the stories, he said, are always about the petty dealer, the small-time thug who sells the guns to the end users. Too little attention, he said, is paid to the largest of the over a thousand producers of these small arms and their ammunition, the large companies that are mostly based in Europe and the United States. 'You see', he said to me, 'I am the criminal, the gangster, the wretched man who is responsible for the blood on the streets. And that might even be true', he said with a wry smile on his face. 'But, I don't make these guns. I only sell them, and that too after they have been sold to many people before I get my hands on them. The people who produce these guns and make a massive profit on them: they are not criminals, but businessmen.'

3

The Palestine Laboratory: An Update

Antony Loewenstein

Antony Loewenstein is an independent journalist, bestselling author, filmmaker, and co-founder of Declassified Australia. In this update to his recent bestselling book, The Palestine Laboratory, *he demonstrates how Israel has long used the occupied Palestinian territories as a testing ground for the most sophisticated weapons and surveillance technology that they have developed. Since 7 October 2023, Palestinians in Gaza have become guinea pigs in a grotesque war of annihilation, with the latest drones, killing machines and arms battle-tested by Israel and its foreign backers.*

The headline in Israeli newspaper *Haaretz* was unsubtle: 'Gaza becomes Israel's testing ground for military robots'.[1] In March 2024, the story explained how, 'in an effort to avoid harming soldiers and dogs, the Israel Defense Forces (IDF) have been experimenting with the use of robots and remote-controlled dogs in the Gaza War. Most of the tests have been with a "robot dog", which is also equipped with a drone.'

Months after the shockwave of 7 October 2023, both the brutal Hamas attack and genocidal Israeli response (for an account of the 2023–24 assault on Gaza, see Chapter 5), the Jewish state's decades-long plan to monetise the occupation has never been clearer. From killer drones to quadcopters and robot dogs to mass surveillance, Israel isn't wasting the opportunity of its onslaught on Gaza to battle-test the most sophisticated forms of inflicting death and injury, and monitoring success rates for potential global clients.

Many nations look at Israeli actions in Gaza with admiration and envy. Don't focus on what they say, even if they verbally oppose Israeli actions, but what they do with their defence spending in the months and years ahead. The Israeli arms industry has never been in better shape.

The most devastating attack on Palestinians in their history, more grievous than the 1948 Nakba, has resulted in the greatest number of civilian deaths and displacement ever recorded. Gaza has become a slaughterhouse with Western backing. Pushing aside the catastrophic intelligence failures on 7 October, and Israel's much-vaunted ring of steel around Gaza melting away in an instant, Israel's defence industry is busy working to erase the dark memories of that day and focus on new opportunities in Gaza.

Take the Israeli company Smart Shooter. After trialling a remote-control gun in the occupied Palestinian city of Hebron,[2] installed in 2022, the firm has become central to Israel's onslaught in Gaza. The IDF uses the firm's counter-drone technology, a tool purchased by other militaries around the world. The corporation's founder and CEO, Michal Mor, told an Israeli newspaper in late 2023 that it had been used successfully for the first time in Gaza.

Smart Shooter was also proud of 'dispersing demonstrations' due to a particular attachment to an Israeli rifle. 'When you don't want to kill but deter, the system will know how to hit, for example, only below knee', Mor said.[3]

During the Great March of Return in 2018 and 2019, when Palestinians in Gaza marched peacefully near the fence with Israel for their rights and freedom, Israeli snipers killed hundreds of Palestinians and injured thousands more (see

Chapter 5). A key goal, according to the snipers themselves, was to maim Palestinians below the knee.[4] One sniper, Eden, claimed to know how many knees he'd hit. He proudly kept the casing of every round that he fired.

This is how the Palestine laboratory works. Tested in Palestine and then exported around the world.

I've spent over a decade investigating Israel's military-industrial complex. The tenth biggest arms dealer in the world, Israel has used its decades-long occupation of Palestine as an invaluable testing ground for tools and technologies to control and repress Palestinians. Once shown to 'successfully' repress this population, the Israeli state and private companies market and sell these weapons, surveillance equipment and repressive tech to over 140 countries around the globe. From India to Finland and Bangladesh to Myanmar, Israeli equipment has become ubiquitous.

The Palestine laboratory is a danger to literally billions of people around the world.

From the early years after Israel's establishment in 1948, the country's leaders recognised that they had to build relationships with other nations. The export of weapons began in earnest in the 1950s and accelerated after the 1967 Six-Day War. Israeli politicians, even some nominally on the left politically, justified this industry as a necessary part of national survival.

But in doing so, the state partnered with some of the most authoritarian thugs on the planet from the Shah of Iran (until the collapse of the regime in 1979) to the dictator Augusto Pinochet in Chile and the apartheid regime in South Africa. Israel didn't hesitate to back and arm governments that were openly anti-Semitic, such as Nicolae Ceauşescu's Romania and Argentina's junta (a state that welcomed Nazi war criminals after the Second World War).

In the modern era, Israel has armed the regime in Myanmar, even after it was found by the UN to have committed genocide against the Rohingya Muslim population, and India under Prime Minister Modi, despite his plans to install a Hindu fundamentalist order in the country.

This presents a danger to all civilians. In February 2024, the Indian state of Haryana unleashed drones on protesting farmers, dropping teargas on them.[5] This tactic was familiar to Palestinians who routinely face this tactic across occupied Palestine.

The leadership in Haryana, including the chief minister and senior Indian police officers, had visited Israel in 2018 and met with Israeli intelligence officials along with a major Israeli arms company, Israel Aerospace Industries.

The trip coincided with the Great March of Return, where Israel dropped tear gas on protesting Palestinians. The Indian officials expressed a desire to 'sharpen' the state's police skills to crush public protests. The chief minister openly declared that he wanted to 'replicate' Israeli actions in his home state.[6]

The use of Palestine as a vital testing ground has become even more brazen since 7 October 2023. Media outlets sympathetic to the Israeli cause have breathlessly reported how many new weapons and tools Israel is using for the first time in Gaza.[7] These include a shoulder-fired missile, night vision, a drone targeting system and a missile defence shield. The stories glorify the new, shiny tools and ignore the people they're being used on.

The only way that Israel's use of Palestine as a laboratory can be stopped, or at least challenged, is through international pressure. There aren't enough Israelis who oppose Israel's endless occupation of Palestine and decimation of Gaza. These global actions could include an arms embargo, holding Israeli soldiers, politicians and military figures to account at an international court and economic boycotts against a Jewish state that still craves legitimacy. It mustn't be allowed to get it.

After killing tens of thousands of Palestinians in Gaza, Israel has lost vast swathes of the global public, especially the young. But the global weapons industry is harder to kill, a multi-trillion-dollar hydra that thrives on worsening conflict from Ukraine to Gaza.

Further Reading

Loewenstein, Antony, *The Palestine Laboratory: How Israel Exports the Technology of Occupation Around the World* (London: Verso, 2023).

PART II

The Impact of the Arms Trade

4

Militarism and the Climate Emergency

Stuart Parkinson

Stuart Parkinson is Executive Director of Scientists for Global Responsibility, a UK-based membership organisation promoting science and technology that contribute to peace, social justice, and environmental sustainability. His particular focus in recent years has been on military carbon emissions. Here he explores the military threat to the climate in some depth. He summarises the key military activities which contribute to the crisis, the available data on the size of the 'military carbon bootprint', and the range of responses from the world's militaries to the problem that they are partly responsible for. He critically assesses the idea that militaries are able to 'go green' – and looks at alternative approaches, including putting more resources into tackling the roots of conflict and insecurity, and conversion strategies for shifting skilled workers from the arms industry to low-carbon industries. Finally, Parkinson also takes a brief look at the other environmental impacts of war.

Militaries use vast amounts of fossil fuels – consumed by combat planes, warships, tanks and other energy-hungry equipment – and these release carbon pollution, making a major contribution to the global climate crisis. However, these emissions are largely hidden. Most governments either conceal them within other national carbon statistics or don't report them at all. Scientific reports barely mention them

– even those by the Intergovernmental Panel on Climate Change (IPCC), the UN's top advisory body on this issue. However, a few independent scientists and non-governmental organisations have uncovered sufficient data to point to a serious problem – and it's a problem that's likely to get much worse as global military spending rises in the wake of the Russian invasion of Ukraine.

The Climate Emergency: A Brief Introduction

The threat from human disruption of the global climate is immense. In 2021, the UN Secretary-General gave a now-famous speech in which he called the latest scientific evidence 'code red for humanity'.[1] He added, 'The alarm bells are deafening, and the evidence is irrefutable: greenhouse-gas emissions from fossil fuel burning and deforestation are choking our planet and putting billions of people at immediate risk. Global heating is affecting every region on Earth, with many of the changes becoming irreversible.'

'Anthropogenic climate change', also known as 'global warming' or 'global heating', is where the global climate system is disrupted from its natural state by human activities. This is mainly due to the burning of fossil fuels, that is, coal, oil and gas. Fossil fuel combustion emits 'greenhouse gases' (GHGs, also known as 'carbon emissions' or 'carbon pollution'), especially carbon dioxide, into the atmosphere and these trap the heat of the sun's rays causing the Earth's surface to heat up more than would naturally occur. This extra heat disrupts the usual climate, causing more extreme weather, especially heatwaves, droughts, and storms, and this, in turn, causes damage to human societies and natural ecosystems. The excess heat also enters the oceans, leading to sea-level rises, increased flooding, and damage to marine life. Through these various pathways, climate change can jeopardise water and food supplies, damage homes, and increase levels of infectious disease. These effects can then lead to political instability, migration, and potentially conflict. It will surprise few to learn that those countries and communities that are at most risk from climate change are those with already high levels of poverty and political instability – and burn the lowest amounts of fossil fuels.

As the UN Secretary-General warned, the atmospheric levels of GHGs are already extremely high. The IPCC publishes regular reports on the scientific evidence and it concluded that carbon dioxide levels in the atmosphere are now higher than at any time in at least the last 2 million years. It also concluded than the average global temperature is probably higher than at any time during the last 125,000 years. This means human civilisation has never experienced climatic conditions similar to how they are now.[2]

In 2015, the world's governments finalised the Paris Agreement, whose aims include 'holding the increase in global average temperature to well below 2°C above pre-industrial levels' and 'pursuing efforts to limit the temperature increase to 1.5°C'. Further scientific research since then – including a special report by the IPCC – has concluded that the global impacts of a 2°C temperature rise would be much worse than those of 1.5°C. The average level between 2011 and 2020 was 1.1°C – and it's increasing rapidly. The IPCC has estimated that global GHG emissions need to fall by at least 43 per cent from 2019 levels by 2030 to give a 50 per cent chance of hitting the 1.5°C goal.[3] Projections based on policies in place by the time of the Glasgow climate negotiations in November 2021 – 'COP26' – showed the world on course for a rise of between 2.0°C and 3.6°C by 2100.[4] Only full implementation of the pledges made at those negotiations – together with favourable assumptions regarding climate uncertainties – would bring the 1.5°C target into reach.

Global climate action since then has fallen far short. One significant factor that has diverted political attention has been the 2022 Russian invasion of Ukraine.

The Military Carbon Bootprint: How Big Is It? And How Is It Hidden?

Military vehicles – whether they travel by air, sea, land, or into space – consume a great deal of energy, mainly through burning oil-based fuels such as kerosene or diesel. The energy efficiency of these vehicles is generally very low due to their high speed or large weight. Hence, they release a lot of carbon emissions when they travel. Table 4.1 gives some examples of the carbon emissions per kilometre of military vehicles compared with an average new passenger car sold in Europe (at the time of writing). As can be seen, the unit emissions vary from 10 times to 5,000 times – and these figures increase further when the military vehicles are operating under combat conditions.

Table 4.1   Carbon emissions of selected military vehicles

Vehicle	Carbon emissions (gCO_2e/km)
Queen Elizabeth class (UK aircraft carrier)	550,000
C-5 Super Galaxy (US military transport plane)	38,000
F-35 Lightning II (US/NATO combat plane)	10,000
Humvee (US armoured truck)	1,100
New passenger car (European average)	110

Notes

Rounded figures calculated using data from various military sources and the European Environment Agency.

'gCO_2e/km' is grammes of carbon dioxide equivalent per kilometre, a standard measurement in this field.

But pollution from these vehicles is only part of the carbon emissions that result from military activities. Direct emissions come from two main sources: 'mobile' – as already discussed – and 'stationary' – that is, the energy used at military bases and at the buildings used by the government policymakers and administrators to manage the armed forces. Stationary energy includes heating and/or cooling of these buildings, and electricity use for lighting and all appliances. Then there are indirect emissions. These include the 'lifecycle' carbon emissions from the manufacture of everything from tanks to tanker aircraft, from uniforms to computer equipment, and from hangars to fuel. Other indirect emissions are due to the impacts of war itself. These include carbon emissions from burning buildings and fuel stores, damaged ecosystems, healthcare of survivors, and post-conflict reconstruction. This total impact has been called the 'global military carbon bootprint' – and Figure 4.1. summarises its main component parts.[5]

The data on the carbon emissions of the military are, in general, very poor. Nevertheless, a few researchers – including myself – have collected together this data, especially for North America and Europe.

For example, Professor Neta Crawford – in a scientific paper published by Brown University – used official data on military energy consumption to estimate the total core carbon emissions of the US military from 1975.[6] She showed that, in recent years, these emissions were larger than national totals for European countries such as Sweden, Finland or Denmark. Researchers at the universities of Durham and Lancaster in the UK have also published similar estimates of US military emissions.[7] Meanwhile, researchers at Scientists for Global Responsibility (SGR) and the Conflict and Environment Observatory (CEOBS) have pieced together military data from the UK and EU nations.[8] In addition researchers from the Netherlands and Ukraine published an estimate of the

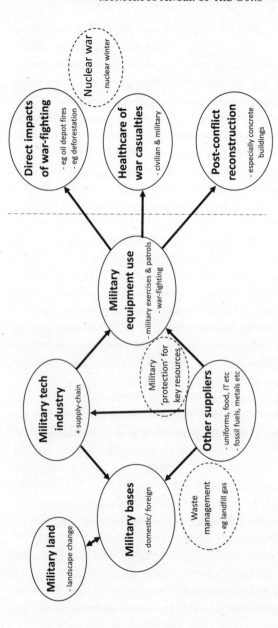

Figure 4.1 The military carbon bootprint: key components

Notes: Arrows indicate flows of materials and/or impacts between different components of the system. Dotted circles indicate activities that have climatic impacts from multiple parts of the system. Activities to the lefthand of the vertical dotted line are components of a conventional 'carbon footprint', whereas activities to the righthand of the line are unique to military activities. The total carbon emissions of both sides are known as the 'military carbon bootprint'.

carbon emissions to date due to the war in Ukraine.[9] It concluded these were equivalent to the level in a small European country.

A calculation of the global military carbon footprint – which I published at the end of 2022 – produced a figure of approximately 5.5 per cent of the total carbon emissions from human activities.[10] This is greater than the level for the whole nation of Russia. The estimate included core and supply chain emissions, but not those from war-related impacts, so the total contribution to climate change is likely to be even higher. Further research to reduce the uncertainty of these estimates is ongoing.

Why is the data so poor? In 1997, after pressure from the US government, the carbon emissions of many military activities were excluded from being reported under the Kyoto Protocol, a major climate treaty. In addition, many of the emissions that were reported were hidden under broader civilian categories. The 2015 Paris Agreement made military emissions reporting voluntary. Therefore, at present, no governments are obliged to report their military emissions, or to do so in a consistent and transparent way. This means that the data on which to base estimates are very sparse.

Figures 4.2a, b and c show some examples of military carbon emissions – comparing the data reported officially to the UN, the core emissions estimated by independent scientists, and the carbon footprint (also estimated by independent scientists). The discrepancies are very large.

Other Environmental Impacts of the Military

Apart from their huge carbon emissions, militaries also cause other environmental damage on an enormous scale. This takes a number of forms, the most common being pollution of air, water and land, direct destruction of ecological areas, and unexploded weapons being left behind after conflict. Militaries are also a key element of the 'extractivist economy', helping to defend fossil fuel and mining interests, especially in nations in the global South or through protection of international trade. A further serious concern is the extreme environmental impact should a nuclear war take place.

POLLUTION, ECOSYSTEM DAMAGE, AND UNEXPLODED BOMBS

When artillery shells, bombs and other explosives detonate during a war, they obviously cause a great deal of death and destruction among the human population. They also cause environmental damage by releasing pollutants into the atmo-

a) France, 2019

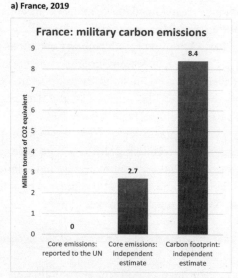

Sources: UN FCCC (2021); SGR/ CEOBS (2020)

Figure 4.2a   Comparison of data for national military carbon emissions

b) UK, 2017/18 figures

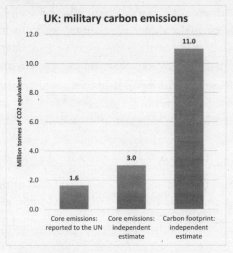

Sources: UN FCCC (2021); SGR (2019)

c) USA, 2018 figures

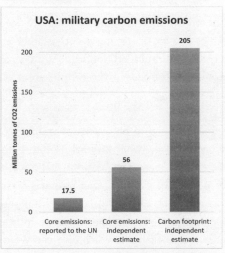

Sources: UN FCCC (2021); Crawford (2019); Parkinson (2021)

Figures 4.2b and c Comparison of data for national military carbon emissions

sphere, the ground (including the soil) and water courses (including rivers and seas). This pollution includes very small particles of the explosives themselves, as well as particles from all that burns in the ensuing fires – including buildings, fuels, forests, and other human infrastructure and natural ecosystems. These pollutants can be extremely toxic to human, animal and plant life, especially if factories and other industrial facilities are attacked. The pollutants can also be dispersed widely by the fires, and some are very 'persistent', meaning they remain a health and environmental threat for years, decades or even longer.

War also leads to direct destruction of environmental areas, including those managed by humans, such as farms, and natural ecosystems, such as forests and grasslands. These can jeopardise human sources of food and lead to major losses of wildlife. Infrastructure for supplying clean water can also be destroyed.

Often major environmental impacts of war are not apparent until the conflict is over or has moved to another area. This is especially true of unexploded bombs, landmines and other leftover weapons. These may make certain areas uninhabitable for years until they are cleared by specially qualified personnel.

But there doesn't need to be a war for militaries to cause serious environmental damage. Militaries often gain exemptions from the environmental regulations that govern civilian society. This means, for example, that military bases – especially those hosted by another country – are often much more polluting than similar-sized civilian facilities. Militaries also often own large areas of land in which they carry out training exercises, and these exercises can cause significant environmental damage.

DEFENDING UNSUSTAINABLE RESOURCE EXTRACTION

Fossil fuels and other minerals have been a key facet of modern industrial economies – including their militaries – so securing access to these resources has been a major political and military priority since the early days of the Industrial Revolution.[11] The history of oil has been especially bound up with military power due to both its high energy density – meaning it is an ideal fuel for the battlefield – and the concentration of oil reserves in just a small number of nations across the world. Securing access to oil has therefore been a key element of many wars fought over the last century or so – not least the two world wars.

In recent decades, developing nations with rich natural resources have been especially plagued by war and dictatorships as different interests struggle for control of those resources. Multinational oil and mining corporations have worked, sometimes covertly and sometimes overtly, with authoritarian regimes to gain access to fossil fuel and mineral reserves – frequently at major cost to human rights and the local environment. Indeed, access to fossil oil and gas has become a major issue in the war in Ukraine. As European nations ramped up sanctions on Russia following the invasion in early 2022, Russia retaliated by restricting sales of oil and gas – on which Europe has a high dependency. The result was a huge rise in international oil prices which helped the Russian economy while damaging economies in Europe and many other parts of the world.

A move away from fossil fuels to, for example, efficient use of renewable energy, would not only help tackle the climate crisis but also reduce the risk of war and its environmental impacts.

FROM NUCLEAR WEAPONS TO NUCLEAR FAMINE

Devastating as the impacts of 'conventional' wars are on the environment, they pale when compared to the impacts of nuclear weapons. The direct impacts are well known from the bombs dropped on the Japanese cities of Hiroshima and Nagasaki at the end of the Second World War in 1945, but further evidence has been deduced from nuclear testing during the Cold War and from computer models of the climate and wider environment since then.

Nuclear explosions initially cause damage through a combination of heat, blast and radiation, with the amount of devastation dependent on the size of the weapon. The intense heat created by a nuclear 'fireball' vaporises the immediate surroundings and causes major fires beyond. This is quickly followed by a blast wave which creates hurricane-force winds which flatten an even wider area. Then radioactive material is distributed far beyond. The explosive size – or 'yield' – of a nuclear weapon is measured as equivalent to a number of tonnes of TNT. For example, the bomb dropped on Hiroshima was equivalent to about 15,000 tonnes of TNT. A typical nuclear weapon currently deployed by the UK military is about 100,000 tonnes, with US and Russian warheads often being around five times larger. The biggest nuclear weapon ever tested measured over 50 million tonnes!

But the most catastrophic environmental impacts of nuclear weapons are not due to their direct effects, but their *indirect* effects. A 'regional' nuclear war – for example, involving around a hundred Hiroshima-sized nuclear warheads exploded over cities and other 'highly combustible' targets – would cause such intense fires, known as 'firestorms', that the smoke would be injected high into the atmosphere, above the cloud level. At this height, the smoke would linger and spread out, blocking the Sun's rays from reaching the ground, and causing a catastrophic cooling of the Earth's surface. This is known as a 'nuclear winter'. Many natural ecosystems would collapse and there would be widespread crop failures. As such, hunger would spread across the globe, in what some have called a 'nuclear famine'. Scientists believe that a 'global' nuclear war – involving most US and Russian nuclear weapons – would lead to an even more severe nuclear winter and famine, likely to end human civilisation. These effects were first investigated by researchers in the mid-1980s – with a host of academic papers updating the early work being published from 2007 onwards.[12]

The Myth of the Green Military

In recent years, some leading military figures have started to highlight the role that global heating can play in making armed conflict more frequent and more severe. Hence, disruption of the climate system is now commonly referred to as a 'threat multiplier'. As mentioned earlier, increasing climate change can damage crops (through heat stress or drought), homes (through storm or flood damage), and land (though more extreme weather in general). These problems can combine with other factors – such as poverty and inequality or ethnic and cultural friction – leading to political instability and at times even conflict. The IPCC – in its latest in-depth assessment report – summarises the evidence on this cycle of violence.[13] It concludes, however, that climate change only currently plays a very small role in increasing the risks – and, to tackle the problem, the focus should be on preventative measures which improve the resilience of society (discussed further in a later section). Nevertheless, militaries are starting to use the climate threat to argue for an even greater role in security strategies – and therefore even greater spending.

But the role of militaries in helping to fuel the climate crisis – due to their huge carbon emissions – is one of the obstacles to their having a large future role. Hence, those militaries that accept the scale of the climate threat – such as the UK and USA – argue that they can play a key role in reducing carbon emissions, by 'going green'. Unsurprisingly, with their huge energy consumption, this is not an easy thing to achieve.

An example of the climate strategies beginning to emerge from the military sectors is the UK Ministry of Defence's *Climate Change and Sustainability Strategic Approach*, published in 2021.[14] Typically, it argues that it 'will seek to use the green transition to add to capabilities' – which, in plain language, means it will try to use low-carbon technologies to give it an advantage on the battlefield. There is no suggestion in this or any similar strategy that nations will, for example, increase diplomatic efforts to find ways to reduce military confrontation and hence give space for the reduction in the current sizes of militaries. Neither is there any acknowledgement of the role in which arms control or disarmament treaties could be used to eliminate some of the high-carbon military technologies currently deployed.

So, the focus is on 'green weapon systems'. For example, the UK Royal Air Force (RAF) has set a target to be net-zero by 2040. A key element of its strategy is to use 'alternative fuels' in all its warplanes and other aircraft – first biofuels and later synthetic fuels.[15]

But there are a number of major obstacles to overcome.[16] First, the current proportion of aviation fuels (both civilian and military) manufactured from biological sources is about 0.01 per cent of the total. The industry is still in its infancy and it will take considerable investment and time to scale it up. Second, there are major environmental limits to how much fuel from biological sources can be supplied. Growing crops to produce such fuel is a virtual non-starter – both because this will compete for agricultural land with food crops and because the lifecycle carbon emissions are often greater than for the fossil fuels they are intended to replace. Using waste biofuels also has very limited potential – as almost all available sources are already being used, especially for road vehicles. This leaves biofuels manufactured from algae – which is still at an early stage of technological development.

Hence interest is turning to synthetic fuels. These fuels are made by harnessing electrical energy to create hydrocarbon molecules using the building blocks of carbon dioxide and water. If the electricity is supplied by renewable energy technologies – such as solar photovoltaic (pv) panels – then the production could, in theory, be ultra-low carbon. Unfortunately, there are two catches. The first is that the technology is barely out of the laboratory. In late 2021, the RAF boldly announced a major breakthrough – it had flown one of its planes on 100 per cent synthetic fuel produced using renewable energy.[17] The catch was that this plane was a microlight aircraft used only for basic training – and the total amount of fuel used in the flight was only 15 litres! The second problem is that synthetic fuels require a very large energy input to create the fuel – making it expensive, and a very inefficient use of renewable energy.

There are major obstacles in other areas too. One area where fossil fuels have been replaced in the propulsion system of a major weapons system is the use of nuclear power in submarines. However, this is extremely expensive and creates radioactive waste which is difficult to manage – even if the vessel manages to avoid being attacked in battle. An added problem for UK nuclear submarines is that the reactor fuel is weapons-grade uranium – so its supply creates major risks of the proliferation of materials which could be used to construct nuclear weapons.

There is one area where low-carbon technologies can be deployed for military purposes in a relatively uncontroversial way: the installation of on-site renewable energy technologies at military bases, for example, solar pv panels.

The overall problem remains, however. In a world where adequate resources are not being found to decarbonise the civilian sector fast enough to tackle the climate crisis, the additional demands of trying to decarbonise energy-hungry military technologies is a distraction we can hardly afford.

Military Spending v Climate Spending

The question of how to pay for the transition to an ultra-low-carbon society is one that has been prominent since the early days of the climate debate. At first, there was consider-able resistance due to the misguided belief that climate-related damage costs would be small. Thankfully, this resistance has reduced, but that hasn't yet led to adequate spending being put in place by the governments and industries of the wealth-ier nations.

The Climate Policy Initiative (CPI) – an international think-tank that monitors financial flows in this area – estimated that a global total of $632 billion was spent in the financial year 2019/20 on action either to reduce GHG emissions or to adapt to the effects of climate change.[18] Just over half of this funding came from governments and other public bodies, with the rest from private sources. Disturbingly, however, it also estimated that the annual spending necessary to keep global temperature change below the 1.5°C target in the Paris Agreement needs to immediately increase to about $3.5 trillion, and then rise to over $4.5 trillion by 2030, with further increases beyond then. If half of this additional funding came from governments, their collective annual spending gap would be around $1.4 trillion in the early 2020s, rising to over $1.9 trillion by 2030.

If we now look at global military spending, using figures compiled by the Stockholm International Peace Research Institute (SIPRI), we find that this climbed to over $2.1 trillion in 2021 – the highest level since the end of the Cold War and, as far as records show, possibly higher than at any time during that period.[19] All this funding came from government sources, the breakdown of which has been covered by Anna Stavrianakis in Chapter 1. Since then, of course, President Putin has ordered Russian troops to invade Ukraine – and many NATO governments have responded by announcing major increases in their military budgets. For example, Germany will spend an additional €100 billion over the next few years and other European nations will collectively spend a similar additional amount.[20]

A direct comparison between international government spending on military forces and spending on climate change shows that military spending is over six times larger (see Figure 4.3). Furthermore, the spending gap between current

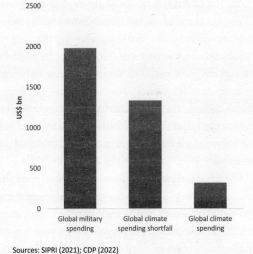

Sources: SIPRI (2021); CDP (2022)

Figure 4.3   Government military spending v climate spending across the world

levels of public climate finance and those necessary to hit the
1.5°C target is equal to about 65 per cent of global military
spending.

Peace and anti-poverty campaigners have, for many years,
argued that even a limited cut in military expenditure by the
world's highest spenders could release funding that would
make a major difference to reaching the UN's Sustainable
Development Goals (SDGs). These 17 aims include eliminat-
ing poverty and hunger, taking urgent action to combat climate
change, and promoting peaceful and inclusive societies.[21]

Changing the Mindset:
From National Security to Human Security

Global threats to human society vary widely in their nature
and scope. During 2020 and 2021, the Covid-19 pandemic led
to approximately 15 million deaths worldwide.[22] This is comparable with the death toll of the four years of the First World
War.[23] The number of deaths associated with the climate
crisis is more difficult to estimate due to the complexities
and uncertainties of the impacts. However, the World Health
Organization (WHO) estimates that between 2030 and 2050,
climate change will likely cause an additional 5 million deaths
due to malnutrition, malaria, diarrhoea and heat stress – with
many more from other causes.[24] If we do not rapidly cut global
emissions in line with the Paris Agreement, this death toll will
rise substantially.

These figures demonstrate the complex nature of threats to
society across the world. Only a small fraction of these could
be challenged by military forces and, in most cases, use of such
forces would have either a very small or a counterproductive
effect. This realisation has led to growing calls for governments to switch their emphasis from providing 'national
security' – with military forces playing the most prominent

role – to providing 'human security' – where resources are spread across government bodies in line with the scale of the threats, and with key roles being given to civil society organisations.

The United Nations has promoted the idea of human security since 1994,[25] and it can be summarised as follows:[26]

- Freedom from fear – including protection from violence and its threatened use, as well as from the existential threats of weapons of mass destruction, and climate and ecological collapse;
- Freedom from want – including provision of decent food, housing and healthcare, and freedom from other forms of physical deprivation;
- Freedom from indignity – including from human rights abuses and other forms of humiliation, such as autocratic rule and racial, religious or sexual discrimination.

In order to create a sustained shift in the security mindset, resources need to be progressively moved away from militaries to civilian agencies. Allocation of resources to these agencies should be proportionate to the scale of the human security threats, so that problems of ill-health, poverty, injustice, and environmental damage are tackled in a timely way.

There are some signs that governments are starting to broaden their approach to security. For example, every few years, the UK undertakes a National Security Risk Assessment and these have highlighted a range of major non-military threats to society, such as pandemics, weather-related hazards, and industrial accidents.[27] However, these assessments have not yet led to a significant shift in resources from the military to the civilian agencies. Indeed, Britain was ill-prepared for the Covid-19 pandemic, and actually slashed its foreign aid budget in 2021 while boosting its military budget.

Changing the Security Culture

A large part of the problem is the nature of military culture, especially in any state large enough to have its own arms industry.[28] It is now obvious that the greatest global challenge to human security is global heating leading to climate breakdown, and military think tanks, to give them their due, will often point to this risk and some have been prominent in highlighting their concerns. The military response, though, is not to argue for rapid decarbonisation but to prepare for the onset of the climate breakdown. While this might include some increase in the ability to respond to flooding, storms and other manifestations, it much more commonly focuses on protecting the state from the instability that will result. In the military culture, this 'defending the realm' is seen as the basic role, so it is not so much a matter of conflict prevention as of responding to the impacts of climate breakdown as they unfold.

Why this attitude persists is partly due to the very nature of what US President Dwight Eisenhower called the 'military-industrial complex', over sixty years ago. As a two-term Republican president and previously the top Allied commander in the Second World War, he warned of a system of the military, arms companies, think tanks and other groups all operating in a largely closed environment, often under conditions of secrecy. Moreover, as the complexes tend to embrace parliamentarians, checks and balances can all too frequently be inadequate.

In all the more powerful states, the system has evolved over many generations and has developed a culture of near immunity to criticism, always able to label critics as potentially unpatriotic. There is, furthermore, an aura of 'hegemonic masculinity' that permeates the culture, along with an expectation that, in most circumstances, the system will remain profitable despite many inefficiencies. Furthermore, the military-industrial complex has a remarkable ability to downgrade or even ignore past failures, while moving on to new challenges, the most prominent recent examples being the highly negative outcomes of the wars in Afghanistan, Iraq and Libya.

Arms Conversion:
Working for a Just and Sustainable Future

Changing this culture will not be easy given the power and influence of military-industrial complexes. However, it is essential if the need for radical decarbonisation is to be accepted, and an important element in this will be the need for arms conversion. In a highly militarised society, a lot of jobs are provided by the armed forces and their supply chains. Therefore, when shrinking the military's role, other jobs need to be created elsewhere in the civilian economy. If a society transitions towards a focus on human security, then there are numerous opportunities for 'economic conversion', including from the arms industry to civilian industries. This is known as 'arms conversion' or 'defence diversification'.[29]

Let's consider the arms industry in more detail. While this industry can provide high-skilled jobs, academic researchers have shown that it is one of the least economically efficient generators of employment. Hence, there is an economic argument for shifting to more productive sectors, such as renewable energy, energy conservation (both within industry and in homes), electric vehicles, and energy storage, which also help tackle the problems of climate change and energy security. As an example of the potential benefits, data from the University of Massachusetts has shown that investment in 'clean energy' has the potential to create 16,800 jobs per $1 billion spent, while military spending at the same level yields only 11,200 jobs.[30]

There are many examples of how this transition might work in practice. Those working in military ship-building can be retrained and re-employed to develop and manufacture civilian ships fuelled using renewable energy. They can also be re-deployed to work on renewable energy technologies that require understanding of fluid dynamics, such as wind, tidal and wave turbines. Electronic, electrical and mechanical engineering offer numerous opportunities for transition, including to renewable energy technologies and electric vehicles. Instead of building and maintaining military bases, those with construction and civil engineering skills could be re-deployed to improve the energy efficiency of civilian buildings.

Throughout history there have been many examples of societies emerging from armed conflicts and going through a 'demobilisation' process. For example, after armistices were declared to end the Second World War, millions of soldiers and industrial workers across the world shifted to civilian work in a matter of months.

Detailed study has been carried out on some of the more recent arms conversion programmes.[31] For example, in Germany in the early 1990s – after the end of the Cold War – military spending fell significantly and systematic efforts were made to move workers into other industries. Government at national and local level worked together with trade unions and companies, and this led to some important successes. One was the Bremen Defence Conversion Programme which operated in a region that was among the most dependent on military funding in the European Community. The programme supported over fifty companies with conversion projects, and saved many thousands of jobs.

Other conversion programmes have been analysed. In the former Soviet nations after the end of the Cold War, and in South Africa following the fall of apartheid, a variety of conversion schemes were run, but they were generally less successful because of a lack of cooperation between governments, companies and trade unions. The same fate befell the worker-led Lucas Plan, proposed in 1986 in the UK. The USA, during times when military spending falls, runs a Defense Industry Adjustment programme. As in the German case above, its success has depended on cooperation between government, companies and trade unions. All these programmes are discussed in more detail in a report by the UK-based Nuclear Education Trust.[32]

As governments and industries develop and implement plans to reduce carbon emissions, trade unionists and other social justice campaigners have emphasised the importance of a 'just transition'. This is where support is provided for workers in fossil fuel and other high-carbon industries to transition to jobs in greener sectors. The support may be, for example, retraining programmes or redundancy packages – and it is important that vulnerable workers are not left behind in the low-carbon transition. A similar rationale can be applied during an arms conversion process to ensure those in the military or weapons industries do not lose their livelihoods during the transition.

Towards a Greener, Demilitarised Future ...

Militaries are helping to fuel the climate crisis, and they have managed to hide the true scale of their impact. They are also responsible for a great deal of other environmental damage – beyond that caused directly to human society. While most militaries are in denial as to the damage they cause, a few have acknowledged some of the problems – but even these have simply responded by claiming they can 'go green' and deploy 'eco-weapons' that will give them a battlefield edge.

But there exist real solutions to these problems. First, we need a shift in the security mindset to prioritise protecting people rather than 'vital interests' – in short, a focus on 'human security' rather than 'national security'. Second, we need more diplomatic effort to find areas of 'common security' between different governments and peoples, accompanied by arms control and disarmament treaties that limit weapons and high-carbon military technologies. Third, we need arms conversion programmes which move government spending and workers from the military sectors into green jobs – allowing us to supercharge our transition to a sustainable society built on justice for all.

Further Reading

SGR, 'Climate change and the military: main outputs', accessed 25 March 2024, https://www.sgr.org.uk/projects/climate-change-military-main-outputs.

5

The Human Cost of the Arms Trade in Gaza

Ahmed Alnaouq

Ahmed Alnaouq is a former Palestinian diplomat who served in the Palestinian mission to the UK and is the co-founder of We Are Not Numbers. Here he writes about his family's experience in Gaza, living under the brutality of Israel's sustained campaign to occupy Palestine, and to suppress and commit genocide against Palestinian people. He writes about how weapons, supplied to Israel from around the world, form a part of the daily reality of life in Gaza. These countries and arms companies are complicit in the 2023–24 Israeli assault on Gaza, a horror that led to the loss of Ahmed's family.

No Longer Innocent

On one of my last days in Gaza four years ago, I was asked in a writing workshop to describe Gaza in just a few words. I replied, 'Gaza is a place where children are no longer innocent.' I understand that this description may be somewhat perplexing or even alarming to foreigners, but to me, it reflects a harsh reality. Several months later, I arrived in the UK to pursue my Master's degree in journalism, yet the image of Gaza's children still lingers in my mind today. Just a few days ago, as I walked to my office in London, I spotted several children playing with their bicycles on the steps of their house. Unable to suppress my thoughts, I found myself drawing comparisons between them and children of similar age in Gaza. While these London children were enjoying their playtime as they rightfully should, our children in Gaza are currently enduring starvation. While the London children are familiar with the names of various video games and amusement parks, our children in Gaza are well-acquainted with the types of weaponry used against them, inflicting terror upon their families. From as early as I can remember, my friends and I had an intimate knowledge of the missiles, helicopters and guns which were a part of our daily reality. Children in Gaza can tell one type of military aircraft from another, just by the sound filling the skies.

Perhaps when I mentioned that Gaza is a place where children are no longer innocent, I was reflecting on my own experiences growing up in Gaza and witnessing the challenges faced by children there. Or perhaps I was observing how my nieces and nephews navigate their lives, or perhaps recalling the stories recounted by my parents about their own childhoods. Consider my father, who was born in 1948 as a refugee in Dair al-Balah. During his birth, tragedy struck our family when his grandfather and his brother were killed by an Israeli bomb dropped from the sky while they were at the market, claiming the lives of 150 people in our city.

On that fateful day, my grandmother not only lost her father and uncle but also gave birth to my father. Although this massacre remains largely undocumented in history my aunt never ceased to speak of the sorrow it brought upon our family.[1] She herself was an only child and was compelled to flee her home in Yaffa to Gaza in 1948 alongside my grandfather. Despite the joy of welcoming a new baby, my aunt, who was just a few years old at the time, recalls the profound grief my grandmother experienced at the loss of her family.

Growing up in Gaza, I was surrounded by tales of my great-grandfather, Ali – stories of his bravery and resilience. I was told that he was the strongest man in our town and that he defied the British army during the Mandate period, resulting in his death sentence. Miraculously, he escaped from prison and sought refuge in Lebanon, where he married a Lebanese woman and lived for many years, before eventually returning to Palestine.

The Six-Day War

When my father was 19 years old, the 1967 Six-Day War erupted, and he couldn't pursue university due to the conflict and the responsibility of providing for his family after his father's passing. At the time, my mother was just 9 years old. She often recounts her memories of the years following the Nakba. My parents described how this war exposed them to new horrors, particularly the introduction of tanks as killing machines. Israel, lacking the capacity to manufacture their own tanks, relied on imports from France, West Germany and the US.[2] Following the war, Israel occupied the Gaza Strip, the Sinai Peninsula, the Golan Heights, and southern Lebanon. For us in Gaza, those years marked the beginning of ongoing horror – the military occupation.

Prior to the war's outbreak, my grandfather, Salem, constructed an underground shelter in his home in anticipation of conflict. It became the only refuge in the neighbourhood. As the war intensified, my grandfather ushered his family into the shelter, and soon neighbours sought safety there too. My aunt, Wesal, now 77, recalls the fear-filled days spent in the shelter, where she heard Israeli soldiers enter their home. Peering through a hole in the wall, she witnessed soldiers indiscriminately shooting people in the streets, with one neighbour tragically executed in his own home. She emphasises the danger they faced, knowing discovery would likely result in their deaths.

Following the Six-Day War, Israel occupied the entire Gaza Strip. My parents witnessed Israeli soldiers digging holes through school walls to shoot Palestinian students for sport.[3] My aunt recalls seeing soldiers celebrate after winning bets placed on injuring Palestinian children, with some aiming for eyes or legs. Among the most horrifying stories shared by my family is the practice of soldiers betting on the gender of foetuses in pregnant Palestinian women's bellies, then cutting them open to find out. Brutality against civilians occurred frequently during the 1967 war, leaving lasting scars on the collective memory of Gaza's inhabitants.[4]

My aunt recounted a harrowing tale of a man in their family shelter who had his entire family killed by Israeli soldiers. The invaders showed no mercy, leaving streets strewn with corpses. Another neighbour endured a different kind of torture; the Israelis murdered his eight children before his eyes, leaving him to mourn them for the rest of his days.

After the war, my father shared with me how the Israeli army continued to find new ways to torment Palestinians, including arbitrary imprisonments. He himself was incarcerated three times, each occasion lasting only a few days. When questioned about the reason for his detainment, he could only answer, 'They just felt like doing it.'

Gaza under Occupation

Israel's takeover of Gaza in 1967 deliberately undermined the local economy, fostering dependency. Many Gazans, including my father, were left with no option but to seek employment in Israel or remain unemployed. Despite being one of the brightest students in his school, my father did not pursue further education abroad, choosing instead to support his family after his father's death. He possessed a photographic memory and fluency in three languages – Arabic, English, and Hebrew. Even at 75, he could still recall lessons from his elementary school days. Like countless other Palestinians, he found himself compelled to work in Israel as a labourer due to the economic stranglehold imposed by Israel's weaponry, which devastated Gaza's economy. I remember my father waking up at 2 a.m. to catch a bus into Israel for work, enduring daily humiliations from his employer and Israeli soldiers at checkpoints. The seeds of resentment and resistance were sown in men like my father, who faced degradation and mistreatment. Palestinian labourers were often detained for hours or subjected to humiliating strip searches by Israeli soldiers for mere amusement. My mother, ever anxious for my father's safety, would spend her evenings waiting by the window for his return.

There's a story my father once shared with me when I was about five, and it has stayed with me ever since. His Israeli boss conveyed a deeply disturbing sentiment, asserting, 'God created only Israelis as humans; the rest of the world were animals, created to serve them. But the early Israelis were disgusted with the animals, so they asked God to transform them into human-like beings. And that's how you all came to be.' This anecdote underscores the dehumanisation many Palestinians face in the eyes of some Israelis. Fast forward to October 2023, Israel's Defence Minister Yoav Gallant imposed a 'complete siege' on Gaza, severing access to electricity, food, water, and fuel, declaring, 'We are fighting human animals, and we are acting accordingly.'[5]

In 1987, escalating harassment by some Israeli militias against Palestinian workers in Israel culminated in the deaths of six Palestinians, sparking the eruption of the first Intifada ('uprising'). The Israeli military responded with harsh measures, including curfews, mass arrests, and violent crackdowns, exacerbating hardships for Palestinians. Schools were shuttered, businesses disrupted, and movement severely restricted, leading to economic strife and social unrest. This period of civil disobedience and resistance fundamentally altered the daily lives of Palestinians, demonstrating their resilience in the face of oppression.

Growing Up

I was born in 1994, the same year the Palestinian Authority (PA) emerged following the signing of the Oslo Accords with Israel. The arrival of the PA raised hopes among Gazans for an end to Palestinian suffering and the attainment of freedom and sovereignty. However, their optimism was short-lived. Despite the Oslo Accords stipulating the establishment of a Palestinian state by 1999, the reality proved otherwise. Instead, the second Intifada erupted in response to Israeli harassment and the invasion of the Al-Aqsa Mosque by the Israeli prime minister.

The second Intifada exacerbated the already dire circumstances for Palestinians. Israel's restrictions intensified, particularly hampering Palestinian movement for work opportunities, leading to widespread unemployment. Many Palestinians, including my father, turned to taxi driving due to limited employment prospects. The uprising, fuelled by Israeli oppression, heightened tensions, violence, and loss of life. Palestinians faced daily confrontations with Israeli forces, checkpoints, and incursions into their communities, leaving deep scars on individuals and communities alike.

When the second Intifada erupted, I was only 6 years old, just beginning my journey to school. On my walks, I witnessed protests and funerals, and the sight of an Israeli tank invading Dair al-Balah, my city, remains vivid in my memory. The second Intifada introduced me to the ominous sounds of killing machines. Tanks, the first vehicles I saw roaming our streets, inflicted death and destruction.

One day, while en route to visit relatives in Gaza City, we encountered a tank blocking the road with soldiers nearby. Confused, I asked my father why it was there. 'To prevent people from crossing,' he replied, adding, 'just because it can.' I couldn't comprehend why tanks invaded our streets and claimed lives every day or two. However, insight came from an Israeli soldier's speech through Breaking the Silence, revealing a systematic strategy of intrusion and intimidation to ensure Palestinians remembered and feared Israeli presence.[6] When I think back on the second Intifada, I recall tanks, M16s, Apache helicopters, martyrs, stones, injuries, and, above all, fear.

Blockade and War

In 2007, Gaza fell under an Israeli blockade, depriving us of essential resources like food, water, gas, and electricity. At 12 years old, I remember my father gathering firewood daily for cooking as borders remained sealed. The blockade plunged us into a primitive existence, with factories shuttered, farming ceased, and medical crises ensued as hundreds of patients succumbed yearly due to border closures.

During Israel's assault on Gaza, starting on 27 December 2008, explosions shook our school as I nervously awaited an exam. The chaos outside evoked apocalyptic thoughts as casualties and destruction mounted. The aftermath saw 1,400 Palestinians killed, 5,000 injured, and 46,000 homes damaged or destroyed.[7] It was during this war that we learned of weaponry we had not encountered before, including the deadly F-16.

The F-16, emblematic of modern military might, instils profound fear and anxiety among Gaza's civilians. It is a fighter jet provided to Israel by the Americans, produced initially by arms producer General Dynamics, and now by Lockheed Martin. Its presence in the sky brings devastating airstrikes and symbolises the persistent violence and instability that have afflicted Gaza for decades. The roar of its engines overhead serves as a constant reminder of the ongoing horror and the vulnerability of life in Gaza. The F-16 is not merely a machine but a symbol of enduring trauma for the people of Gaza.

Then Israel also used different types of weapons on Gaza. During this 2008–9 war, we saw for the first time the use of white phosphorus, an internationally prohibited chemical weapon, intensively employed against the civilian population in Gaza.[8] My uncle's house was targeted multiple times with white phosphorus. Fortunately, he wasn't at home; otherwise, he and his family would have been killed. However, it was well-documented that Israel bombed a UN school with white phosphorus, killing and wounding over a dozen Palestinians seeking shelter.[9] Additionally, during this war, Israel introduced drones to Gaza and utilised them extensively. These drones have become another tool of control against Palestinians, not only for surveillance but also as killing machines, targeting and bombing civilians. Even after the war ended, these drones continued to hover above our heads day and night.

In 2014, Israel launched yet another war on Gaza, more severe and brutal than before, resulting in the deaths of more than 2,300 people. This time, my brother was among those killed by Israel. He was targeted with an F-16 plane and cut to pieces.

In 2018, Palestinians in Gaza, fed up with the ongoing situation and the 13-year siege imposed on them, called for an end to the blockade and demanded their right of return. They decided to march peacefully at the fence between Gaza and historic Palestine. Tens of thousands of Palestinians protested every week for two years. However, the Israeli army responded with live bullets and tear gas. As a journalist reporting from the scene, I lost count of how many times I was teargassed or shot at, but I survived. Unfortunately, some of my colleagues did not. Israel killed two journalists during the March of Return, along with many paramedics and over 300 Palestinian protesters (for more on the March of Return, see Chapter 3).[10] Israel employed different types of weapons against the protesters, including butterfly bullets that penetrate bodies and then explode, resulting in over 300 amputations.[11]

In 2021, Israel launched another war in Gaza, killing hundreds. This time, we witnessed a new type of killing: massacres. For the first time, Israel bombed entire buildings on top of their inhabitants. My colleague Zainab Alqolaq was among those whose homes were bombed by Israel, resulting in the loss of 22 of her family members. She was injured and buried underground for six hours. Hearing her story, I couldn't fathom her pain and suffering and how she managed to survive: until the following war occurred.

The Family Cost

In October 2023, Hamas launched a military operation against Israel, killing around 1,200 Israelis and foreigners.[12] Israel responded with a genocide. A massive, unprecedented war on Gaza, one that could even surpass the Nakba of 1948.

On 22 October, an Israeli fighter jet dropped a bomb on my home in Dair al-Balah, Gaza, killing 21 members of my family – my father, 2 brothers, 3 sisters, a cousin, and 14 nieces and nephews, all under the age of 13. Here are their names:

My father, Nasri Alnaouq, aged 75. My sister Walaa, 36, and her children: Raghd, 13; Eslam, 12; Sara, 9; and Abdullah, 6. My sister Alaa, 35, and her children: Eslam, 13; Dima,

12; Tala, 8; Noor, 4; and Nasmah, 2. My sister Aya, 33, and her children: Malak, 12; Mohammed, 9; and Tamim, 6. My oldest brother Muhammad, 35, and his children: Bakr, 11, and Basema, 9. And Mahmoud, 25, a human rights activist who had just been admitted to a Master's programme in Australia. My little brother.

Initially, three members of my family – Shimaa, Omar, and Malak – survived the bombing with wounds. Unfortunately, after a few days in the hospital, Malak succumbed to her severe burns. She was killed along with all her siblings and mother. Her father, Yousef, is the only survivor.

When Malak passed away, her father Yousef sent me a message on WhatsApp: 'Malak is martyred.' I responded, expressing my condolences. He replied, 'I am body no soul. I died a thousand times every day as I watched my daughter, my firstborn, die.' He then shared some final memories of Malak, bringing tragic but somewhat comforting closure to her story.

The other two survivors of the house bombing were Shimaa, my sister-in-law, 33 years old, and my nephew Omar, 3 years old. Both were injured but recovered after a few days. When Shimaa regained the ability to speak, she recounted the terrifying experience of the bomb's impact. She shielded Omar with a blanket to protect him from smoke inhalation as they lay trapped under the rubble. Miraculously, they were eventually rescued by neighbours.

'Muhammad wasn't just my husband,' Shimaa said. 'He was my father, my mother, my sisters, and brothers. He was my universe, and nothing in the world could replace him. And nothing could make up for my loss. My children were all so special. We had dreams for them, hoped to build a bright and meaningful future. And then, in a moment, all of my world collapsed. With one bomb, I lost my husband, my children, my home, and my family. I am Shimaa, I am destroyed.'

Shimaa's devastation mirrored my own, as well as that of my two other sisters who were not in my home at the time. My older sister, Doaa, had been there with her four children just one day before the bombing, but fortunately, they had left due to overcrowding. When I called Doaa afterward, she broke down, listing the names of our lost loved ones. Unable to contain my grief, I pleaded with her to stop.

In that moment, I empathised with Zainab Alqolaq and understood the depth of her pain, a feeling beyond words. I pray that such tragedy never befalls anyone else in the world. As the death toll of Israel's latest assault on Palestine surpasses 30,000 at the time of writing, in March 2023, I want to remind the world that every one of those deaths represents a parent, a child, a sibling or a loved one. We are not numbers.

6

Undermining the Chance for Peace in Yemen

Mwatana for Human Rights

Mwatana for Human Rights is an independent Yemeni organisation that documents violations of international humanitarian law and international human rights law committed by parties to the conflict in Yemen and publishes the results of its investigations. Here they take us through an overview of the conflict in Yemen, its historical context, and how it is being fuelled by Western arms that prioritise never-ending – and therefore profitable – warfare over any potential peace process. They share their perspective on how the arms trade undermines peace efforts and has created an entirely man-made humanitarian disaster in Yemen, while those driving it face no accountability. They lay bare just how devastating the war has been for the Yemeni people, the pattern of violations of international law by all parties to the war, and what is required on an international level to bring not just peace but also accountability, reparations and justice.

Introduction

Yemen's armed conflict began in September 2014, when Ansar Allah, generally known as 'Houthis', and forces loyal to former president Ali Abdullah Saleh took control of the capital Sana'a by force. In March 2015, Saudi Arabia and the United

Arab Emirates (UAE) began military operations in Yemen. According to the Yemen Data Project, up to March 2022 the Saudi/UAE-led coalition conducted 25,054 airstrikes, which have resulted in massive destruction in Yemen and left thousands of civilian casualties, including women and children.[1]

The regional rivalry in the Middle East has caused Yemen to pay a heavy humanitarian price, with the Saudi/UAE-led coalition supporting the internationally recognised Yemeni government that is fighting the Iran-backed Houthis. Western countries, especially the United States (US) and the United Kingdom (UK), are supplying arms to the Saudi/UAE-led coalition, in part due to Iran's involvement in the armed conflict in Yemen. These Western weapons have been used in countless attacks on Yemen, many of which violate international law. The parties to the conflict, including the supplying countries for the Saudi/UAE-led coalition, show little to no respect for the laws of armed conflict, including agreements that prohibit the sale of weapons to the violating parties who caused the deaths and injuries of civilians. A clear pattern of repeat violations has been well established.

Armed conflict in Yemen has been fuelled by the global arms trade, and this trade is directly complicit in the loss of civilian life and widespread infrastructure damage that have resulted from the war. The arms trade undermines peace efforts and causes untold damage, all while making vast profits for the companies involved, who remain seemingly immune from accountability.

Civilians in Yemen have suffered hugely from this armed conflict. After nine years of war, Yemen is still facing one of the world's worst humanitarian crises. While the number of people relying on humanitarian assistance has decreased compared to previous years, 18.2 million people, over half the population, still need to rely on humanitarian assistance in 2024.[2] Only half of Yemen's health facilities are considered operational,[3] and a huge number of healthcare facilities and schools have been destroyed by airstrikes and ground shelling.

We would like to deliver a clear message to all societies around the world that the crisis in Yemen is man-made. There is hope that the international community will pressure the seller countries to stop selling weapons to the parties that commit grave violations in Yemen, as well as pressure the warring parties to sit at the table and negotiate over the outstanding issues and put an end to this disastrous war.

Background and the Development of War

Yemen is a country located in the south-western part of the Middle East, south of Saudi Arabia. In the Middle East and North Africa, Yemen ranks among the poorest countries and has the lowest human development indicators.[4] Much of Yemen's ongoing humanitarian crisis results from long-standing and complex local and regional dynamics. Meanwhile, corruption, severe poverty, and the absence of state institutions and the rule of law have ravaged the country. Yemen is also severely impacted by the climate crisis.

As part of the Arab Spring uprisings in the Middle East and North Africa in early 2011, protests began in Yemen, initially against unemployment, economic conditions, corruption, and government proposals to amend the constitution. The protesters' demands then escalated to calls for the resignation of Yemeni President Ali Abdullah Saleh. The Gulf Cooperation Council brokered a power transfer agreement in Riyadh on 23 November 2011, under which Saleh transferred power to his vice president, Abd-Rabbu Mansour Hadi.

Yemen's Comprehensive National Dialogue Conference opened on 18 March 2013 in Sana'a, with the goal of bringing together all political parties in Yemen to begin a process of reconciliation and transitional justice. It lasted for ten months until 25 January 2014, ending with the deepening of a political dispute over the division of Yemen into six regions.

The armed conflict began on 21 September 2014, when Ansar Allah 'Houthis' and Saleh forces took control of Sana'a. The Houthis began as a religious and political rebel group in northern Yemen, became a party to the conflict in Yemen and are now the de facto authority in much of the country. During March 2015, a Saudi/UAE-led coalition began military operations against Houthis and Saleh forces in support of the internationally recognised government of former president Abd-Rabbu Mansour Hadi. The coalition also blocked imports into the country by air and sea. Most parts of Yemen, especially in southern governorates, continued to see heavy fighting between the parties to the conflict. In December 2017, the alliance between Saleh and the Houthis collapsed, with armed clashes in Sana'a, leading to Saleh's assassination.

In May 2017, Aydarus Al-Zubaydi, backed by the UAE, established the Southern Transitional Council (STC) to unite all social and political forces in the south for secession from Yemen. In 2018, the STC's forces ousted the government from Aden (the temporary capital of Yemen) and the surrounding area. Saudi Arabia intervened to reinstall the government and drew up the Riyadh Agreement of 2019.

Several rounds of peace talks continued to attempt to produce a sustainable ceasefire agreement. One of the most important negotiated ceasefire agreements, centred on the port city of Hodeida, was reached in Sweden on 13 December 2018, but did not translate into a pathway toward peace.

In February 2021, the Houthis intensified their attacks on Marib, the last northern stronghold of the internationally recognised government, which was the bloodiest and longest battle of the war. In the aftermath, the Saudi/UAE-led coalition forces increased their use of airstrikes, including against

Sana'a, while the Houthis attacked several Saudi Arabian and Yemeni areas with missiles and drones.

As of October 2021, the United Nations (UN) Human Rights Council revoked the mandate of the Group of Eminent Experts on Yemen to investigate violations and abuses in the Yemen war. Reports suggest Saudi Arabia used 'incentives and threats' to pursue a shut-down of the investigation.[5]

Yemen's armed conflict now involves several warring states and non-state armed groups. Parties directly involved in hostilities include state members of the Saudi/UAE-led coalition, the regular armed forces of the internationally recognised Yemeni government and non-state armed groups like the UAE-backed STC, and the Joint Forces on Yemen's west coast. They are all in a military confrontation with the Houthis, who have taken control of Yemen's densely populated north-western regions including the capital Sana'a.

On 7 April 2022, the Presidential Leadership Council (PLC) was formed by presidential decree in Riyadh, Saudi Arabia, to succeed the then-President Abd-Rabbu Mansour. Rashad Muhammad Al-Alimi chairs the council, which consists of eight members and has all the powers of the president and vice president. The UN Security Council highlighted this announcement of the peaceful transfer of presidential powers and welcomed the creation of the PLC.[6]

In April 2022, the UN Special Envoy for Yemen, Hans Grundberg, announced a two-month truce between the internationally recognised government backed by the Saudi-led coalition, and the Houthis. There were then two further extensions, but the truce expired in October 2022. All offensive military operations in Yemen and across its borders were suspended under the truce. As part of the agreement, fuel ships were allowed to enter the ports of Hodeida governorate, and commercial flights were also allowed to fly from Sana'a airport to predetermined destinations. Additionally, the two parties agreed to meet under the auspices of the UN Special Envoy to open roads in Taiz and other governorates.[7] The parties in Yemen released nearly 900 conflict-related detainees in April 2023 following a plan agreed upon by the parties to the conflict at the last meeting of the Supervisory Committee on the Detainee Exchange Agreement. The Supervisory Committee is co-chaired by the Office of the Special Envoy of the Secretary-General of the UN to Yemen and the International Committee of the Red Cross (ICRC), with the membership of the parties to the conflict.

Since the official truce expired, violence has not returned to pre-truce levels. In December 2023, parties to the conflict committed to a set of measures to implement a nationwide ceasefire, improve living conditions, and engage in preparations for the resumption of an inclusive peace process.[8] This would include the opening of access to Taiz, as well as an easement on continued restrictions on Sana'a airport and the port of Hodeida, Yemen's main shipping lifeline. As of March 2024, the UN Special Envoy was engaged in efforts to stabilise the de facto peace process and develop a roadmap to end the war.

However, the UN's efforts are complicated by regional and national developments. In November 2023, the Houthis began attacking commercial ships in the Red Sea in response to Israel's conduct of hostilities against Palestinians in the Gaza strip. Consequently, an American and British-led military coalition has increased naval operations in the Red Sea and launched several airstrikes against targets in Yemen since January.

In a February 2024 UN Security Council briefing, the UN Special Envoy noted a 'sense of foreboding' along frontlines, with reports of clashes, mobilisations and casualties.[9] At the time of writing, the situation both nationally and regionally remains volatile.

The Impact of the Conflict

For years through the war, various international agencies described Yemen as the world's worst humanitarian crisis. By the end of 2021, the conflict was estimated to have cost Yemen's economy $126 billion[10] and, according to estimates by the United Nations Development Programme (UNDP), 377,000 people had been killed, of whom nearly 60 per cent died due to indirect conflict-related causes, such as lack of access to food, water and healthcare.[11] In September 2023, the UN Food and Agricultural Organization (FAO) estimated in a representative survey of Yemeni households that 71 per cent of households were moderately or severely food insecure.[12] Five million children under 5 are estimated to require treatment for acute malnutrition in 2024.[13]

People struggle to access food, safe drinking water and adequate health services. The war in Ukraine has further threatened food supplies, as almost half of the imported wheat used to come from Ukraine and Russia.[14] In some Yemeni governorates, mainly in Taiz, 25 per cent or more of people now live in areas where the availability of water, sanitation, and hygiene has completely collapsed.[15] Other critical infrastructure, such as roads and bridges, has been widely damaged. Almost 90 per cent of the population has no access to publicly supplied electricity. Access to health services relating to gender-based violence remain virtually non-existent, with less than 5 per cent of health facilities providing clinical management of rape or other forms of gender-based violence. Landmines and explosive remnants of war continue to impede farming, kill civilians, and prevent displaced people from returning home.

Only half of Yemen's health facilities are considered operational, with many lacking staff, equipment, and basic medicines, especially in hard-to-reach areas. The armed conflict and its many and changing active frontlines, economic decline, and natural disasters such as floods, are placing further stress on the health system by exacerbating existing vulnerabilities.

Many schools have been affected by the war in terms of their educational systems, educational processes, and physical structures. Two thirds of all Yemeni teachers have not been paid in years. In addition to a large number of students dropping out of school, the armed conflict has limited access to schools for those displaced. During the truce, attacks on schools reduced; however, as of October 2023, 2,426 schools remained destroyed, partially damaged, or used for non-educational purposes, for example as shelters.

In September 2021, Mwatana and Global Rights Compliance (a not-for-profit organisation specialising in international humanitarian, criminal and human rights law) published a report entitled *Starvation Makers* that sheds light on the impacts that warring party attacks and other conduct have had on Yemenis' lives.[16] It concluded that members of the Saudi/UAE-led coalition and the Houthis used starvation as a method of warfare. The conduct of the coalition severely impeded civilians' access to food and water, and they acted in spite of the widespread knowledge of the dire humanitarian situation in Yemen, where people, including children, were dying from starvation. Members of the Saudi/UAE-led coalition and the Houthis were either aware of the virtual certainty that, following their conduct, starvation would occur without humanitarian intervention – or this was their intention.

The armed conflict in Yemen has been devastating for the country's civilians. In addition to destroying hospitals, homes, markets, and transport infrastructure, weapons have caused the death and injury of thousands of civilians, with survivors often pushed into poverty. The catastrophic humanitarian crisis in Yemen is the result of the arms trade's role in prolonging the Yemeni conflict.

Arms sales create big business for Western countries, but they come at the expense of human rights and reduce the likelihood of achieving stability. At present, the global arms trade is a substantial financial and political deterrent for the international community to encourage in a meaningful peace process. Peace and stability efforts in Yemen must be supported by the international community, not discouraged through arms sales.

Pattern of Violations

Since the outbreak of the armed conflict in Yemen in late 2014, warring parties have been gravely violating the laws of war (for a discussion of the legal frameworks at play, see Chapter 14). Mwatana has documented thousands of incidents, some of which amount to war crimes, including airstrikes, ground attacks, landmines, attacks on hospitals and schools, denying access to humanitarian aid, arbitrary detention and torture, and assaulting public and individual freedoms.

The sale of weapons and ammunition to conflict parties is a key factor in the deterioration of the conditions in Yemen. The clear pattern of violations demonstrates that continued arms sales to warring parties contributes to international crimes, and it is doubtful that the governments and executives that export weapons are unaware of this fact.

AIRSTRIKES AND THE ARMS TRADE

Since 2015, Saudi Arabia and the UAE have led military operations in Yemen. According to the Yemen Data Project, between March 2015 and April 2022 the Saudi/UAE-led coalition conducted nearly 25,054 airstrikes, which have resulted in around 19,226 civilian casualties.[17] There have been more than 1,000 airstrikes documented by Mwatana which have resulted in civilian casualties, and severe damage to vital civilian assets such as hospitals, schools, and other places essential to civilian survival.[18] The targeting of civilians in war constitutes a direct violation of international humanitarian law.

Despite this evidence, the US, the UK and various members of the European Union continue to support the Saudi/UAE-led coalition, providing them with weapons, munitions, training and operational support. From 2010 to 2019, around 19 per cent of arms imports to Saudi Arabia came from the UK, and around 60 per cent from the US.[19]

While arms sales from Western countries such as the UK, US and France to Saudi Arabia and the UAE long pre-date the current conflict in Yemen, these sales have only increased since the mounting evidence of international crimes in Yemen. Since the start of the military campaign of the Saudi/UAE-led coalition in March 2015, the sale of more than £11 billion worth of British arms has been authorised to Saudi Arabia. The US also has a long history of dealing weapons to Saudi Arabia: between 2013 and 2017, Saudi Arabia and the UAE purchased more than a quarter of US arms exports.

Among the most commonly used weapons in the war are the Typhoon and Tornado fighter jets, which are the result of joint production systems involving several European companies, such as BAE Systems (UK), Airbus Defence and Space (Germany and Spain), Leonardo (Italy) and Panavia Gmbh (Germany). These aircraft are also equipped with European bombs and missiles, including the Brimstone and Storm Shadow missiles manufactured by MBDA (UK and France), as well as the Paveway IV bombs produced by Raytheon UK, and the Rheinmetall Italia bombs of the MK 80 series. Targeting devices that enable the launch of these bombs are provided by the French company Thales and others.

In some cases, the only guide to finding out the companies involved is to find remnants of exported weapons at the sites of the air strikes, many of which violate international law. Mwatana, the University Network for Human Rights, and the

Dutch peace organisation PAX published a report in September 2021 titled *Day of Judgment*,[20] which documents 27 Saudi/UAE-led coalition attacks: weapons remnants indicate that in 22 incidents, a US-made weapon was likely used; in 2 incidents, a UK-made weapon was likely involved; and in the last 3, weapons found were joint-made by the US and the UK. The suspension lug for a US-made bomb used in one of the attacks was produced in Italy.

These 27 coalition airstrikes include 16 attacks on civilian gatherings, civilian homes, and a civilian boat; 5 attacks on educational and health facilities; 5 attacks on civilian businesses; and an attack on a government cultural centre. They killed at least 203 people and injured at least 749. At least 122 children and at least 56 women were among the dead and wounded. Many of the attacks appear to have taken place far from any potential military target. Others caused harm to civilians that vastly outweighed any likely military benefit.

Moreover, many arms companies and military contractors in the UK and US supply the personnel and the expertise necessary for maintenance, training and support services to the coalition forces. The conflict is not framed as a British war, and yet British bombs are being dropped by British planes, which are maintained by British personnel and flown by British-trained pilots. In 2019, a former BAE Systems worker revealed how crucial this support is: '[w]ith the amount of aircraft they've got and the operational demands, if we weren't there, in 7 to 14 days there wouldn't be a jet in the sky'.[21] It is hard to deny that these countries, thousands of kilometres away, are complicit in the horrors of the war in Yemen.

ATTACKS ON HEALTHCARE FACILITIES

The warring parties in Yemen have repeatedly attacked an already collapsed medical sector in extremely dangerous humanitarian conditions, worsened by the outbreak of Covid-19 and other diseases such as cholera.

A report, published by Physicians for Human Rights and Mwatana in 2020, documents 111 attacks on health facilities and medical personnel in Yemen between March 2015 and December 2018.[22] Attacks on medical facilities and personnel have had a particularly acute effect on the civilian population. The warring parties have damaged or destroyed health facilities in airstrikes and shelling, occupied medical facilities, and assaulted medical professionals, among other abuses. These attacks have been a determining factor in the collapse of Yemen's health system.

ATTACKS ON SCHOOLS AND EDUCATION

Education has been severely eroded as a result of grave violations committed by the parties to the conflict, which caused material damage to schools as well as death and injury to students and teachers.

In August 2020, Mwatana produced a report entitled *Undermining the Future*, which analyses warring parties' attacks on schools and education facilities between March 2015 and December 2019.[23] The study is based on more than 600 interviews with witnesses, victims' families, parents, and education workers conducted in 19 of Yemen's 22 governorates. Mwatana documented more than 380 incidents involving schools and educational facilities in Yemen. The documented incidents can be put in four main categories of attack. First, the impact of Saudi/UAE-led coalition airstrikes on educational facilities – Mwatana documented 153 coalition airstrikes on or impacting schools. Second, attacks during ground fighting – Mwatana documented 36 ground attacks on or impacting schools. Third, military use and occupation of schools – Mwatana documented 171 incidents of military use and occupation of schools. In addition to these three primary patterns, Mwatana documented 20 incidents of other forms of abuse impacting schools, examples of which are included in the report's final section.

In January 2021, Mwatana released a study called *War of Ignorance* based on data collected from students in 137 government schools between February and April 2020.[24] It highlights the conflict's many negative impacts on students: 81 per cent of respondents in the main sample of 400 students had to stop studying for varying periods due to the armed conflict. Students reported a variety of causes which prevented access to education, including direct damage to schools and the use of schools as military barracks, shelters for displaced people and centres for aid distribution.

Of the displaced students surveyed, 67 per cent said that military confrontations caused their displacement. Other reasons included exposure of homes to ground shelling, airstrikes on homes, and lack of job opportunities in the original community.

DENIAL OF HUMANITARIAN ACCESS

Yemeni civilians have limited access to food, medicine and fuel, essentials for survival. The Yemeni economy is heavily dependent on imports. Taiz city's eastern crossings remain closed by the Houthi group, as well as roads in Marib and Hodeida. Due to Saudi coalition restrictions on air, land and seaports, humanitarian aid has been impeded.

On land, Mwatana has documented hundreds of instances of denial of humanitarian aid and essential materials for the survival of the civilian population. Actions obstructing access include looting, hindering projects and interfering with their implementation, engaging in air strikes and ground attacks, and assaulting humanitarian workers by threatening, kidnapping, and detaining them.[25] All parties to the war have committed these violations, the large majority of the instances documented in detail by Mwatana have been attributed to the Houthis. Notably, in 2023, Houthi forces continued to close vital routes into Taiz.[26]

At sea, the blockade of shipping, both humanitarian and commercial, into Yemen has for years contributed gravely to the humanitarian crisis. The sea blockade has been imposed by the Saudi/UAE-led coalition. Access to Yemen's main ports and the airport in Sana'a, previously virtually completely blockaded by the coalition, has improved but not yet been fully restored after the initial truce. Yet, while according to the figures from the UN Verification and Inspection Mechanism for Yemen from 2022, the year of the truce, average monthly imports of fuel increased compared to the two previous years,[27] they remained at less than half the necessary import levels as calculated in 2015.[28]

The blockade was imposed using weapons made or designed in the West. The Saudi and UAE navies are made up of French, British, German, Italian, and Swedish-made ships and fitted with Western arms.[29] In many cases they were supplied with weaponry at the same time as Yemenis were being deprived by the basic necessities of life using these very ships.

Accountability and Reparation

Yemen has yet to see credible accountability or reparations despite repeated cycles of violence. Since 2011, when Yemenis rose-up against long-time president Ali Abdullah Saleh, none of the wide range of perpetrators that have committed or enabled grave human rights abuses and serious violations of international law in Yemen have been held accountable. Civilian victims continue to wait for reparations addressing the significant harms done to them. This overwhelming envi-

ronment of impunity has facilitated the abuses that continue
to be carried out by local, regional and international actors in
Yemen.

Throughout the current conflict, Mwatana has documented
international law violations, some of which amount to war
crimes, by parties to the conflict in almost all of Yemen's governorates, including violations committed by the Houthi armed
group, the Saudi/UAE-led coalition, the internationally recognised government, the UAE-backed STC and Joint Forces,
and other armed groups and forces active on the ground.
Other countries – including the US, UK, Iran, France, Italy
and Germany – have continued to provide support to the
warring parties in Yemen.

The Saudi and UAE-led coalition, the internationally recognised government of Yemen, and the Houthi armed group
have all made promises to provide aid to civilian victims of
their abuses. Mwatana for Human Rights and the Allard K.
Lowenstein Clinic at Yale Law School published *Returned to
Zero: The Case for Reparations to Civilians in Yemen*, which
describes the assistance offered as 'grossly inadequate'.[30] This
report examines the international legal obligations of states and
non-state armed groups to provide reparations in Yemen, the
promises that warring parties have made to provide assistance
or redress to civilians, and the most significant mechanisms
that warring parties have set up to respond to civilian harm
since the conflict began. It calls for the warring parties to fulfil
their 'legal and moral responsibility' to provide the reparations owed to the people of Yemen. In 2023, Mwatana released
The Struggle for Justice report describing both the impunity
of the parties to the conflict and the avenues for accountability.[31] These include the domestic judicial systems of the parties
to the conflict, the International Criminal Court, and foreign
domestic courts in countries that supply arms into the conflict.
Mwatana has been a part of several legal challenges relating to

arms sales, notably in France, Italy and the UK. Of the cases brought in a number of jurisdictions, so far partial successes have been recorded in the UK and Belgium. In Belgium, courts have called for the suspension or annulment of several contested licences for the export of arms,[32] whereas in the UK new export licences to Saudi Arabia could not be granted for approximately one year as a result of litigation in 2019–20. However, a number of cases are still pending as of February 2024, including at the International Criminal Court. The fight for accountability will be the focus of Mwatana's work going forward in our quest for justice for the people of Yemen.

7

The Scourge of Arms
in East Africa

Tabitha Agaba and Ian Katusiime

Tabitha Agaba is a researcher and an advocate whose work focuses on transnational organised crime, crime based illicit financial flows and corruption. Ian Katusiime is a Ugandan journalist, researcher, governance consultant and foreign policy analyst. Here they explain the long-term effects of the Lord's Resistance Army war in northern Uganda and the widespread and varied crises it caused in the region. They also tackle the attendant post-conflict crises, the attempts at conflict resolution and Uganda's response to the resulting refugee situation. They examine the general impoverishment wrought by arms trade, trauma, its impact on the most vulnerable — women and children — and the inevitable outbreaks of disease occasioned by war and insecurity.

Uganda

The greatest tragedy the nation of Uganda has faced is the twenty-year insurgency waged by the Lords' Resistance Army (LRA) led by a former altar boy, Joseph Kony. The LRA had visions of ruling Uganda based on some form of Christian fundamentalism. An estimated 100,000 people were killed and as many as 2.5 million were displaced in the conflict which centred around the Acholi sub-region in the northern part of the country.

Although the war ended in 2006, its scars remain seared in the nation's conscience. Thousands of children were orphaned and women left widowed. Families were destroyed in unimaginable ways: girls were abducted on a vast scale and turned into sex slaves and teenage wives for rebel commanders, while boys as young as ten were conscripted as child soldiers.

The war also took a grave toll on the schooling system. Schools in Acholi went through phases of displacement, forced to relocate to Gulu town or other 'protected areas' to escape the fighting.[1] In Gulu, government soldiers had some control and many non-governmental organisations (NGOs) set up a host of social services. There were also 'amalgamation schools' like Gulu High School where many teachers and students converged.

The war led to another scourge on the social fabric of the country with the creation of camps for internally displaced people (IDPs), established in the Lango region between 2002 and 2004.[2] An estimated 2 million people were living in these camps by 2006, at the time the war was ending. In addition, nearly 800,000 were still waiting for the infrastructure of their abandoned villages to be put back together.[3] The harsh reality of war ensured that hundreds of thousands of Ugandans spent some of their prime years sheltered in IDPs scavenging for food, water, safety and other basic necessities.

The weapons that sustain insurgencies like those waged by the LRA are not tanks and fighter jets, but small arms and light weapons (SALW). These include revolvers, AK47 rifles, and shoulder-fired missiles sometimes described as Man-Portable Air Defence Systems (MANPADS). The proliferation of these weapons is the reason the conflict was able to drag on for twenty years.

Seventeen years after the guns fell silent in the LRA war, the Acholi region in Uganda has tried to rebuild a life for its citizens. Monumental challenges remain as victims of the war live with the trauma. Some of those with deep scars were victims of rape during the violence.

For schools in Gulu, the epicentre of the LRA war, teachers received training on dealing with students with war trauma, and peace clubs were introduced in schools as a form of psycho-social support.[4]

Sudan

There were widespread reports that the LRA was being supported by Sudan, then under President Omar el Bashir, who supplied them with arms and logistics.[5] For a long time, Uganda and Sudan were hostile to each other, and these tensions played into sustaining the war, perpetuating the suffering and hardship in the Acholi community in northern Uganda.

In turn, Uganda backed anti-Sudan rebels: the Sudan People's Liberation Army (SPLA), who eventually governed South Sudan after secession from Sudan in 2011. These interlocking conflicts have led to a vicious cycle of displacement and created a refugee influx in the East African region, where Uganda currently hosts 1.5 million refugees.

Another conflict in the region is the Darfur conflict in western Sudan. February 2023 marked 20 years since that war began and those fleeing from the war face the same quandary as those fleeing war elsewhere: how to return to villages they called home years ago. A steady supply of ammunition, weaponry and funding enables and facilitates these conflicts.

South Sudan

South Sudan, the world's youngest country, still struggles to forge a stable nation. In 2013, war broke out, pitting President Salva Kiir against his sacked vice president, Riek Machar, after a power struggle between the two exploded in public leading to death and destruction in the country just two years after independence.

Now in its thirteenth year of independence, South Sudan has yet to build a unified army that can support its stability even as it faces other socioeconomic challenges.[6] Lying in a volatile region, the Intergovernmental Authority on Development (IGAD) has tried to come to the rescue of South Sudan with its initiatives as a regional body.[7] In addition, the IGAD region is home to 4.8 million refugees and asylum seekers.[8]

The aftermath of the conflict in South Sudan is felt deeply across the whole region, as in Uganda, where a serious refugee crisis has emerged. The West Nile region in the northern part of Uganda has borne the brunt of this as the largest refugee hosting community in Uganda. In March 2019, then IGAD Executive Secretary Mahboub Maalim said Uganda was the best example of refugee inclusivity in local and national settings because of its refugee settlements plan as opposed to 'refugee camps'.[9] Uganda insisted on using the term 'settlements' because it gives refugees free rein. Although Uganda's progressive refugee policy and response to the crisis have been widely praised, this has not prevented tensions rising between the refugees and the host community.

There have been attempts to forge peace in South Sudan. Years after long-lasting negotiations between the warring parties, a landmark peace deal was signed in 2018 between the belligerent parties in a peace pact known as the Revitalised Agreement for the Resolution of the Conflict of South Sudan (RARCSS).[10]

Nairobi Protocol

The Nairobi Protocol for the Prevention, Control and Reduction of Small Arms in the Great Lakes Region and the Horn of Africa was deployed in 2004 in an attempt to deal with gun violence in the region. Uganda, Sudan and South Sudan are 3 of 15 states that have adopted the Nairobi Protocol. Its path was forged by the 2000 Nairobi Declaration on the Proliferation of Illicit Small Arms and Light Weapons in the Great Lakes Region and the Horn of Africa.[11]

Article 3 of the protocol instructs states to 'adopt such legislative and other measures as may be necessary to establish as criminal offenses under its national law the following conduct, when committed intentionally: illicit trafficking in small arms and light weapons; illicit manufacturing of small arms and light weapons; and illicit possession and misuse of small arms and light weapons.'[12]

The Nairobi Protocol also calls for the strengthening of operational capacity among member states to combat illicit circulation and trafficking of small arms. The Regional Centre on Small Arms (RECSA) was created to implement the Nairobi Protocol in full force. Uganda has partnered with the US and RECSA to destroy excess arms and light weapons in its territory as a State Party to the Nairobi Protocol.[13]

While international laws and treaties seem good on paper, their impact has not been felt in the slightest, and the arms trade has continued unabated. From its impact on women and children, to the widespread impoverishment it causes, to the health and environmental crises it brings about in the areas it ravages, the severe impact of the arms trade is felt in East Africa and across the world.

The Impact on Women and Children

The displacement brought about by conflict exacerbates the vulnerabilities felt in societies, and often sees a rise in rape, child marriages, and impoverishment.

Children are used as tools in war through threats, coercion or manipulation.[14] In some cases, boys end up as child soldiers after being taken up by warlords. An analysis by the African Centre for the Constructive Resolution of Disputes says that 40 per cent of child soldiers globally are in Africa.[15] Not only are these boys deprived of their childhood, but they frequently end up committing war crimes. Meanwhile, girl children experience horrors of their own while forced to act as servants and/or wives of the warlords.

Women fare similarly when they are recruited into armed struggles: some as caretakers and some on the frontline of battle. In *'If You Don't Cooperate, I'll Gun You Down'*, an Amnesty report published in 2022,[16] several women shared their experience of sexual violence in South Sudan. Many of the victims described the crimes being perpetrated by government soldiers. While narrating her story, one woman described being given the option of being raped or being murdered alongside her children.[17]

This is an example of how the arms trade destroys human development; it acts as a catalyst, fuelling conflicts with a mass influx of weapons.

Women and children suffer another blow due to the arms trade when governments engage in arms purchases rather than facilitating healthcare budgets. A lack of adequate healthcare services leads, among other things, to maternal and infant mortality.

In 2022, a report by World Vision noted that of the 27 million people facing acute food insecurity in the Democratic Republic of Congo (DRC), 15.8 million were children.[18] A United Nations report on children and armed conflict in the DRC released in November 2022 reported that between April 2020 and March 2022, there were 7,616 violations against 6,073 children.[19] At least 1,249 children were victims of multiple violations, with children abducted to be recruited or otherwise used, killed, maimed, or forced to endure sexual violence. Children are even victims of armed violence when at school: the report noted that 929 children were attacked across 281 incidents in schools and hospitals. Responsibility for 93 per cent of all violations was attributed to armed groups.

When the insecurity created by war prevents families from growing or otherwise sourcing their food, this also has dire consequences. Plan International notes that adolescent girls and young mothers face an increased risk, since adequate nutrition plays a vital role in supporting the growth of their bodies ahead of and during pregnancy.

> These girls and women will be at increased risk of miscarriage and maternal mortality and face risks of stillbirth, new-born deaths, low birth weight and stunting for their children, leading to an intergenerational cycle of malnutrition.[20]

As the arms trade continues to make vast profits for the manufacturers and brokers, its consequences continue to impact human beings, years and even generations after the initial destruction of life.

The Arms Trade and Impoverishment

The arms trade has a socioeconomic ripple effect, exacerbating impoverishment as funds that should be invested in education, healthcare and agriculture end up earmarked for the purchase of arms. As a result, economic gaps are created and worsened.

During a war, assets such as livestock that would have been accumulated by households are stolen by the fighting groups, along with their land that could be used for agriculture to provide food and income, further diminishing their ability to support themselves and their communities.[21]

In February 2023, Oxfam reported that the majority of African governments reduced their investment in agriculture and increased their expenditure on arms.[22]

Most African governments depend on agriculture to feed their population, create employment opportunities and earn revenue to support their budgets. Less investment in the field means less output. Less output means less food, which leads to a food crisis, causing increased malnutrition and possible starvation. UNICEF noted that between April and June of 2023, 7.76 million people would face the risk of severe starvation in South Sudan.[23]

Governments consciously investing in agriculture and other key sectors, rather than arms, would be a huge step towards addressing food insecurity and improving the quality of life of their citizens.

Health Crises Created by the Arms Trade

Similarly, the arms trade has created a health crisis, both directly and indirectly: indirectly, because the extravagant expenditure on arms comes at the expense of proper healthcare investment. The money that could be used to procure ample medicine, staff and equipment in hospitals instead goes to the purchase of arms. This leaves the healthcare centres under-equipped to handle patients.

The direct impact of the arms trade on healthcare comes from the use of arms in war, causing physical and mental destruction, and a resulting strain on healthcare systems. The destruction of war comes in the form of injury and death, as well as damage caused while people flee for safety, denied access to basic needs such as clean water, shelter and adequate food. The lack of adequate clean water encourages the spread of hygiene-related diseases such as cholera and typhoid, which can also lead to death if not treated quickly and effectively.

Effective treatment is, of course, highly difficult, since there are no safe medical centres in most war zones, and those that exist quickly become overrun.

In 2022, it was reported that most African governments had increased military spending despite the challenges presented by Covid-19. Quoting SIPRI, *The East African* newspaper noted that: 'In 2021, military expenditure in sub-Saharan Africa totalled $20.1 billion, 4.1% higher than in 2020, but 14% lower than in 2012.'[24] Uganda spent $1.066 billion dollars, an 8 per cent increase from 2020.[25]

In most cases, governments invest more in the arms trade than other sectors, supposedly in a bid to protect their countries: however, this logic doesn't hold up, as many of these countries aren't involved in war directly. Instead, such governments use the arms trade as a mechanism to facilitate corrupt practices and benefit a few individuals in positions of power.

International Law and the Arms Trade

Countries frequently violate international humanitarian law when they purchase arms and resell them to those that are at war.

A European Union arms embargo has been imposed on Sudan since 1994, and then extended to include South Sudan when the country divided.[26] Arms embargoes are meant to encourage warring factions to protect civilians and seek peace: they 'prohibit the supply or transfer of arms and related materiel to specific areas or actors'.[27]

However, South Sudan has still been able to access weapons through neighbouring countries, in particular Uganda. In 2018 it was reported that Uganda helped South Sudan to acquire weapons and ammunition by buying weapons from Bulgaria, Romania and Slovakia and providing 'end-user assurances', before breaking those assurances by transferring the weapons to South Sudan.[28] While Uganda was lauded for sending troops to South Sudan to avert the deadly civil war that broke out in 2013, this also implicated Uganda as a catalyst for the violence wracking its northern neighbour.

In November 2018, a report by Conflict Armament Research indicated that a network of Ugandan and US companies had procured military equipment that was headed to South Sudan.[29] The report stated that the 'weapons funnelled through Uganda to South Sudan were in violation of an arms embargo imposed on the country by some European Union member states'. The weapons were manufactured in Bulgaria, Romania and Slovakia.

SALW are used in most war zones and trade in them is often illegal under various national laws. However, ease of concealment among ships' legitimate cargoes, and of transport by light aircraft landing in remote airstrips, makes these laws very hard to enforce. The widespread use of brokers, front companies and other intermediaries, accustomed to evading national and international restrictions, further complicates enforcement. In resource-rich areas controlled by armed groups, payment for weapons may take the form of access to the raw materials: hence the term 'conflict diamonds' in places like Angola, Sierra Leone and the DRC.

Over the years, countries in the Eastern Africa region (DRC, Rwanda, Uganda, South Sudan, Somalia and Sudan) have all experienced conflict directly or indirectly. This has contributed to governments' urge to engage in arms proliferation. However, this cannot justify the purchase of weapons given the effects that arms have on the purchasing countries and their citizens.

B. Arneson, Director of the Global Arms Trade and Corruption Program at the World Peace Foundation, asserts:

The arms trade is driven by money and power. It cloaks its transactions under the guise of security, primarily to advance its own interests. If it were not for this dynamic, the acquisition of unnecessary or outdated weapons would cease, ultimately challenging the notion that the arms trade contributes to our collective safety.[30]

The gun violence and arms trade in Africa has led to a militarisation that is being taken advantage of on the scale of great power politics, as shown by the US/China militarisation of Africa.

US/China Militarisation of Africa

The US militarisation of Africa through the US Africa Command (AFRICOM) has without doubt led to a surge in gun running on the continent. AFRICOM was set up in 2008 and, although it is headquartered in Germany, it runs a string of operations through its bases on the African continent.

According to *The Intercept*, there were 29 US military bases in Africa at the last count in 2019, and over a dozen of those were permanent bases.[31] Of those permanent bases, one was in Entebbe, Uganda, and two were in Kenya – signalling how East Africa has come under the yoke of US military influence over the years. Another significant example of US militarisation in Africa is Niger, which hosts a large drone base in the city of Agadez.[32]

The construction of the Niger base, which cost $100 million, and the long-standing US military presence in the country, have led to the emergence of local jihadists who are wreaking havoc on the Nigerien population. *The Intercept* reported that Niger has one of the largest US security assistance programmes, totalling over $500 million since 2012.[33] Its arms procurement has also been blighted by systemic corruption.[34]

China has not sat idly by as the US spreads its military influence. There has been a proliferation of Chinese military contractors in Africa, such as DeWe Security Service Group, Overseas Security Guardians, Hua Xin Zhong An Group and Frontier Services Group. These are state-owned military contractors who provide security to Chinese infrastructure projects like mega-dams, railways and other Chinese businesses in Africa.

In 2021, Poly Technologies, a Chinese defence contractor, worked on programmes with Special Forces Command (SFC), an elite unit of the Uganda Peoples Defence Forces (UPDF). Poly Technologies sold a number of armoured personnel carriers to SFC.[35] Poly has done work in other African countries like Benin, Egypt, Namibia and Zimbabwe.

Another Chinese contractor, Norinco, has also supplied weapons to Uganda: namely VN2C infantry fighting vehicles.[36] One of the VN2Cs was displayed at a ceremony where President Yoweri Museveni joined 543 graduates who had successfully completed the Armoured Crew Course Level 3, at the Armoured Warfare Training School (AWTS) in Mubende, Uganda.

Djibouti offers a snapshot of the US/China military competition, where the two superpowers have military bases just 6 kilometres apart in the country – the only country in the world that hosts military bases of both nations.

Arms harm people far more than they help to resolve the conflict at hand. The long-term impact, and what goes on in the arms trade, have far-reaching consequences that are often ignored by leaders who claim they are needed as a safety precaution. Ultimately it is the people in these African countries who suffer the consequences, while the arms companies make the profits.

8

Arms Trade in the Land of Gandhi: The Military-Industrial Complex and Its Impact on India

Binalakshmi Nepram

Binalakshmi Nepram was born in Manipur in the North Eastern Region, and is currently a Fellow at the Asia Centre at Harvard. She is an Indigenous scholar, published author and peace builder, spearheading work on making Indigenous and women-led peace and disarmament meaningful to our lives. Her chapter examines the magnitude of arms proliferation in today's world and its impact on India. She analyses the rise in gun violence and conflict across India, alongside the growing Indian defence industry and military spending. She delves into the significance and limitations of the United Nations Programme of Action on Small Arms and Light Weapons and the Arms Trade Treaty. Finally, the chapter highlights the important work of Indigenous women of Manipur in Northeast India leading peace and disarmament initiatives.

A Weaponised World

In the origin stories of the world passed down by our ancestors, weapons were not an overwhelming feature. How did the world come to a point where an estimated 1 billion small arms are in circulation across the world?[1] The international arms trade is out of control.

For the first time in 1992, the severity of rampant arms proliferation was highlighted with the establishment of the United Nations (UN) Register of Conventional Arms. Resolution 50/70 called for the formation of a panel to study the issue.[2] The first significant international attempt to address light weapons proliferation was in January 1995 by the Secretary-General of the UN, Boutros Boutros Ghali, who coined the term 'micro-disarmament'. Since then, the UN has developed the UN Programme of Action on Small Arms and Light Weapons (2001) and passed the international Arms Trade Treaty (ATT) in 2014.

Arms Trade in the Land of Gandhi

India is the birthplace of Mahatma Gandhi, the founder of modern non-violence. The UN declared that his birthday, 2 October, would become the International Day of Non-Violence. The India that existed at the time of independence championed peace and disarmament. However, the India of today is very different. While many know of the country's economic rise, not many know of a weaponised India that is arming itself to the teeth. Every year, hundreds of arms companies come to New Delhi and Bengaluru to sell their wares at an international arms bazaar. India is currently the second most heavily armed nation in the world, and the majority of its firearms – an estimated 71.1 million guns – are in civilian possession, with a further 3.9 million held by the defence forces of the government.[3] As of 2023, there were 1.3 million arms-licence holders in the state of Uttar Pradesh alone.[4,5]

India's Defence Industry

India has one of the largest defence industries in the world. In 2023, the country's defence spending rose to a staggering $72.6 billion, 13 per cent more than initial estimates.[6] India is ranked as the fourth most powerful military in the world with an estimated total military personnel of 5,137,550.[7] Additionally, India is currently the world's biggest arms importer.[8]

India is also now poised to increase its arms exports and is developing closer ties with other international arms suppliers to achieve this. The government of India has ushered in phased liberalisation of the defence industry, commencing reforms in the field of foreign direct investment (FDI), the Ordnance Factory Board (OFB), and establishing defence production in Uttar Pradesh and Tamil Nadu.[9] These measures were aimed to strengthen India as an arms exporter.

In a report published by the UN in May 2023,[10] it was mentioned that since the military junta seized power in Myanmar in February 2021, companies within India (both private and state owned) have exported at least $51 million in arms to Myanmar's military. According to the report, 22 suppliers based in India, including Bharat Dynamics, Bharat Electronics and Yantra India, were involved in this. India's defence production rose more than 12 per cent, reaching $12 billion in 2023.[11]

Lack of Regulation of the International Arms Trade is Hurting India's Citizens[12]

Several years ago, I met Javed, a brave 28-year-old Kashmiri with whom we worked on addressing the issues caused by arms proliferation. In Javed's own words:

Any weapon has only one purpose … to destroy something. My legs are lifeless; I have no sensation in them. Only the wheelchair ensures my mobility. Everything that Kashmir had in the past has been ruined in the last 15–20 years. There has been so much armed conflict … so many guns, so many weapons … they are freely available … that all humanity is destroyed. Today a human being has no value.

Javed was shot in the spine by a single bullet from a foreign-made pistol.

Nilu Dalauja, an Indigenous woman from Karbi Anglong, Assan (Northeast India), recounts her story:

It was a Monday morning when 200 militants came. They started firing guns for over an hour. They killed people, they killed cows, and they even killed our goats. We lost everything that we had in minutes …

Nilu is a survivor of the 2005 Assam Karbi–Dimasa ethnic conflict that claimed over a hundred lives in Northeast India. I also met a brave mother, Ima Sinam Chandrajini from Malom Village, who passed away in 2022. In November 2000, her two sons and her sister were shot dead by Indian paramilitary personnel in Malom Village, Manipur. The testimonies are endless.

Democracy at Gunpoint: Proliferation of Small Arms and Light Weapons in India

India is part of a region that is flooded with arms. The primary source for the proliferation of weapons in South Asia was the Soviet-Afghan war in the 1970s–1980s. Weapons were dumped into Afghanistan and were smuggled from there into South Asia. The known countries of origin of illicit arms uncovered in Northeast India are China, the US, Russia, Belgium, UK, Czech Republic, Pakistan, Afghanistan, Thailand, Cambodia and Bangladesh. Many of these weapons have ended up in the hands of non-state actors in India.

The arrival of these illicit small arms and light weapons (SALW) is driven by a host of factors, including the spread of low-intensity conflicts. The weapons play a pernicious role and adversely affect the security of the country. India's northeast is one of the most affected zones, characterised by large numbers of insurgent outfits, in addition to a variety of transnational criminal activities that have increased the demand for small arms. This demand is met promptly by a supply from China, Myanmar, Thailand, Cambodia and, to some extent, Bangladesh, supported by an intricate web of relations and agreements that cut across regions, communities and countries. Several political parties in India now use money, muscle power and guns to win elections and get access to power – 'democracy at gun point'. Violent ethnic conflict erupted in Manipur in May 2023, supported by an influx of guns. Now human and drug trafficking in the region is rife, over 200 people have died, 5,000 homes have been burnt and 70,000 people displaced.[13]

Arms Controls in India

India's domestic policy on SALW is regulated under the Arms Act (1959) and Arms Rules (2016), as well as various amendments.[14] This legislation and various executive instructions from central and state governments have created, at least on paper, a mechanism for control and regulation of SALW in India. The Arms Act (1959) and Arms Rules (2016) cover all aspects of lawful possession and of the manufacture, sale, transfer, transport, import and export of arms and ammunition, and lay out penal provisions for violations. The provisions of the Arms Act and Arms Rules seek to classify firearms and other prohibited weapons so as to ensure that dangerous weapons are not available to civilians and that weapons for self-defence can be possessed by citizens in special cases only.[15]

In reality, these laws do little to prevent arms still being easily available in India. Arms continue to fuel ongoing conflicts – actors in Manipur and Kashmir, as well as the Naxalites (a Maoist revolutionary movement), have been able to get hold of foreign-made weapons through middlemen. The two warring communities in the recent Manipur conflict were heavily armed with sophisticated illegal weapons. Eventually, the Indian military created 'buffer zones' to stop the heavy firing.

India is also home to 'cottage industry' pistols, known as 'kattas', produced using a variety of ordinary items, including plumbing pipes and jeep steering columns. These home-made guns lack the 'quality' of foreign-made weapons and are a disappointing, but readily available, second choice for men who want to achieve power through fear and violence.[16]

The Arms Trade Puts Women in India in the Firing Line

Women in India are increasingly paying a heavy price for the unregulated multi-billion dollar trade in small arms. Large numbers of women suffer directly and indirectly from armed violence. Women are particularly at risk of certain crimes because of their gender,[17] and guns also affect women's lives when they are not directly in the firing line. Women become the main breadwinners and primary carers when male relatives are killed, injured or disabled by gun violence. Women are displaced and forced to flee their homes for an uncertain future, and then face starvation and disease as they struggle to fend for their families. These dangers are all too prevalent for women in India.

The Historical Emergence of Women's Disarmament Movements in Manipur, Northeast India

For more than a century, women have mobilised in support of peace and disarmament. There have been examples of women's organisations and movements working at the national, regional and international level with a primary focus on peace and disarmament. It started as early as 28 April 1915, when nearly 1,200 women from warring and neutral countries came together at an International Congress for Women to protest against the First World War. Indigenous women from Manipur, Northeast India were an integral part of this process.

Mothers have often organised in order to protect their children, such as the Mothers of the Plaza de Mayo protesting the 'disappearance' of their children in Argentina. In Sri Lanka, a group of more than 2,000 women from across the country directly affected by the civil war – their sons, husbands missing/missing in action, killed, or disabled due to the war – formed the Association of War Affected Women (AWAW). On 14 May 2023, women and mothers from various conflict zones of the world came together in India and the US to form the International Mothers Association for Peace.

Women of India, Peace and Security

The UN Security Council Resolution 1325 on women, peace and security was adopted in October 2000. This resolution was a monumental turning point in recognising women's direct contribution to disarmament. The resolution acknowledged in international law a tradition of women actively advocating for peace and disarmament at every level. Building on this, Indigenous women from Northeast India, led by Manipur Women Gun Survivors Network and the Control Arms Foundation of

India, worked to develop India's first National Action Plan on Women, Peace and Security in 2015.

The Manipur Women Gun Survivors Network, and the Northeast India Women Initiative for Peace organised network meetings to address and respond to gender-based violence in conflicts across the eight states of Northeast India. Women leaders across the eight states and youth survivors of violence congregated in 2015, 2016, 2020 and 2023 for the Northeast India Women Peace Congregations. These congregations consist of consultative meetings aimed at ensuring participation of women in peace processes, peace talks and decision-making forums; ensuring prevention of violations of women's rights in conflict; and bringing a much-needed focus on peace and development in the region.

The Origin of the Manipur Women Gun Survivors Network

A third area of work for responding to arms proliferation in India takes the form of direct intervention in the lives of gun survivors. The Manipur Women Gun Survivors Network (MWGSN) is the first initiative of its kind in India to offer victim assistance to women gun survivors. The idea for the MWGSN came from an incident on 24 December, 2004. That Christmas Eve, 27-year-old Buddhi Moirangthem was dragged from his car battery workshop in Wabgai Lamkhai village in Manipur by three gunmen and shot dead. Even today, his then 24-year-old widow Rebika Akham does not know who the killers were or why they killed her husband. Days after the incident, 4,500 rupees were contributed by committed people to buy a sewing machine for Rebika. This was the first ever intervention of MWGSN and it enabled her to secure a living by stitching clothes. The Manipur Women Gun Survivor Network was formed in 2007 to help women like Rebika Akham. MWGSN attempts to lift women above the trauma and agony faced in conflict. It helps women survivors of gun violence to find ways to heal the scars in the community caused by decades of living under the shadow of a gun.

Strengthening Civil Society

The most important activity going forwards is to strengthen the role of civil society, and women in particular, in peace initiatives. In 2001, after the UN addressed the issue of small arms and light weapons with the launch of the UN Programme of Action on Small Arms and Light Weapons (UNPoA), meetings were organised on the issue in five different Indian cities which called upon the government of India to implement the UNPoA. However, even as India kept submitting report after report to the UN on the small arms issue, claiming that it was adhering to UNPoA, the work never materialised on the ground. In response, civil society mobilised and in 2004 formed the Control Arms Foundation of India (CAFI) in New Delhi. The aim of the foundation is to address issues relating to the proliferation of small arms and light weapons, particularly as they affect women, children and the elderly, and to create a movement where defence and security issues are examined.

CAFI proposes new ideas for thinking about security: for instance, looking at women-led disarmament policies and programmes to make human security a fundamental right, and to make sure the disarmament movement is meaningful in people's lives. The formation of a strong civil society organisation directly addressing the issue of small arms is one of the most effective actions taken by women in India to combat gun violence. CAFI also undertakes advocacy work with Indian disarmament officials, parliamentarians and think tanks, and is part of a network of NGOs. They have conducted mass awareness programmes and have made three films on gun control issues and organised photo exhibitions related to gun violence. At a time of the backsliding of democracies and the rise of warlordism and conflicts, the only way to save the planet and its people is to work together to ensure that we hold accountable the permanent five members of the UN Security Council who produce 88 per cent of the world's weapons. The arming of the world must stop. The arms must be laid down.

9

The Market of Death as Seen from Latin America

Ana Penido

Ana Penido is a Brazilian political scientist, with a Master's in Strategic Studies and a PhD in International Relations. She is currently a FAPESP postdoctoral fellow in Political Science at Unicamp in Brazil, and a researcher at Tricontinental: Institute for Social Research and the International Defense and Security Study Group (GEDES). Here she shares her perspectives on how the arms trade functions as a tool to continue the legacy of colonialism, keeping countries in the 'periphery' dependent, both financially and strategically, on the global economic 'core'. She also explores how the prevailing narrative that defence spending is inherently linked to a country's 'development' leads to the misguided pursuit of independence through arms in the global South. She shows how this instead leads to a further dependency on international finance, assimilation into the global order, and the diversion of public funds away from the public good. Finally, in Latin America, she demonstrates how this military expansion has bled into public and political life, as armed forces are conceived as a 'civilising' internal force, leading in some cases to military coups and the suppression of political opposition.

With some exceptions, few inter-state conflicts with direct use of force have occurred in South America. The scarcity of wars, added to the fact that no country in the region has nuclear weapons, has led to the continent being known as the 'zone of peace'. Yet, that label does not signify the absence of violence, but rather that violence happens predominantly within these countries. In fact, the region boasts the highest murder rates in the world, according to various United Nations (UN) reports.[1]

The murder rates are supported by a huge number of fire-arms: in Brazil, the country with the most homicides in the world, there is one armed citizen per hundred, who collec-tively possess almost six times more weapons than the 360,000 weapons under the control of state-wide security forces.[2] In other words, there are many more armed citizens than the entire ranks of the armed forces: but for the arms industry, the question remains how to sell pistols to the remaining 99 per cent.

Furthermore, in a continent afflicted by a wide variety of problems, social wealth is directly linked to the purchase of arms. The death market is supported by the global South's strategic dependency on the US, resulting in military guard-ianship over democracy, in increased economic dependency and in the killing of nationals by the military in the fight against drug trafficking.

Continuing belief in an inherent connection between defence spending and 'development', order and progress, has led to the ringfencing of a military budget that could have more socially and economically efficient uses, particularly in peripheral countries in which projections indicate that deaths from hunger (aggravated by financial speculation in agricul-tural commodities and the Ukraine crisis) will exceed those from the Covid-19 pandemic.

Weapons and Violence in a Non-war Situation

The global arms trade has many humanitarian impacts, such as the dislocation of refugees, the violation of international laws of war, and the problem of disactivated arms, such as landmines. But in Latin America, the weapons responsible for the social tragedy are different: light arms predominate. In December 2020, there were 2,077,126 legal private firearms in Brazil.[3] In 2020, Brazilians spent R$150 million ($27 million) importing firearms, 34 times more than in 2016.[4] Brazil also broke records in arms exports. In 2020, the manufacturer Taurus registered a 78 per cent increase in revenue, hitting R$1.77billion ($320 million).[5] 'Non-lethal' arms manufacturers, like Condor, accompany the general growth of the arms industry.

In pure numerical terms, of the total homicides registered worldwide, 29 per cent were in Latin America – a region that accounts for only 8 per cent of the global population.[6] The World Health Organization (WHO) considers rates above 10 homicides per 100,000 inhabitants to be epidemic levels.[7] The world average in 2021 was 6.1; Latin America registered 14.8 violent deaths per 100,000. Of the five most deadly countries, three are in Latin America and the Caribbean: Jamaica (48.6 per 100,000), Honduras (41.2) and Venezuela (40.1).

Nigeria, India, Mexico, the United States, and Brazil are responsible for 33 per cent of homicides on the planet. These deaths are predominantly concentrated in the big urban centres. According to 2021 data from openDemocracy, 38 of the 50 most violent cities in the world are in Latin America; Brazil and Mexico stand out.[8] Another fundamental piece of data is that the profile of those who are most often killed and most often die is well defined: men, youth, poverty-stricken and black people. The Brazilian figures are remarkable: 76.2 per cent of victims are black, 54.3 per cent are poor, and 91.3 per cent are male.[9]

A first hypothesis is that violence is a product of poverty. In reality though, even when poverty rates fell across the region, this was not accompanied by a decline in homicides.

A second hypothesis would be the lack of state investment in public security. This also has no basis because, according to the Inter-American Development Bank, the total spent on security relative to total public spending in Latin America is double the average of 'core' countries, such as the Triad states of the United States, Europe, and Japan.

A third given explanation rests on the lack of punishment. Even with the prison population of the Americas (excluding the US) growing by 121 per cent since 2000, according to the World Prison Brief,[10] in reality, the conviction rates for homicide are low (24 convictions per 100 victims in 2016). A fourth element which helps explain this reality is the easy access to firearms; this theory is well proved in the literature. According to UN data cited by Instituto Igarapé, firearms were used in three out of four homicides committed in the region in 2017.[11] A fifth potential reason for the high levels of violence advanced by Instituto Igarapé was accelerated urbanisation in the region.

Finally, it should be noted that there are two other issues underlying the problem that add to possible causes and explanations. First, the adherence to the US doctrine on how best to tackle the problem of drug trafficking does not dampen the ongoing struggle between different groups for the profits of this trade. While Brazilian security forces (both armed forces and police) are deployed to combat drug trafficking from a security point of view, at its heart the issue is a public health concern. The motives of the trade are eminently commercial, and some of those involved in the trade are active or retired members of the security forces themselves. Therefore, different cartels and criminal networks will continue to compete – violently – for the profits from this trade, unless interventions tackle the root causes of drug misuse and make the sector unprofitable.

Second, highly militarised police forces account for part of the security problem, rather than its solution. Many are involved in various human rights violations and crimes: deaths linked to police violence in Latin America are comparable to those generated by armed conflicts across the globe. Moreover, their involvement in crime such as drug trafficking further contributes to public insecurity. With the justification of the proliferation of ever more sophisticated weapons by drug trafficking groups, the police are also acquiring more heavy-duty weapons every day, preparing for urban warfare. This only increases violations of human rights, as civilians are murdered in violent clashes, classified as necessary collateral damage of police operations. Once again, police and military forces in Latin America become part of the security problem, rather than the solution.

Weapons and Colonialism

It is possible to find additional, long-standing reasons for the combination of external peace with internal violence on the continent. In Europe, the process of centralisation and legitimation of nation-states took place in tandem with the growth of their capacities for coercion. According to American sociologist Charles Tilly, as war grew more complex, rulers needed to professionalise their armies, increasing their capacities for organisation, mobilisation, and arms.[12] In order to do this, tax systems, an administrative bureaucracy, and finally, a central authority, were created. As the revolutionary socialist Rosa Luxemburg shows, militarism is a province of capital accumulation.[13] Faced with (real or fictitious) imminent conflict, capitalist countries extracted from the proletariat the revenues necessary to maintain armies, transferring the masses' purchasing power to the state, which in turn transformed that revenue into armaments and stimulated new areas of capitalist production.

A different path is followed by 'peripheral' countries, or states with a colonial past that are exploited and kept dependent on the wealthy imperial 'core'. At the time of their independence, the hierarchical international system was already consolidated, such that the recently independent countries were incorporated on terms unfavourable to their overall mode of functioning. Internally, the state used force to hold down the prices of extracted raw materials that were sold into the international market. The organisation of this force was financed externally, by means of international loans and foreign exchange derived from exports of commodities. In sum, Latin American state construction was linked more to the economic interests of its export sectors than it was to the enterprise of war, as it was in the European case. In an attempt to keep up, the periphery asked for loans from the core in order to buy weaponry produced by the core that was then used to oppress the workers in the periphery who produce surplus value for core countries.

In regions with few inter-state conflicts this happens even more, as there is not enough demand for military goods to stimulate the national arms sector. As Rosa Luxemburg had already indicated, military demand 'presupposes a big industry of the highest order. It requires the most favourable conditions for the production of surplus value and for accumulation.'[14]

South American armed forces were formed by the importation of European military models – especially those of France and Germany – and consolidated by direct and indirect military operations over the period 1885 to 1926.

Author Alain Roquié alerts us to the idea that, in Latin America, '[t]he modern armies were state forces that guaranteed internal order and the uninterrupted exploitation of the mineral and agricultural riches desired by Europe'.[15]

Thus, professionalisation of the armed forces in the periphery served as insurance for international investors, who wanted to keep wages down and to keep the underpaid workers from becoming a threat to the local owners and managers of the raw material extraction industries.

After the Second World War, US influence was implanted, consolidated, and – building on previous neocolonial structures – deepened. Military thinking in the periphery retains the rationalities and strategies formulated externally over time.[16] The 'universalisation' of weaponry systems led to technology becoming ingrained as a strategic element.[17] A recipe for military success was created: the greatest amount of equipment and the most advanced technology wins wars. This becomes the eternal search for the sword that slices through everything, now in the form of the dazzling speed of the aircraft.

Armaments and Dependency in Latin America

Since the 1970s, some South American countries have begun to produce their own arms. In the 1980s, international cooperation in manufacture intensified and, in the 2000s, there was a peak in military growth, in militarism, and in the domestic production of armaments.[18] South American military spending is concentrated in five countries: Argentina, Brazil, Chile, Colombia, and Venezuela. Together, they were responsible for 88.2 per cent of spending in the continent between 1980 and 2016, for 77.8 per cent of arms imports.

The acquisition or manufacture of a weapon doesn't only produce a stand-alone artefact but also the organisation of staff, military hierarchy and recruitment – the 'relations of force'.[19] Arms production is a consequence of technological advancements in society, and of civil–military relations. The relations of force interact with the social development of each society. Political scientist Keith Krause postulates that the top-level producers expand the technological frontier through innovation; the second level reproduces these sophisticated weapons and adapts them to the specific demands of the market; such that the third level is restricted to copying and reproducing already existing technologies, unable to capture the underlying process of innovation or adaptation.[20]

In copying core countries, the production model used in the periphery allows countries to enjoy military-industrial advantages without having to go down the long path of domestic production. However, this creates a disconnect from the necessary social relations for their manufacture and use, and does not diminish the continent's dependency on the core. The advancements bolster only those industries – like arms – that ultimately benefit the global North. Moreover, one look at the data is enough to demonstrate Latin America's insignificance in this sector: there is only one Brazilian firm – Taurus – in the top hundred arms producers, and it mainly produces small arms.

Strategic dependency is not just about the imposition of force or an exclusively economic relationship, but is also the result of the capacity of the powers to colonise the global South's thinking. This benefits the internal elites of both the core and the periphery.[21] In the global South, the narrative goes that military superiority guarantees victories, and that investment in military technology is not only necessary but that some technology may also have some social 'dual' use. Thus military investment is seen as a way to carry out both the policing and repression of working classes and to take care of national defence.

The result of this mentality was the production of arms in the periphery states through the use of foreign credit in the 1970s, or based on the commodities boom that financed neo-developmentalist policies in the 2000s, including in the military sector.[22] Taken from industry, the funds directed to armaments become a tool for the maintenance of economic dependency, besides the fact that the prioritisation of primary goods exports in the 2000s had the effect of de-industrialisation.

In reality, the arms trade in Latin America has absorbed the continent into the heavily militarised international order. The economic impact of this has been the strangling of fiscal resources, the increase in debt, the scarcity of investment in public health and welfare, and a new dependency on the import of arms (and their maintenance thereafter). In sum, there is an immense social wealth available in the periphery, but it is wasted on sectors that are more destructive than productive of human life.

In Addition to Economic Dependence, a Strategic Dependence

Our understanding of war and peace in the global South often comes from uncritically employing concepts proposed by thinkers of the global North. These theories, formulated to resolve the problems of the North, do not always apply easily to the South. Dossier 50 of Tricontinental: Institute for Social Research[23] argues that the international division of labour manifests itself in the roles played by the armed forces of the periphery. While the militaries of core countries concentrate on the world's major geopolitical conflicts, notably the growing confrontation between the US/NATO on the one hand and China and Russia on the other, the militaries of the Latin American periphery focus on the control of internal order, and eventually on peacekeeping missions, usually under US aegis.

In a 1993 article, political scientists Alexander Wendt and Michael Barnett proposed four types of militarisation standards.[24] The first two are organised with regard to factors of production: the capital-intensive (modern and high-tech armaments for professional soldiers) and the labour-intensive (non-conventional forces, grounded in popular participation with highly mobile troops and light weaponry). The last two standards are established by dependency on external sources: auto-centric and dependent militarisation. The authors also identify the concept of militarisation-by-invitation, which occurs in regions of high strategic interest for arms-manu-facturing powers, as is the case of Israel.[25] Successful popular wars were based on labour-intensive and self-sufficient strate-gies, as outlined it Table 9.1.

Table 9.1 Comparison between technocratic and self-sufficient militarisation[26]

Military sector	Technocratic armed forces (conventional; oriented towards industrialised countries)	Militia/popular army (self-sufficient; dissociated from industrialised countries)
Budget	Large amounts of currency	Small amounts of currency
Infrastructure	Diversified, specialised	No specific military infra-structure. Minimum logistic system
Arms and equipment	Modern, capital-intensive systems: tanks, aircraft, warships with extensive tactical radii, mobile tank divisions; partially constructed and assem-bled locally, occasionally exported	Simple: anti-tank and anti-aircraft missiles, light infantry, predominantly local production, varied supply lines, maritime equipment for the protection of the coast
Specialists from industri-alised coun-tries	Various	None

Military sector	Technocratic armed forces (conventional; oriented towards industrialised countries)	Militia/popular army (self-sufficient; dissociated from industrialised countries)
Alliances	Association; bilateral accords; usually with no formal alliances, but neutrality is maintained in the expectation that foreign aid will be received in the case of a crisis	Principally neutral; non-aggression treaties
Armed forces	Professional; specialised troops in the three forces	Militia system; labour-intensive with non-traditional organisation; above all oriented to economic, not military, functions
Mobilisation	Permanent mobilisation of professionals, limited reserves; troop movements to the front and to battlefields	During peacetime, limited degree of mobilisation; total mobilisation of the population in case of war; popular mobilisation in areas where people live and work
Command	Hierarchical, centralised	Democratic, decentralised
Strategy	Defensive and offensive, including the possibility of pre-emptive attacks	Defensive, reactive, territorial defence to prevent occupations
Importance of militarism	Expansion of the armed forces' role	Almost total participation of the population

The different strategic models impact on civil–military relations: in Latin America, disputes between different sections of the military permeate political organisation. One effect of external modernisation was the construction of armed forces that consider the development of their country unworthy of them, so they assume the internal responsibility of 'civilising, educating, inspiring and modernising' their countries. They are soldiers, therefore they are strongly interventionist, and perceive their capacity for government of public matters as superior to that of the civilian sector. This is one of the main motivations for the profusion of military coups on the continent. In some measure, despite formal independence, they continue to act as colonial armed forces.

Author Frederick Nunn highlights that the US has involved itself in South American domestic military engagement, most recently in Colombia and Venezuela.[27] The second half of the twentieth century saw the establishment of military dictatorships throughout the continent, such as in Brazil, Chile and Peru, among others, and with that came the repression of political enemies of the state. This, however, pre-dates the establishment of the National Security Doctrine, and has long been part of Latin America's history. The suppression of opposition has taken on different political hues, depending on the country and the historical moment: established enemies range from Indigenous peoples, communists, unionised workers, or, more recently, feminists and environmentalists. Unlike in Europe and the US, the varied enemies of the state remain within the borders, and are used to justify domestic repression rather than international warfare. Time and time again, militaries align with the conservative elites, and citizens critical of the dominant regime are understood as enemies of the homeland, and therefore become the object of military confrontation.

In contemporary Latin America, the main enemy constructed by the US that feeds militarism is not terrorism but drug trafficking, and it is due to this conflict that the humanitarian tragedy makes itself felt most deeply, as the figures at the start of this chapter indicate. After the Cold War, it became necessary for the US to invent a new enemy that would continue to drive the arms industry. The attacks of 11 September 2001, offered the answer that the USA was looking for: the new global enemy was terrorism. This led to direct wars, as in Afghanistan and Iraq, and several indirect aggressions against different states, under the justification of hunting terrorists. It is certainly not true that the Middle East is more stable, or more pro-American, than before the hunt began. On the other hand, this failure was compensated with economic gains for the re-heated arms industry.

In Latin America, instances of terrorism – other than the state terrorism practised by military dictatorships – are few and far between. The enemy of choice, therefore, was drug trafficking. The US was successful in transforming a public health issue into a major security problem, which justified an increase in spending within the US and the imposition of military spending targets on Latin American countries, especially Colombia. Thus, the Latin American armed forces armed themselves to carry out the 'war on drugs', as an auxiliary force for the US Army.

The arms trade, and those whose interests it protects, are hugely influential on the world stage, especially in countries in the periphery. They determine what should be protected, from what or from whom, and how. They create and maintain regimes in which the population is treated as a threat to the security of the state, and not its principal resource. They impose the militarised mentality of the global North on the South, superseding the will of the popular masses in their own countries. They do all this while creating vast profits for their own. Latin America has the challenge of cutting the strings of its dependency to prioritise the welfare and development of its people. It is not possible to do so without cutting arms spending.

PART III

Global Campaigns Against the Arms Trade

10

Stop the War Coalition:
A Mass Movement against
Weapons and War

Lindsey German

Lindsey German is a long-time socialist and campaigner. She went on her first demonstration against the all-white South African rugby tour in 1969. She is the convenor of the Stop the War Coalition, which she helped form in 2001. She has organised hundreds of protests and activities against war, imperialism and oppression. Her publications include several books on women and a jointly authored People's History of London. *Here she recounts the history of the Stop the War Coalition, formed in the UK in response to Bush's 'War on Terror', and how it mobilised a mass movement of opposition to the military expansionism of the 2000s. She demonstrates the importance of a movement that places individual conflicts against the wider context of imperialism and the nature of the arms trade, showing what connects them and why it is important to stand against them. She also shares her thoughts on how these anti-war campaigns politicised an entire generation, leading to a shift in British politics in the 2010s, and how this movement remains resilient in its opposition to militarism and the arms trade.*

Following the end of the Cold War, the world grew hopeful for the possibility of a 'peace dividend', an economic boost that would arise from a reduction in defence spending. Many thought that lessons had been learned and that the world would return to a more peaceful norm. Instead, the twenty-first century ushered in a new period of conflict and instability, and defence spending and arms production has never been higher than at the start of the 2020s.

The Stop the War Coalition was formed in September 2001 against a background of the events of 9/11. Our argument was that the 'War on Terror', called by then US President George W. Bush in response to the terrible attack on that day, would lead to far more deaths and conflict than we had so far seen. We were told that it was impossible to build a broad anti-war movement, given the impact of the attacks, but we were overwhelmed by the response from sections of the left, trade unions, the peace movement and, most notably, the Muslim community, which is considerable in Britain and was, in its majority, opposed to Western foreign policy especially over the Middle East.

Bush's War on Terror, launched initially against Afghanistan but then moving rapidly to target Iraq, took military conflict onto another plane. It gave a massive boost to the arms trade, led to a growth of active conflict wars, to the forging of new and strengthening of old alliances between powers, and to a changed political configuration in the Middle East.

It also led to the strategic decision in many countries to expand so-called 'defence' spending – really used for directly offensive military expansionism – and to advance more interventionist policies. The UK government under Prime Minister Tony Blair took a lead in this. Its 1998 Strategic Defence Review talked of 'force projection' and of the need to have a pre-emptive military strategy.[1] Blair's Chicago speech on the 'doctrine of the international community' in the middle of the Kosovo war in 1999 made the case for the necessity of military intervention to avoid humanitarian disasters.[2] After 9/11 this

was expanded to include developing specific forces to inter-
vene in international crises.

But Blair's open zeal for the War on Terror also helped to
create a mass opposition in the form of Stop the War. One of
the strengths of the coalition was that it involved people from
different backgrounds and political orientations, all united by
a common goal. It placed specific campaigns over wars and
conflict – whether in Afghanistan, Iraq or Palestine – in a
wider context of imperialism, resource wars over oil, and the
nature of the arms trade.

The resulting involvement of many different forces in the
coalition led to exceptionally large demonstrations across
Britain. We brought 2 million onto the streets on 15 February
2003, as part of a worldwide movement of up to 30 million.
It was an unprecedented coalition which reached deep into
British society and mobilised large (and often overlapping)
sections of the Muslim community, the unions, and the peace
movement, including many who had never protested before.
School students struck in their tens of thousands, and on the
day that war broke out there were mass acts of civil disobedience – with roads from the port of Dover to the Mersey
Tunnel blocked by protesters, and strikes and walkouts across
hundreds of workplaces.

Any mass movement is made up of hundreds of thousands
of people who do often small things to contribute to a wave
of protest. This is what gave Stop the War its power. We held
thousands of public rallies, spoke at trade union meetings,
held school student meetings, occupied colleges, blocked
roads, protested at air bases, debated with pro-war MPs, gave
out leaflets, booked coaches, convinced friends and families.
It was an astonishing democratic process which transformed
politics in Britain for some months and has a considerable legacy. It was all the more remarkable given that these
protests took place under a Labour government and so there

was no official opposition support (although many Labour MPs openly opposed the war). This was unlike the other main belligerent countries such as Italy, Spain and the US, whose leaders hailed from their respective conservative and right-wing political parties.

Despite all this we didn't stop the war. That would, in my opinion, have required mass industrial action to prevent the movement of equipment for war and to bring the country to a halt, something still sorely needed to this day (see Chapter 12). Many of us were aware of this need, but the movement would need to have been much more embedded in local workplaces and unions for that to succeed. However, the movement had a long-term impact on public opinion in Britain, as did the deaths of British soldiers in Iraq and Afghanistan. There remains to this day strong anti-war feeling, reinforced by the defeat in Afghanistan in 2021.[3]

It was also a major factor in creating distrust in politicians. The anti-war movement helped bring about the demise of Blair himself, who was forced to promise to resign during the 2006 Lebanon war, when again hundreds of thousands turned out on the streets. That war galvanised large numbers, in part because it touched on the key issue of Palestine due to Israel's role, and in part because it demonstrated Blair's addiction to war and his determination to be at the forefront of the belligerents. The memory of Iraq was still raw – and we had since seen the atrocities in Fallujah and Abu Ghraib, and noted the total absence of weapons of mass destruction.

Such was the failure of intervention – and the scepticism about claims for it – that in 2013, then-UK Prime Minister David Cameron's plan to bomb Syria was met with a temporary development of backbone on the part of the parliamentary Labour Party.[4] The attempt was defeated. This did not, of course, mean the defeat of warmongering or militarism. There continued mainly covert and proxy interventions in Syria, an ongoing presence in Afghanistan and, from 2015, the war in Yemen (see Chapter 6). But the nature of the interventions has changed; it is difficult now for the US and British governments to sign up to full-scale invasions and occupations of the sort we witnessed in Afghanistan and Iraq. Instead, the emphasis is on remote forms of warfare, coupled with proxy interventions and wars carried out by allies.

The current war in Ukraine presents challenges for the anti-war movement in the UK – 'our' government is not responsible for the invasion, which instead came from Russia. The proxy aspects of this war can be seen by very big movements of arms from all the NATO countries to Ukraine, paid for from our taxes and bringing further profit to the arms industry. This changes the nature of the conflict as it is much more clearly a conflict between major powers possessing nuclear weapons. There is a clamour from governments across the developed world to spend even more money on 'defence' because of the war in Ukraine: Germany, for instance, committed in 2023 to effectively doubling its defence spending. This – at a time of great personal hardship for millions of its citizens – should be opposed.

The answer to war in Ukraine and elsewhere must be to call for a ceasefire and to promote peace. This, however, would not be a profitable solution for the arms trade, and it is therefore no coincidence that diplomacy is not the first choice for the UK and other militarised nations.

Arms sales are rising at an extraordinary rate, with the people of Yemen – where war has raged since 2014 – at the receiving end of some of the most devastating consequences.[5] This war has served as a grotesque and bloody experiment in the use of weapons. The relationship between the British government, BAE Systems and the Saudi government is at the heart of it.[6] The war in Yemen is a forgotten war. While we see daily reports on our television screens of the war in Ukraine, there is virtually nothing about the misery and devastation in Yemen, described as one of the worst humanitarian disasters in the world, combining war, a man-made famine and disease to afflict the population.

The political impact of the Ukraine war has been to move the UK Labour Party further to the right, and make it harder to organise within and around the Labour Party in opposing the current war. The general atmosphere generated by politicians across the spectrum and by the media has been to dismiss those opposing NATO expansion and escalation of the war as Putin apologists. The Trade Union Congress also narrowly passed a motion calling for more defence spending.

However, the anti-war movement, and especially the huge mass protests over Iraq, had a profound effect on many people, including younger generations experiencing their first protests. This has encouraged them to campaign on a range of issues, including those closely related, such as arms sales and justice for Palestine, but also on a range of other issues. The surprise success of Jeremy Corbyn in winning the Labour leadership in 2015 is attributed in large part to his role in movements including Stop the War, of which he was chair for a number of years. This in turn speaks to how war and militarism, and the associated mobilisation in 2002–3, politicised so many. His apology for the Iraq war, which was made on the same day as publication of the Chilcot Report,[7] was a high point of his leadership, and one of the main lines of attack on him from the media was over his opposition to war and to imperialism – which tells us a great deal about how vital these issues are to the British establishment, and how threatened they are by popular opposition.

Many of those who supported this shift in UK politics have become disillusioned with electoral politics and are turning instead to support campaigns like Stop the War. Still today, a broad section of the UK population are turning up, sometimes in their hundreds of thousands, to protest against the unchanging militarism and indefensible foreign policy positions of their governments. It is vitally important that voices of dissent on this question are heard. Despite the difficulties we have faced, we are determined to keep campaigning. It is obvious that those who control the system – the politicians, the industrialists, the arms dealers – have every intention of maintaining a society addicted to war. We have every intention of fighting back.

11

Direct Action against
the Arms Trade

Palestine Action

Palestine Action is a direct-action network of groups and individuals formed with the mandate of taking action against the sites of Elbit Systems and other companies complicit in Israeli apartheid, calling for all such sites to be shut down. Here the organisation's founders set out how they saw a need for a militant arm to the Palestine solidarity movement, disillusioned by the established political process and the likelihood that Britain will ever willingly step back from its colonial, strategic and economic interests around the world. They explain how direct action finds successful targets and forces those with power to change their minds, not by appealing to their consciences, but by using sustained disruption tactics to make it unprofitable and undesirable for them to operate. Finally, they delve into the victories that Palestine Action have already won against Elbit Systems, damaging not just the reputation of the Israeli arms giant, but also its very ability to operate.

Established Politics is Pointless

With several well-funded non-governmental organisations working within England and Wales to provide solidarity with the Palestinian people, why did we feel it necessary to start a militant arm to this movement?

Frankly, many members of these organisations have, over the years, become disillusioned with the lack of progress. No matter how many people came out to protest, no matter how many people signed petitions or lobbied their representatives, their governments, and every government before them, would not be persuaded to sever its lucrative links with Israel's apartheid regime.

And why would they? Britain has been complicit in driving the colonisation of Palestine right from the get-go through the Balfour declaration, a public statement issued in 1917. The statement, which consisted of just 143 words, had fateful consequences. Lord Balfour, the foreign secretary at the time, promised to build 'a national home for the Jewish people' in Palestine — a land that wasn't his to give away.[1]

When the First World War ended, the League of Nations established a British Mandate for Palestine in 1922, giving Lord Balfour the opportunity to make good on his earlier promise. The British imperial forces burnt down Palestinian villages to prepare the way; with this came arbitrary killings, arrests, torture, sexual violence including rape, the use of human shields and the introduction of home demolitions as collective punishment to repress Palestinian resistance.[2,3]

The British were initiating the ethnic cleansing of Palestine, fulfilling the Zionist aim to build a 'home' over the top of what were Palestinian communities, towns, villages, farms and ancestral land, rich in heritage, culture and ancient archaeological sites.[4]

The Palestinians refer to this time as the Nakba — which translates into 'the great catastrophe'. In 1948, over 500 Palestinian villages were demolished and erased from the map; over three quarters of a million Palestinian people were expelled; many were massacred and buried in mass graves hidden beneath the all-new Zionist entity. Since that date, Britain has worked hand in hand with the Israeli government to pursue its colonial project: the result is an apartheid state where the Palestinians who remained or fled to other areas live without rights, without recognition and under perpetual, brutal subjugation.[5]

In autumn 2023, an even more horrifying onslaught began. A genocide, broadcast over social media, has (at time of writing in spring 2024) seen the majority of the population of Gaza displaced and their homes destroyed (see Chapter 5). Despite the International Court of Justice ruling that Israel is plausibly committing a genocide, and arms export laws forbidding the shipping of weapons when there is a risk they will be used to violate international law, the British political and media establishment has continued to support Israel and the arms exports are still flowing.

Pleading with the oppressors who created this murderous state to suddenly gain a moral conscience and return what has been stolen from the Palestinian people is futile. Politics as usual, diplomacy and impassioned pleas have all failed. The only way we, as activists, can disrupt the lethal ties between Britain and Israel, and dispel the myths, is through direct action.

Elbit Systems

Palestine Action's key target is Elbit Systems – Israel's largest arms firm, which develops just about every type of airborne, land and naval munition you can think of, not just for Israel to use to sustain its vicious apartheid regime, but for other foreign militaries, including Britain's.[6]

Formed in 1966,[7] Elbit Systems formed as a tool to help maintain Israel's domination over historic Palestine. The oppressive Israeli regime requires ever-advancing technology to surveil, control, oppress and attack the Palestinian population and to outsmart a growing and more savvy resistance.

DRONE WARFARE

Today, Elbit supplies 85 per cent of Israel's military drone fleet, deployed over Gaza and across the West Bank.[8] Israel's occupation of Palestine has provided it with a trapped human population on which to test out new and experimental armaments. Documenting their lethal effectiveness then enables Elbit to market its weapons openly, brazenly even, as 'battle-tested' or 'combat-proven', giving them a competitive edge in the global arms trade. This marketing 'knowledge' allows the company to sell their weapons to the world's most repressive regimes.[9]

Elbit's 'Hermes' drones form a crucial part of Israel's military arsenal, which is used to entrench the illegal blockade of Gaza and attack Palestinian families, schools, hospitals and homes.[10] The Hermes drone was then modified to create the 'Watchkeeper' drone for the British military.[11] A subsidiary of Elbit now boasts that the Watchkeeper has clocked-up over 100,000 hours in Afghanistan and Iraq,[12] and the drone has been used to stop migrants seeking refuge in Britain.[13]

Elbit's weapons were out in full force during Israel's bombardment of Gaza in May 2021 — a massacre that killed over 200 Palestinians, including 67 children. It provided ample opportunity to deploy the world's first state-of-the-art Artificial Intelligence drone swarms. Rather than a single drone operated by one soldier, a whole swarm of drones could now work autonomously and communicate with each other.[14]

'We operated day and night in cooperation with unit 9900, Elbit and the Administration for the Development of Weapons and Technological Infrastructure … to perfect the system,' admitted an Israeli general. 'We carried out more than 30 operations.'[15]

Palestine Action

Palestine Action was born out of a necessity to drive Israel's arms trade out of Britain. This meant going straight to the source, disrupting and damaging the weapons and infrastructure that supports their manufacture. Activists have blockaded the entrances, climbed onto Elbit's roofs and stormed their sites, causing damage to its property both inside and out, all with the aim of disrupting this business of bloodshed.

We are not a protest group. We are a direct-action movement. A key phrase that informs our approach comes from the late great David Graeber who said: 'Protest is like begging the powers that be to dig a well; direct action is digging the well yourselves and daring them to stop you.'[16]

We are not begging anyone. We are taking action! We act more than we talk. We stormed the headquarters of Elbit Systems UK in London and used our now-iconic red paint to deface the building and bring a visual symbolic representation of what this company is all about, bloodshed — summed up in a chant we often use 'Your profits are covered in Palestinian blood.' In our first week, in the summer of 2020, we targeted Elbit Systems five times.

DOES IT WORK?

It works because it stops the factories and offices from opening. It prevents the workforce from doing their jobs. When you damage the property and the products being made, it takes Elbit weeks to repair its premises and its stock. It costs them money; it eats into their blood-soaked profits. A company like Elbit can only survive if it is accruing funds to make and design new munitions so it can continue the brutal subjugation of the Palestinian people. Repairing windows, replacing

doors, hiring lawyers for court cases, re-fencing and redeco-
rating is not where it wants its financial surplus to go.

Although we are standing on the shoulders of giants who
have used direct action in the past, including the Palestinian people themselves, the Raytheon 9 in Derry,[17] those who
brought an end to apartheid in South Africa, and many others
around the world – we also knew that the time was ripe to
build a solid and more sustained movement. We had witnessed
previous direct actions and the explosion of interest in such
tactics – Extinction Rebellion, for example, was already in
motion: their rapid growth proved that this was the right way
forward.

And so, considering those who inspired us, we work on five
key principles to run a successful direct-action campaign.

1. *Disruption*. To win, you must disrupt the security of 'busi-
   ness-as-usual'. This can take many forms, from simple
   blockades to lock-on devices, to locking activists' arms in
   reinforced tubes, to more sophisticated contraptions built
   into vehicles. The crucial goal is to delay the police from
   removing activists for as long as possible, thus increasing
   the disruption. Some have occupied factory roofs or gone
   inside buildings to damage machinery or other infrastructure – anything that serves to disable the company from
   reopening.
2. *Sustained actions*. Many of us had been involved in actions
   against Elbit prior to the launch of Palestine Action, but
   these were one-off events, occurring once every six months
   or even less. We needed to up our game and become a
   regular and imposing presence in order to force the third
   important element of a successful campaign: creating a
   dilemma.
3. *Creating a dilemma*. In simple terms, this means making it
   unprofitable for the company to operate. If action is being

taken day in and day out, the company cannot get back to work and continue with their evil trade. Their dilemma is whether to continue operating from the site or give up trying. Some past one-off actions resulted in no arrests. This was a sign that there was no dilemma – therefore there was a need for a greater level of disruption, whether in terms of more damage, or more frequent actions.

4. *Sacrifice*. This is not a popular concept in Western secular culture. However, this principle works when people see activists prepared to risk their safety and liberty for a cause. It forces people to stop and question why people would be prepared to do that and further validates the purpose behind the action. It's also a worrying concept for your target, who will understand how far people will go in order to stop them.

5. *Focus*. Going after one company is key. We also hit secondary targets, such as site landlords, managing agents and suppliers, but concentrating your efforts on one target will help create the essential dilemma and keep your actions sustained and focused. It helps that Elbit is literally one of 'the worst of the worst' – it kills; it's an easy target for people to feel strongly about. Going hard after one company that is crucial to the Israeli subjugation of Palestinians, again and again, is a winning strategy.

A STRATEGY TO WIN

And win we have. By sticking to these principles and keeping things simple, we have built a diverse, inclusive, grassroots movement, even involving the communities living around the factories. In March 2024, we forced Elbit to sell their Tamworth factory after our sustained direct action saw their profits slashed by 75 per cent.[18] We have forced them to sell their subsidiary in Oldham at a massive loss.[19] We have forced them to abandon their HQ in London[20] – it was apt and symbolic that the first person to storm their office was a Palestinian and the final nail in the coffin for this particular site was an action that involved two Palestinians, one of whom was born in Gaza.

Then, the Minister of State for Defence Procurement, Alex Chalk, confirmed that the Ministry of Defence was kicking Elbit out of one of their most lucrative contracts, worth £160 million, to deliver training for Britain's nuclear submarines and was negotiating Elbit's departure from a second contract, worth £123 million. Alex Chalk justified this decision by explaining that Elbit fell short of 'operational sovereignty standards' for the UK's highest capabilities.

As Elbit have obtained special 'List X' status in the UK, they are obliged to report every single security breach to the Ministry of Defence (MOD). That meant every time we broke into one of their factories, defeated Elbit's security and occupied their buildings, the MOD's estimations of Elbit's security capabilities was reduced. So while we were causing severe disruption to our target, we also damaged their reputation both among the general public and the defence sector itself.

The consequences of Elbit's actions are usually felt most strongly by the Palestinians. The role of direct action is to ensure that there is at least a financial cost felt by Elbit itself, until Palestinians are no longer paying with their lives. The great Palestinian writer Ghassan Kanafani, assassinated in 1972 by Israel's Mossad spy agency, famously said: 'the Palestinian cause is not just the cause of Palestinians but of every revolutionary.... wherever you strike imperialism, you damage it and you serve the world revolution.' Mark our words, Palestine Action will continue to strike.

12

Workers against the Arms Trade

Lorenzo Buzzoni

Lorenzo Buzzoni is an investigative journalist and documentary filmmaker based in Italy working at Investigate Europe. He writes about the industrial action taking place across Europe and how workers are striking back to prevent their work from enabling the delivery of weapons into conflict zones where international laws are repeatedly being violated. He specifically describes action to prevent weapons entering conflicts in Gaza, Ukraine and Yemen, and how there is desperate need for a functional arms export control mechanism in the European Union.

31 October 2023. At least six Israeli airstrikes hit residential areas in the Jabalia refugee camp in northern Gaza, killing more than 50 people and injuring about 150.[1] The Israeli military justified the bombing, saying it had targeted the camp to kill Ibrahim Biari – a key Hamas commander linked to the group's October 7 attack on Israel.

'I condemn the killing of civilians in Gaza and I am dismayed by reports that two-thirds of those who have been killed are women and children',[2] said the UN Secretary-General, António Guterres, in response to the attack. He reiterated his call for an immediate ceasefire and urged all sides to respect international humanitarian law (for more on this assault on Gaza, see Chapter 5).

Bombardments killed at least 8,525 Palestinians, including 3,542 children, in that first month alone, according to Hamas health ministry figures issued before the strikes on Jabalia.[3]

On the same day of the airstrikes on Jabalia, Belgian transport workers' unions called on their members to refuse to handle military equipment being sent to Israel. 'While a genocide is underway in Palestine, workers at various airports in Belgium are seeing arms shipments in the direction of the war zone.'[4]

The Belgian unions said that loading or offloading these weapons would mean supplying organisations that kill innocent people. For this reason, they refused 'to contribute to the murder of innocent victims and call for an immediate ceasefire'.

About two weeks earlier, Palestinian trade unions had released an urgent call for international trade unions to take action to halt the arms trade to Israel.[5] 'As Israel escalates its military campaign, Palestinian trade unions call on our counterparts internationally and all people of conscience to end all forms of complicity with Israel's crimes – most urgently halting the arms trade with Israel, as well as all funding and military research' says the statement.

The Belgian transport unions were the first workers' organisations in Europe to boycott arms exports to Israel in response to this call. Other logistics arms workers in various European countries immediately followed the Belgian example.

On 6 November, in Barcelona, Spain, port workers decided not to allow war materials to be sent to the conflict in the Gaza Strip. They did this 'for the sole purpose of protecting the civilian population, regardless of territory. No reason justifies the sacrifice of civilians.' The dockworkers consider it a collective 'obligation' to defend the Universal Declaration of Human Rights 'tooth and nail', and criticise the many countries that seem to have forgotten they signed the Declaration.[6]

Two days later, transport workers' trade unions in Italy, Turkey and Greece make a joint statement demanding the governments of their countries halt the transfer of arms from their ports and stop support to Israel, which is murdering the people of Palestine. 'The history of transport workers has always been clearly on the side of peace, against fascism, racism, against any occupation and oppression of peoples. For this reason, we cannot tolerate the transformation of the ports, airports, ships, and trains of Europe into centres of trafficking of death'.[7]

On 10 November, hundreds of dockworkers and human rights activists blocked the port of Genoa, Italy, with a march to the offices of Israeli shipping company ZIM, pledging to block arms shipments and calling for a halt to Israel's Gaza genocide.[8] Meanwhile, more than 400 trade unionists in the UK, under the banner of Workers For A Free Palestine, blocked the entrance to the BAE Systems factory site in Kent, where some central components of the fighter jets that Israel is using to bomb Palestine are made before they are shipped to Israel and become a part of the killer fighter planes.[9]

Ukraine

The action of European workers in strikes and boycotts to stop the transport of Western arms to conflict zones does not concern only the war in Palestine, as shown by the widespread cases that happened in 2022, at the beginning of the war in Ukraine, when railroad workers in Greece blocked a shipment of US tanks to Ukraine for more than two weeks,[10] as well as in Pisa, Italy, where airport workers refused to deliver weapons, ammunition, and explosives to Ukraine, passed off by the authorities as 'humanitarian aid'.[11]

'We don't want to get our hands dirty with blood, nor do we want to be accomplices in wars with our working hours.

The fact that I go to work to bring food to my daughter and contribute to the death of other children in another country is madness to me,' said José Nivo,[12] leader of the Collective Autonomous Port Workers (CALP), a dockers association in Genoa, Italy.

Saudi Arabia

The CALP workers were among the first promoters of the battle against the Bahri 'war ships'. Bahri is a company controlled by the Saudi government which ships weapons produced in Western factories to Saudi Arabia via Belgium, Spain, France and Italy.

Arms exports are often legal, but international treaties and many national laws prohibit international transfers of weapons that could be used to commit war crimes, such as direct attacks on the civilian population, and Saudi Arabia is deeply involved in a war in neighbouring Yemen since 2015, a conflict in which there have been repeated violations of international law (see Chapter 6). The conflict in Yemen has led to one of the world's most significant humanitarian crises, and yet arms sales to the Saudi/UAE-led coalition continue from Western countries, including the US, the UK, France, Germany, Italy, Canada and others. Saudi Arabia was the second main importer of major arms at global level in the period 2018–22.[13]

The first coordinated protest between workers from various European ports against Barhi ships occurred at the French port of Le Havre in May 2019. The French media outlet Disclose revealed that one of these ships was on its way from Antwerp to the French port of Le Havre to load eight CAESAR cannons, an artillery piece made up of a mighty gun mounted on an all-wheel-drive truck chassis manufactured by Nexter, a state-owned French defence company. The

CAESAR 'is one of the most powerful weapons France has sold to Saudi Arabia'.[14]

The public reaction was immediate. The French NGO ACAT lodged an appeal with the French courts. 'Faced with the illegality of these deliveries according to the arms trade treaty, signed and ratified by France, because of the possibility of these weapons being used in Yemen against civilian populations, ACAT filed a summary order to block the delivery of the weapons,' the organisation wrote in a statement.[15] So the ship continued its journey without docking in France. But the protest spread and the dockers teamed up, reporting the presence of weapons in the holds of Bahri ships.

Thus, when the Bahri ship *Yanbu* docked at the port of Genoa on 20 May 2019, it was greeted by a banner reading 'Ports closed to weapons, ports open to migrants'.[16] The suspicion was that the cargo ship was in Genoa to load war materiel: four electric generators produced by the Teknel company of Rome, used to power communication, command, and control centres for air and land operations. This material is 'dual-use', technology for civil use that can also be used for war operations.

The *Yanbu*, blocked by the dockers' strike for eight hours, could not carry out loading operations and left the port without the generators. The dockers' action was praised by Pope Francis, who, in November 2019, returning from a trip to Asia, told the story of the dockers of Genoa. 'The dockworkers said no. They were good! And the ship returned to its home. A case, but it teaches us how to move forward.'[17]

'We won the first battle. We have prevented the loading of direct weapons in contexts of blatant violation of human rights,' says Riccardo Rudino,[18] a dockworker of the CALP. 'Now, we have to win the second round. We must prevent even the mere transit of arms to countries in conflict.'

Italian law prohibits the transit of arms 'to countries in a state of armed conflict', 'to countries in which a total or partial embargo on war supplies has been declared', and 'to countries whose governments are responsible for serious violations of international human rights conventions'.[19] However, Bahri ships have continued to carry arms from Genoa to Saudi Arabia, like the fighter helicopters photographed in the ship's hold by the CALP dockers in November 2022.[20]

The dockworkers' struggle struck a blow against the arms trade and laid the basis for the creation of a European network between logistics unions and activists from Spain, Italy, France, Germany, Greece and Ireland that share information and civil disobedience strategies, and have planned an 'international day of struggle against the trafficking of arms from ports'.[21]

International solidarity

When the Palestinian trade unions launched an appeal at the beginning of the war in Palestine, support came from several countries, including Canada, Colombia, Japan, Brazil, South Africa, the USA, India, and even Israel. 'We call on all other trade unions worldwide to emulate that example, refuse to build weapons intended for Israel and to load or unload such weapons', said Israeli citizens and activists in political organisations in a joint statement.[22]

On 26 January 2024, the International Court of Justice (ICJ) in the Hague stated that Israel is 'plausibly' committing genocide in Gaza,[23] and in February UN experts urged other states to immediately halt arms transfers to Israel, including export licences and military aid.[24] Still, 'United States and Germany are by far the largest arms exporters to Israel, and shipments have increased since October 7, 2023. Other military exporters include France, the United Kingdom, Canada and Australia', the experts noted.

Although the Arms Trade Treaty (ATT) prohibits the international transfers of weapons that could be used to commit war crimes, such as direct attacks against the civilian population,[25] and the European Common Position on Arms Exports, in turn, prohibits EU states from authorising arms transfers in such situations,[26] researchers agree that the weak link in all arms trade international treaties and national arms control laws is the lack of enforcement.[27] 'We have one common position on arms export of the EU, but we have 27 national interpretations, 27 export systems, and an increasing divergence in actual exports of Member States,' said Green MEP Hannah Neumann at the European Parliament.[28]

'We want a strict, transparent and coherent EU-level arms export control mechanism, which includes sanctions in case of violations by EU Member States,' declare the Greens/EFA, a political group of the European Parliament proposing an EU regulation to improve arms export control. 'The advantage of a regulation (in comparison to a Common Position) is that the Commission would have a duty to control the respect for the procedures described in the regulation, and, ultimately, to involve the Court of Justice of the European Union if its principles are violated.'[29]

When the Belgian workers took action as the killings in the Gaza war intensified at the end of October 2023, the lack of a meaningful arms export control mechanism was all too evident, and yet it was a first step in building support from unions in other countries. Workers have taken powerful solidarity actions throughout history, such as the Rolls Royce factory workers in Glasgow, Scotland who refused to service fighter jets heading to Pinochet's Chile.[30] When regulations and the law fail to protect human rights, workers have the power to step in, to build a bigger movement and to unite workers across borders fighting against the arms trade. Mass industrial action could turn the tide and ensure that those responsible for our failed arms export controls are held to account.

13

Student Campaigns against the Arms Trade

Carmen Wilson

Carmen Wilson is the Director of Operations for Demilitarise Education (dED_UCATION/dED), a community and guide for modern-day peacemakers, working to see universities break ties with the global arms trade and become champions for peace. Her chapter explores youth campaigns against the arms trade, beginning with the need to demilitarise higher education, followed by a brief global history of youth demilitarisation campaigns and the context they work within today in the United Kingdom. It then discusses the challenges and the work being done to overcome them. She argues that policy reform, divest-to-reinvest and long-term accountability are crucial to address the pressing need for university partnerships to promote peace and sustainability.

There are many defining moments in a young person's life. For some, one of these moments is receiving a university acceptance letter, kickstarting a potential career and ultimately setting the stage for the jump to adulthood. However, this hope for a bright future – and trust in the universities to get them there – is directly undermined by university partnerships with the arms trade. These partnerships come in the form of investments, research projects undertaken with arms companies, and projects and events aimed at funnelling students into careers in all aspects of the arms trade. As a society, we must set expectations for higher education institutions to be free of manipulation from the military and defence sector, and to care more about their students than their bottom line.

There exist deep institutional ties between US universities, defence companies and the Pentagon. Over the last twenty years, universities around the world, and especially in the UK, have followed this pattern, becoming increasingly marketised and acting more like companies than a trusted place for students to grow into confident and capable individuals.[1] However, society is not being taught the realities of the military-industrial complex in academia. University–(arms) industry partnerships are instead presented as 'innovative' opportunities that enable global competition and set participants up for future labour markets. Students can no longer trust that their universities have their best interests at heart when they continually choose profit and commercial interests over ethics, integrity, sustainability, and social justice.

Peace Movements of the Past

Prominent historical examples of student peace movements include the activism in opposition to the Vietnam War. Many American students opposed the increase in military and arms research partnerships and recruitment. From October 1964, the University of California at Berkeley saw over a decade of dissent, with students occupying the campus for so long that the National Guard were sent to remove them.[2] In similar attempts to quash protests the National Guard killed four students at Kent State University in Ohio in 1970.[3] Two years earlier, as part of a growing global crackdown against anti-war activism, at least four students were murdered by police and military troops in Mexico City.[4] In the mid-1970s, following the anti-war protests of 1968, the British government planned with universities to repress student opposition to the military and the arms trade.[5] Across continents, student peace activism continued to strengthen efforts to combat increasing militarism. In the post-Cold War era, student campaigning occurred around the world including in Brazil, Colombia and Mexico.[6,7] The Greenham Common women camped at the gates of a nuclear base from September 1981 to 2000 in Berkshire, and Britain saw a 30,000-strong strong demonstration by women in December 1982,[8] while a 1983 Campaign for Nuclear Disarmament protest was Britain's then-largest peace demonstration with 300,000 people turning out.[9] These actions paved the way for the post-9/11 UK and global youth and student opposition to the Iraq and Afghanistan wars.

In the early twenty-first century, campaigns continued in opposition to increasing militarism, with particular efforts in the US to decolonise curricula.[10] Current efforts continue to push back against the militarist curricula of South Sudan[11] and in the post-Apartheid struggle in South Africa.[12] Across the US, the Dissenters group is running a #DivestfromDeath campaign,[13] with 2022 action against Raytheon at the University of Massachusetts, Amherst.[14] US campaigns continue to target the militarisation of policing, including policing of university campuses, and counter-recruitment on campuses. In Australia, Wage Peace Disrupt War focuses on weapons company infiltration of STEM programmes,[15] and notable examples in Europe include youth campaign group Changemakers in Norway, German resistance to the promotion of a military ethos in schools,[16] and the growing Spanish peace movement.[17] Student peace movements are also active in South Korea,[18] and peacebuilding projects with university students in India are growing.

dED_UCATION

On 12 September 2017, London was set to welcome the likes of Saudi Arabia to buy weapons from British arms manufacturers like BAE Systems. Student Jinsella Kennaway, dED_UCATION's co-founder and executive director, realised that every two years the London ExCeL centre hosts one of the world's largest arms fairs, Defence and Security Equipment International (DSEI). Yemen faces the brutality of British weapons being unlawfully used by Saudi Arabia and its military coalition in conflict zones.[19] The Campaign Against Arms Trade (CAAT) took the fight to the British government, who have 'refused to stop arms sales to Saudi Arabia, despite overwhelming evidence of violations of international humanitarian law in Yemen'.[20] Jinsella attended the Stop the Arms Fair protest and watched weapons entering the centre as police arrested protesters who were blocking the road trying to prevent more British weapons being sold.[21] Upon returning to the University of Manchester, she began building dED_UCATION to raise awareness about the arms fair, soon discovering that the problem was more deeply rooted than she first thought.

UK universities are currently profiting from the destructive nature of war and benefiting from partnerships with the military and defence sector. While student demilitarisation campaigns have existed in the UK for decades, they've struggled to sustain momentum due to fast student turnover. Co-founders Jinsella Kennaway and Mélina Villeneuve officially formed dED_UCATION in April 2019 as an organisation that acts as a central source of knowledge, education, and support, connecting campus campaigns and creating a national benchmark for peace.

Current UK Context

dED works in a global network building on the demilitarise education movement and spreading transformational support to campaigns across UK universities. Demilitarisation campaigns have had some important wins in the past 15 years, often in concert with mobilisation around key social justice issues. Notable campaigns include the University College London (UCL) group Disarm UCL, who used the university's ethical investment policy[22] to campaign in 2021 for a student union motion to end UCL's relationship with arms companies.[23] Given that UCL received thousands of pounds in direct payments from companies like BAE Systems, General Dynamics and Raytheon (2018–21),[24] in direct contradiction of their ethical framework and fossil-free commitment, Disarm UCL exerted pressure on the university to match the words of the policy with divestment action, to little success.[25]

Some universities now have legitimate ethical investment commitments to exclude arms, notably the University of Southampton[26] and the University of St Andrews.[27] Despite this, Southampton receives millions in research partnerships funding from arms companies.[28] The University of Leeds, facing a campaign from the Palestine Solidarity Group involving Freedom of Information requests, direct action, online petitions and an open letter to the vice chancellor, ended investments in arms companies tied to the Israeli military.[29] Solidarity played a huge role, bringing student societies and solidarity groups in the wider Leeds community together to target arms companies like Airbus and banks providing finance to the Israeli military, such as HSBC.[30]

This campaign has inspired other student activists and elected Student Union representatives (called sabbatical officers) to campaign in universities across the UK, including for pensions divestment at Leeds Beckett University[31] and campaigns at the universities of Manchester, Newcastle, Birmingham, and King's College London.

This anti-militarism activism continued in 2022, with several student groups, like Demilitarise Lancaster and Glasgow Against Arms & Fossil Fuels, being re-established and many existing groups organising powerful actions across the UK, including occupations of buildings and disruptions of career fairs.[32]

This experience illustrates that we need to continue to strengthen student-led actions and to work in solidarity for efforts to be taken seriously and to be sustained long term.

Ending UK University Partnerships with the Global Arms Trade

dED_UCATION sees universities as being at the forefront of societal transformation. We attempt to harness community, research, and media to break the ties between universities and the arms trade and refocus those energies on peace. Getting our demilitarisation model into universities across the UK will launch the process to create lasting institutional change in favour of peace and make clear that university partnerships with the defence sector will not be tolerated. This requires supporting students to investigate, expose and end harmful partnerships. We maintain data relating to these activities on our universities and arms database, which enables students to understand the overall issue and movement, and to seek solidarity, support and insight from others engaged in similar struggles.

dED_UCATION began out of a need to support youth campaigns working to end their universities' unethical ties to the global arms trade. University leaders need to understand that this change is not only necessary but also beneficial to their institutions. They must work closely with students to understand their needs, and the ethics and values that underlie those needs, as there is currently a chasm between the ethical expectations of students and the actions of their universities.

With many universities already committed to going fossil free and to decolonise, the door has opened for further commitments to change investments, partnerships, and policies. As of December 2022, a total of 100 UK universities have committed to divest funds away from the fossil fuel industry and reinvest in sustainable options.[33] This commitment cannot be upheld unless it also includes a commitment to demilitarise: you cannot claim to be 'fossil free' if you invest in the business of war, which contributes more to the climate catastrophe than any other industry. New ethical policies to exclude fossil fuels and some arms companies often include subjective language and myriad loopholes.[34] We need a rigorous ban, preventing all arms trade involvement in any recruitment, research, and investment across education, which is why we're calling for universities to sign the Demilitarise Education Treaty.[35] This treaty is a public commitment for UK universities to plan and implement ending their financial, academic, and research partnerships with arms companies, and to establish clear policies and accountability mechanisms to sustain their commitment long term to replace unethical arms partnerships with ones in peaceful and renewable industries.

Solidarity across struggles is also crucial: most recently, the Demilitarise Education movement has joined other movements fighting for climate action and sustainability, addressing the cost-of-living crisis and rent strikes. Movements like People and Planet and a range of Boycott, Divestment, and Sanctions initiatives have paved the way for student voices to make themselves heard and for ethical reform.

While universities used to be a home for those fighting for social justice, the higher education environment has become increasingly hostile to progressive causes. Despite solidarity efforts and generations of resistance, there's more work to be done in demilitarising our educational institutions. Administrators continue to show their complete disregard for upholding ethics, but we need to continue to hold them accountable – and to apply pressure on universities to invest their resources in peace – through research, campaigning, and direct action.

Universities hold undeniable power to shape society and the demilitarise education movement is here to make sure this power is used in favour of peace, not war.

14

Strategic Litigation against the Global Arms Trade

Valentina Azarova

Valentina Azarova (PhD) is a researcher and practitioner from the Feminist Autonomous Centre for Research (Athens) and Emergent Justice Collective centring movement law/yering, transformative justice and abolition feminism as responses to interpersonal, societal, and international violence. The chapter begins with a critical overview of the laws being invoked in strategic litigation efforts concerning arms transfers since the Arms Trade Treaty, often with the aim of exposing the brokenness of licensing systems. Then, in reflecting on the experience of domestic legal struggles against arms transfers that violate international law, the structural obstacles in accessing remedies faced by survivors of mass and structural violence are considered. Domestic legal cases – and the lack of transparency, oversight and accountability they enable for established arms supply relations – are discussed as legal and bureaucratic transnational processes that contribute to the permissive and unaccountable modus operandi of the global arms trade, fuelling and enabling violence. Finally, the chapter concludes by reflecting on a justice and accountability agenda that encompasses the vision of anti-militarist, non-violence, and peace movements, and seeks the transformation of the political (and legal) economy of the global arms trade.

Introduction: Strategic Litigation and the Arms Trade

In the early days of the conflict in Yemen – an ongoing site of humanitarian catastrophe, atrocity, and human suffering – the UN and leading human rights experts called for a ban on all arms sales to the warring parties, citing extensive and mounting evidence of war atrocities. Yet since the Saudi-led coalition entered the conflict in March 2015 – several months after the Arms Trade Treaty (ATT) came into force – the Yemen conflict has been fuelled by ongoing arms supplies from Western states and corporations. A number of ATT State Parties maintained or increased mission-critical arms supplies to Saudi Arabia and the UAE – relationships which may amount to indirect involvement in the Yemen conflict – despite the buyer's systemic violations of and disregard for international law.

In the absence of other avenues for accountability, especially for primary perpetrators of international crimes in Yemen – that is, both the Saudi Arabia and UAE-led military coalition and Yemeni actors – the scale and significance of the arms supplied into the conflict has produced the most extensive body of domestic legal cases based on the ATT. In unprecedented, concerted efforts, civil society actors, including survivors' groups, have attempted to use the ATT and related international laws in the domestic courts of arms-supplying states. Their aim is to contest, restrain, and ultimately halt the supply of weapons that fuel the violence in Yemen. These increasingly coordinated legal challenges have occurred in at least nine European countries, as well as North America and South Africa, and have reached the prosecutor of the International Criminal Court (ICC). This unique legal effort to hold state and corporate actors to account, and to focus on arms suppliers as a way to support an end to the violence, has served as a test of the strength of the ATT. These cases have exposed the political and economic interests embedded in both the law and the practice of its implementation, and thus the role of international and national law in the reproduction of violence and irresponsibility. This chapter critically examines the legal practice and policy, enabled by international and domestic arms control law, that legitimises the role of exporting states in structural violence, as revealed by the experience of transnational litigation around the Yemen conflict.

When the ATT was being drafted, the political and economic interests of state and corporate actors heavily influenced the text of the final document. This is demonstrated by the current landscape of the arms trade, in which arms-supplying companies and states are enabled to continue a range of highly problematic practices unchecked. Not only were the rules enshrined in the ATT highly compromised throughout its negotiation and drafting, they were further watered down during their domestic implementation by states. The legislation that adapts the ATT into domestic law, and the licensing systems and procedures they establish, have not prevented – nor provided the means to effectively challenge – licensing decisions that are unlawful under the ATT and other international laws.

The surge of litigation may have disincentivised, but it has not stopped exporting states from continuing (and in some cases increasing) arms transfers to the Yemen conflict. The 'rearming' commitments around the war on Ukraine – with arms being provided without conditions and despite known diversion of weapons beyond the reported user; and the continuous supply of weapons to Israel for use in its sustained assault on Gaza – have had extremely negative effects on the regulation of the arms trade. Mindful of the particular limits of these legal instruments, strategic litigation against the arms trade has equally focused on exposing the structural biases and political interests that underpin them, with a view to identifying much-needed systemic law and policy reforms.

The Fractured Legal Landscape of Arms Trade Strategic Litigation

The ATT's drafting and negotiation quickly fell hostage to corporate and state lobbies and the interests of foreign interventionists, producing a system that in effect legitimises even clearly unlawful arms transfers. The treaty's adoption resulted in minimal change to domestic laws and procedures, gave domestic licensing authorities a wide margin of interpretation, and made domestic courts and, to a lesser extent, parliaments the principal oversight authorities. In other words, in the absence of an international supervisory body for the ATT, domestic authorities could single-handedly decide on how to implement the ATT, including by setting aside the application of certain international law rules, such as those on state responsibility, which were meant to be applied with and complement the ATT. At the domestic level, arms export control decisions are governed by administrative and public law and procedure which places the burden on claimants to investigate and prove the exporting state's wrongful conduct. This fractured legal landscape offers a limited number of legal grounds and pathways for challenging domestic authorities' licensing decisions.

As the main enforcers of the implementation of *international* arms control law, domestic licensing authorities have provided a stamp of legality also for arms transfers that appear to be 'unlawful' as they are destined for serial offenders of international law. They do so based on high-threshold, politically skewed interpretations of terms like 'seriousness' and 'risk'. Stopping an arms export from the outset requires a very high threshold to be met, including that the state has knowledge of the likelihood of exported arms being used for the commission of genocide, crimes against humanity, breaches of the Geneva Convention, attacks on civilians or war crimes (Article 6(3) of the ATT). Similarly, risk assessments under Article 7, concerning possible *serious* violations of international law which may also arise at any point during the lifespan of a licence, have been widely discretionary in particular in the definition of what constitutes 'serious' violations. Crucially, post-export reviews of existing licences (some last up to a decade) are not mandatory (only recommended), even if new information about such concerns is available to the supplying country after the export of the weapons.

These critical shortcomings are compounded by a number of silences in the treaty that *exclude* certain types of meaningful controls:

- no prohibition on facilitating, fuelling or maintaining protracted conflict and violence (arms can 'contribute to or undermine international peace and security' [Article 7(1)(a)]);
- no time-limit on the length of licences, including post-sale activities such as training and maintenance;
- no regulation of a company's activities through its subsidiaries in most countries, allowing companies to avoid national restrictions by using foreign subsidiaries;
- limited controls for joint projects, intra-European and other non-sensitive licences (so-called 'open' or 'extant' licences), and no controls over the actions of international organisations, such as the Organisation for Joint Armament Cooperation (OCCAR) with member states including Germany, France, Italy, Spain, the UK and Belgium; and
- no requirement to publish in a timely manner all information about newly issued licences (except in the form

of periodic, broad reporting to parliament), nor the reasons for licensing decisions.

Despite concerted efforts and increasing ingenuity by civil society actors, these biases structurally preclude the possibility of effectively challenging even licensed transfers that contribute to egregious violations and harmful realities of protracted violence. The domestic laws that implement the ATT in effect circumvent states' obligations under other international laws that prohibit assistance and aid to another actor's violations, despite the fact that the ATT makes clear that its provisions are without prejudice to states' existing obligations under other international treaties (Article 26 of the Treaty).

The ATT's purpose was to prevent complicity by defining the scope of arms trade relations that amount to 'wrongful assistance' to serious violations, which would inform judicial reasoning and government legal advice on licensing decisions. The definition of wrongful assistance or complicity is found in the rules of international law on state responsibility, which prohibit states from aiding and assisting any wrongful acts by other states. These also include a set of special rules on aggravated violations, such as so-called 'serious breaches of peremptory norms' or fundamental principles that require states not to aid, assist or recognise 'as lawful' such wrongful acts and their consequences, including by refusing arms export relationships and deals in situations that would validate such acts (codified in the International Law Commission [ILC] Draft Articles on State Responsibility). Special rules on complicity are also found in international humanitarian law (IHL) and human rights law (IHRL), such as the obligation to ensure respect for IHL by all states including arms recipients (see Common Article 1 to the Geneva Conventions), and the IHRL requirement that arms-supplying states ensure that their actions do not harmfully impact the right to life, for example, decisions to license arms transfers by its corporate nationals.

In practice, domestic regulatory regimes are much less effective than the ATT's envisaged prevention framework for arms transfers that wrongfully assist serious violations of international law. In particular, the pre-transfer and the post-transfer controls implemented by domestic export control systems are much less robust than what is arguably required of states under either the ATT or other international laws on wrongful assistance, which barely inform the advice provided by government lawyers to licensing authorities. The very laws that are intended to regulate complicity and wrongful military assistance are therefore in practice backgrounded and silenced, including in the context of domestic legal cases challenging certain arms transfers. In other words, in this 'zone of non-responsibility', states and corporate actors can effectively export to whomsoever they want, regardless of the purpose for which the arms are used and their contribution to systemic harm and violations of IHL and IHRL.

Most domestic judges consider these issues to fall outside the scope of their jurisdiction and thus consider such legal questions to be resolved as part of the licensing decision-making process. This is a fundamental flaw that undermines their ability to demand the review and even revocation of licences that enable wrongful assistance, in line with the ATT and other international laws.

This is closely linked to another structural regulatory 'silence': the limited regulation of corporate actors, especially in the absence of post-export controls. Under the UN Guiding Principles on Business and Human Rights, the Organisation for Economic Co-operation and Development (OECD) Guidelines on Multinational Enterprises, and the 2019 OECD Due Diligence Guidance for Responsible Business Conduct, states are required to adopt 'regulatory measures' that require businesses to engage in human rights due diligence (HRDD) to ensure that their operations do not adversely impact human rights throughout their, downward and upward, supply chains.

The Information Note on 'Responsible business conduct in the arms sector' issued by the UN Working Group observes that rarely do arms-supplying states and companies apply HRDD procedures to arms transfers, and concludes by calling upon them to 'Ensure that the complexity of HRDD processes is commensurate with the business's position in the arms sector value chain and its risk of causing or contributing to human rights abuses'.[1] These (soft) law international standards also require that home states provide survivors of wrongs by their business with access to an effective remedy (arguably irrespective of the 'legality' of the transfer), which invites the very discussion we turn to next concerning the accessibility and quality of domestic avenues for transnational litigation to challenge the harmful contribution of arms supplies.

The Experience of Unaccountability: Strategic Litigation against Arms Transfers to the Yemen Conflict

With little to no regulation or oversight by international authorities, domestic bodies and processes are an essential pillar of the implementation and enforcement of the ATT, and the main form of recourse against breaches of the ATT and related international laws. In most countries, domestic judicial oversight is also the only form of external post-export control, other than the generic, limited and sometimes non-existent forms of parliamentary oversight. Due to the absence of accountability for the principal wrongs and perpetrators in the Yemen conflict, the surge in ATT-based domestic proceedings since 2016, seeking relief against unlawful arms supplies, has become one of the only ways to pursue legal accountability and remedies for communities affected by the mass and structural forms of violence (the latter often being slow and indirect) fuelled by arms supplies. This experience has exposed the various access barriers – including a systemic lack of transparency, restricted jurisdictional scope and limited scope of review available before domestic jurisdictions.

Prime among these is the unwritten presumption of national security-based secrecy, a structural entry-level hurdle that has either completely barred proceedings from being initiated (e.g. in Spain), limited the arguments that can be put forward to challenge the state's claims (e.g. in the UK), or resulted in more limited claims and repeated filings due to delays and infrequency of the release of information about issued licences (e.g. in Belgium). In most countries there is no publicly available information about the full scope of items transferred, let alone the reasoning behind licensing decisions; partially available information is often released too late, making such challenges dismissible or obsolete.

Most claims are filed without proper information on the scope and duration of arms sales and export licences, and most of the information we know about such processes and decisions was obtained through proceedings, such as in the Italian and Canadian cases. In all jurisdictions, the government can refute challenges to arms transfers by relying on classified information, at best in closed proceedings with Special Advocates (particularly in the UK), and otherwise in a limited government position with a laconic reference to 'privileged' information (e.g. Canada). Violations of the right to information and freedom of expression may be considered by the European Court of Human Rights due to Spain's abuse of Franco-era secrecy laws to classify licences and Belgium's refusal to release information about arms transfers in a full and timely manner.

The restrictions on the jurisdictional scope of what courts are allowed to review and adjudicate on is a further key set of barriers to access. In some jurisdictions, such as France and the US, courts cannot challenge licensing decisions because they are deemed 'acts of government' that are immune from judicial scrutiny. Whereas, in common law jurisdictions such as the UK and Canada, the scope of what can be judicially challenged and reviewed is limited to the procedural validity of how a licensing decision was adopted, in a manner that is highly favourable to the licensing authority. In other words, it is a public law review standard in which the court considers whether to interfere with the government's licensing decision-making process, for example, by ordering it to reassess a decision (often with no substantive guidance). The threshold for such interference is whether the public authority's decision to grant a *specific* set of licences to a given buyer country is 'rational', based on the advice it received and the potential misuse of the type of arms. Despite abundant information about serious violations in certain contexts, and while the information governments offer about arms transfers is at best scarce, civil society and survivors bear an inordinate evidentiary burden in having to show that the licensing authority had erred in assessing the risk of misuse.

Where cases are admissible and allowed to proceed, most courts have set astronomically high thresholds to establish illegality and wrongfulness (specific to the licence, often meaning they do not establish precedent). Domestic proceedings have revealed just how easily exporting states can use changing interpretations of their arms control law to diminish 'overriding' risk to suit their interests. The evolution of the UK's position in response to the CAAT proceedings is an illustrative example. On 7 July 2020, four years after the start of proceedings and a year after the Court of Appeal ordered the UK government to reassess its policy of approving arms sales to Saudi Arabia, the government released a 'revised methodology' which limits its risk assessment to the review of 'specific conduct' (excluding general conduct and attitude towards international law) and whether it amounts to patterns of violations as opposed to mere isolated incidents that 'occurred at different times, in different circumstances and for different reasons'. Despite the UK's government having recorded at least 518 incidents from 2015 to July 2020 in which the Saudi-led military coalition violated the laws of war (averaging 1.5 incidents per week; see Chapter 6), the government was adamant that 'the prohibitive risk threshold was not met'. The new position also disregards the clear rule that so-called 'overriding risk' cannot be mitigated through assurances or privileged information about the buyer state, in this case Saudi Arabia's 'genuine intent and the capacity to comply with IHL'. This view effectively gives 'legal' cover to highly violative 'general' conduct and 'attitude towards' international law.

On 6 June 2023, the UK's High Court dismissed the second judicial review claim brought by CAAT challenging the government's new position to renew arms sales to Saudi Arabia. The Court itself noted '"the deliberately high threshold" of irrationality that CAAT must prove', and further stated that 'judicial review is not an appeal against governmental decisions on their merits'. This time the Court again agreed with the government that the Saudi-led coalition's 'improvements' in adhering to IHL over the course of the war shows that they were willing and able to comply with IHL, and that the number of IHL breaches recorded 'is consistent with a limited number of errors, well within the margin that would be expected in a conflict of this nature'.[2]

This tactic of deflecting serious concerns arising from the buyer's likely end-use of a given export is, alas, not unique to the UK. France and Canada have also regularly referenced classified assurances and privileged information to dismiss the presence of 'overriding risk' of the arms misuse, despite overwhelming evidence of serious violations by arms-buyers.[3] During proceedings, the Canadian government revealed that to reach a sufficient threshold of 'risk' it required proof of misuse of the specific Canadian-manufactured weapons by the buyer, and not only similar types of weapons, as understood by ATT experts. In Belgian courts, the assessment of risk has been based on the location of the armed forces unit that would use the weapons and their violating conduct, and not on the quality of the armed forces unit's 'general' conduct. The fact that the scope of judicial review in civil law jurisdictions is limited to the examination of specific licences, has enabled some governments to easily reissue annulled licences (e.g. Belgium).

While these definitions of an unlawful transfer are narrower and more restrictive than those ostensibly found in the ATT, the presumed conformity of domestic law with international law in some states (e.g. the Netherlands, Italy), and the inability to invoke international laws directly before domestic courts in others (e.g. Canada), has meant that no domestic court has been called to review whether domestic law provisions or decisions conform with the state's obligations under the ATT or other related international laws. An attempt to refer a question concerning the application of the European Union (EU) Common Position (an instrument of Common Foreign and Security Policy) to the Court of Justice of the EU, in the course of French domestic proceedings, was denied.

In a second strand of domestic cases under domestic criminal and civil law, the restrictive nature of what is allowed as evidence and substantive argument effectively limits the scope of judicial oversight to a narrow category of acts, that is, knowingly assisting in the injury caused by a supplied weapon's use. Such proceedings are lengthy, costly, and in no case have they resulted in the termination of sales to a certain buyer. The criminal filing to the Italian prosecutor in April 2018, charging managers of RWM Italia (an Italian subsidiary of the German arms manufacturer) and officials of the Italian Arms Export Authority with complicity in murder and personal injury through gross negligence, is based on an RWM Italia munition found at the site of an airstrike in Deir al-Hajari, Yemen, that killed a family of six in October 2016, that was said to have been exported from Italy in November 2015. The Italian public prosecutor's motion to close the case in October 2019 was overturned on appeal in February 2021. The proceedings, however, are believed to have influenced the Italian parliament's 1 February 2021 decision to cancel a shipment of more than 12,700 bombs to Saudi Arabia; the first permanent revocation of an existing licence since Italy's 1990 law on arms exports came into force. The Judge for Preliminary Investigations in Rome dismissed the case in March 2023, accepting that the licences had been issued in violation of the ATT but maintaining nonetheless that it 'could not be proven that the company profited from the abuse of power'.[4] This case has since been filed against Italy before the European Court of Human Rights, citing claims of failure to investigate the crimes of homicide and personal injury, and seeking access to justice for victims of war crimes committed with weapons produced in and/or exported from Europe, as required under the right to life (Article 2 of the European Convention on Human Rights).

The latest strategic litigation efforts seek to call into question the organised complicity enabled by domestic arms export controls laws by requesting the ICC prosecutor to investigate government and corporate officials from five European countries who have supplied arms to parties to the conflict in Yemen, in full knowledge of their involvement in war atrocities. This pending communication before the ICC Office of the Prosecutor (under Article 15 of the Rome Statute) by a coalition of rights groups led by the European Centre for Constitutional and Human Rights (ECCHR) mounts a strategically important structural critique of domestic arms export control laws and oversight mechanisms. Mindful of the limits of criminal measures as forms of justice, and of the ICC as an institution, such a legal intervention also calls on regional and international bodies to review their more limited role in the implementation and enforcement of the ATT and other related international laws.[5] Similar efforts include the filings before the European Court of Human Rights, mentioned above, on information and the right to life; various initiatives at the European level to harmonise controls, including resourcing the EU Working Group on Conventional Arms Exports (COARM) and a draft EU regulation on arms export controls; and advocacy before the UN Working Group on Business and Human Rights, which led to the issuance of an Information Note on 'Responsible business conduct in the arms sector'.[6]

Remedial Limits and Denial of Justice: Legal Mobilisation within the Political Economy of the Arms Trade

By 2023, civil society actors involved in litigation have become well-acquainted with domestic ATT regimes and their capacity to avoid making determinations of 'prohibitive risk' that would require the review and suspension of arms exports.[7] Domestic proceedings have been the main pathway for non-governmental legal advocates to expose the government's legal position and challenge the justifications brought by government lawyers. Social justice actors have been disheartened by the legal outcomes of licensing challenges, due to the ways in which they have encouraged irresponsible arms exports, resulting in denial of justice for survivors and communities affected by violence fuelled by arms supplies. By deflecting responsibility and artificially narrowing what is challengeable, governments have enabled themselves to subtly renew licences and amend policies to circumvent the effects of protracted legal proceedings. The various procedural and substantive barriers to effective oversight and review of domestic licensing processes has prevented the possibility of effectively challenging even those transfers that may both breach ATT end-use prohibitions and attract responsibility for wrongful assistance. The Arms Trade Litigation Monitor, a near-comprehensive observatory of international, regional and domestic legal efforts to challenge the arms trade, offers detailed documentation of these efforts,[8] and of the status quo, in which domestic systems appear to be entrenching the very problem that the ATT regime intended to redress: the disparities between domestic export controls and their consequent ineffectiveness as controls on the global arms trade.

What do these legal and political struggles – in the courtroom, parliaments and other regional and international bodies – against irresponsible arms supplies tell us about the possibilities for accountability in the global arms trade? What is the transformative potential of mobilisation based on existing law? Which actions has it exonerated and legitimised? Which aspects of the broader anti-militarist social justice agenda has it sidelined, silenced or denied? What is the justice which we seek and have not had access to as regards the systems that enable the arms trade and its links with militarism, and hence the fuelling of mass and structural violence? In what ways is the justice and accountability that is available to survivors and affected communities through existing mechanisms constrained and obstructed by the very systems that purport to control and remedy the harms of the arms trade?

The ATT was established in the (far from naïve) hope that an international project of its kind could begin to redress the role of the global arms trade in enabling and perpetuating mass and structural violence. The experience of strategic litigation by civil society has exposed the impunity of those who profit from war economies, whereby even the most apparently prohibited arms supply relationships are protected from and enabled by international law. Such legal struggles have revealed that the choice to arm warring parties involved in war atrocities and responsible for serious violations of international law is consistent with the political preferences that underpin the ATT regime. Licensing decisions may be the work of bureaucratic state authorities, but such processes are contingent on deep-seated politics that privilege arms supply relationships and their political economy over the lives and wellbeing of those they continue to gravely harm.

The transformative potential of legal interventions from within this system is obviously limited. In relying on existing forms of recourse, we are left with challenges that essentially avoid making decisions about the legality of buyers' and suppliers' conduct; that launder the role of arms suppliers in fuelling violence; and that avoid reviewing inter-state defence cooperation relations, and their devastating socioeconomic and developmental implications. The political contribution of domestic strategic litigation has been to expose the policy preferences embedded in the politico-legal practices deployed by licensing systems that sanction, legitimise and normalise neoliberal militarism. The focus on domestic proceedings has narrowed the possibilities for and visions of justice and accountability for the grave systemic harm caused by arms supply relationships. The reliance on such limited legal forms reinforces the impunity of arms suppliers and silences the potential for a transformative anti-militarist social justice agenda. This includes the social, economic and political ties that underpin arms supply relationships and intersect with the structural causes of conflict and the global systems of inequality.

Given the near impossibility of directly challenging, let alone transforming, the interests that underpin and drive the arms trade, arms trade litigation often distracts from the need to mobilise against the political economy of the arms trade and its legal systems. It also takes away from the felt urgency around the need to enhance the means and capacity of the international system to pursue systemic and intersectional justice that addresses the root causes of mass and structural violence.

Conclusion: Liberatory Lawyering against the Arms Trade

Given the limited scope of what is reviewable under the current law governing the global arms trade, truly liberatory lawyering should seek social transformation that would reimagine current laws and prefigure new anti-militarist futures that are unavailable under current conditions underpinning arms trade litigation. Liberatory lawyering is a commitment to centring restorative and transformative justice and accountability that can challenge the violence of the underpinning racial, economic, and representational inequalities of liberal justice systems.

A liberatory lawyering agenda for the arms trade should draw on anti-war, and peace movements' social and political visions, and aim to reimagine international public policy that promotes neoliberal militarism and endorses exploitative policies of globalisation.[9] What would it mean to fully align the licensing system and its review mechanisms with the values and politics of anti-militarism and non-violence struggles? What are the conditions of possibility in international law for prohibiting arms sales that fuel and enable mass and structural violence? How does this link to questions around the ways in which the international community responds to violence with violence and in ways that reproduce it? How can we create justice processes that pursue a broader and fuller social transformation vision and agenda? Such questions need to be discussed collectively in a different kind of forum, where survivors, affected communities, social movements, and other civil society actors, can meet each other and create a space, such as peoples' tribunals in which we can act from a grounded place of critical reflection.[10]

How do we frame and position our interventions against certain arms licences and transfers in a manner that is critically conscious of the ways in which these very systems enable and endorse militarism, and the harmful socioeconomic and developmental impacts of arms suppliers as conflict actors? By focusing on the entangled complicities of arms suppliers, lawyers can begin accounting for some of the ways in which these roles and responsibilities condition and fuel violence and how certain resources can be redistributed towards reconstruction and development.

To pursue real social transformation with regard to the arms trade, our daily struggles against unlawful arms transfers need to centre a broader social justice agenda that seeks to end militarism and war economies, resource our ability to respond to violence in ways that prioritise non-violence and anti-militarism, and expose and counter the international laws that enable violence and maintain global inequalities. This is particularly urgent given the surge in militarism around the ongoing arming of Ukraine and Israel and its entanglements with international justice mechanisms, which have undermined arms control laws and the responsibilities of arms suppliers in relation to transformative reparations.

The more pointed, and hence limiting, struggles against 'unlawful' arms transfers critically invite us to (re)imagine the ways in which the international system could respond to violence in transformative ways. This includes shifting away from the current (over)use of conflict management tools, which include arms export controls, which make an exception of certain 'illegal' forms of violence and contributions thereto, only to enable other forms of violence. To avoid this, arms trade accountability efforts should be situated and contextualised within broader struggles, transformative reparations for the colonial root causes of mass and structural violence and be grounded in an affective politics that centres social transformation and that resists and counters its particular conditioning in/through law.

15

Lynchpin of the Pacific: Ending the Militarisation of Hawai'i

Kawena'ulaokalā Kapahua

Kawena'ulaokalā is a community organiser rooted in the Hawaiian independence movement and union organising. Here he demonstrates how resistance to the arms trade can strike concrete blows to the military-industrial complex, using the case study of how the Hawaiian sovereignty movement managed to get the Red Hill fuel storage facility shut down for good. His chapter explores how the US uses the occupied Hawaiian nation as its testing grounds for weapons of war, threatening the lives and communities of the Indigenous people; how those people have been forced from their land and their homes for military gain; and how they are fighting back, not only to further their own struggle, but to launch the first blow against US imperialism that has repercussions all across the world.

In the ever-expanding global arms trade, certain regions of the world have become demarcated as sacrificial testing grounds for weapons of war. Paramount among these regions is the Pacific Ocean. The territory of the Pacific Islands combined, including the water where people have voyaged for generations, is the most expansive region on Earth. And yet, because of the vast distances between islands, many consider it sparsely inhabited. For thousands of years, Pacific Islanders have crossed vast oceans to make even the more remote islands a thriving home. The military-industrial complex has determined that those engaging in these incredible human endeavours are expendable. The arms industry was readily willing to displace, discard, and annihilate all that Pacific Islanders have accomplished in these waters. Indeed, since the advent of colonialism in the Pacific, Western powers have seen the Pacific as their testing ground for weapons and their staging ground for wars of imperialism. Hawai'i especially has fallen victim to such political machinations. For much of Hawai'i's history since Western contact, Hawai'i has had to deal with the fact that Western powers only see value in its strategic and military worth, while the Indigenous people of Hawai'i strive to protect our home and end the proliferation of the arms trade on our land.

When the United States was eyeing the Pacific as the next stage in its 'manifest destiny',[1] it sent General John Schofield, Commander of the US Military Division of the Pacific, to the Hawaiian Kingdom on a secret mission to scout out a location for a new base. In 1873, Schofield sent a secret communiqué to General William Sherman, commanding general of the United States Army, that spoke of 'Pu'uloa, now known as Pearl Harbor: 'It is the key to the Central Pacific Ocean, it is the gem of these islands, valueless to [Hawaiians] because they cannot use it, but more valuable to the United States than all else the islands have to give.'[2] This would culminate with the illegal invasion of the Hawaiian Kingdom by US Marines in 1893, the overthrow of the kingdom in support of a cabal of sugar barons and other capitalist elites, as well as the establishment of the Pearl Harbor naval station as the heart of United States military power in the Pacific. Since 1959, the occupied Hawaiian nation has been falsely claimed as a US state and is the headquarters of the Indo-Pacific Command,[3] the largest command area of the US military on the planet. The United States military controls over 200,000 acres of land in Hawai'i and is seeking more.[4] From massive bases like Pearl Harbor and Kāneāohe Marine Corps Base to weapons training areas like Pōhakuloa or Mākua Valley, there is no part of Hawai'i undamaged by the presence of the US military.

These bases were acquired by evicting the communities who already lived on the land, many of whom died without ever getting to return to their homes. In the case of Mākua Valley, amid the aftermath of the Second World War bombing of Pearl Harbor, the US Army told the evicted residents that they could return to their homes after the end of the war, and then instead used those homes as bombing targets under the guise of 'national defense'.[5] The US military still controls Mākua Valley. To this day, the US military has a dominating presence on the landscape, already squeezing out the working-class and poor people confronting an unaffordable housing market and forcing many into homelessness. The occupation of Hawai'i is not for defensive purposes; nearly every US war in the Pacific and Asia has used Hawai'i as a thoroughfare, staging area, or base of operations. From the Second World War to Korea and Vietnam, it is famously said within the Hawaiian sovereignty movement that 'when the United States goes to war, Hawaiians lose more land'. This legacy continues today: we see major transfers of US troops and weapons through Hawai'i to reach the Middle East and Asia, where the United States enacts its hegemonic foreign policy agenda paired with the construction of new military facilities. In addition, the United States uses the vast water territory of the Pacific Islands to control shipping and navigation in the Pacific and to give its navy ease of access to threaten its opponents. Situated in a central location in the Pacific, Hawai'i is weaponised as the lynchpin of US imperialism. This reality highlights the importance of the Hawaiian sovereignty movement in combating US imperialism in the Pacific – by removing the United States from the islands that they believe to be their fortress.

The United States' death grip on the Pacific has been spread by its imperialist policies, but it has also been a means of capitalist profit. For too long the Pacific has been used as an 'isolated' weapons testing and training ground for the imperialist powers of the world. From nuclear testing in the Marshall Islands[6] and Tahiti[7] to the testing of agent orange in Hawai'i and Guam,[8] the people and environment of the Pacific Islands are viewed as disposable and yet their geographical location is approached as an integral part of the strategy of the imperialist powers. In this way, the United States generates profit through the sale of these weapons as well as the introduction of the military-industrial complex to these regions. Pearl Harbor is, unfortunately, a site of great harm not only for Hawai'i but the world, due to its hosting of the US Pacific fleet. Hawai'i's strategic location, of which Pearl Harbor is a focal point, is the reason why the Red Hill storage facility was chosen to store the jet fuel that ultimately poisoned the Hawaiian water supply, and why American military action is able to launch around the world.

The US military has seized vast swathes of land to become firing ranges and other weapons training areas. Sacred places like the island of Kahoʻolawe, Pōhakuloa on Hawai'i Island, and Mākua Valley on Oʻahu, are now riddled with the scars of military activity. This military activity and infrastructure supports not only the US military's war crimes and acts of aggression but also those of its allies. This is accomplished through the training of other nations' militaries on Hawaiian land and waters, training them to suppress people's movements and resistance through exercises bombing Hawaiian land and polluting Hawaiian waters.[9,10,11]

Every two years the US military hosts the Rim of the Pacific (RIMPAC), the largest military exercises in the world, in Hawai'i. The United States and over 20 other nations practice invasions, suppression of resistance groups, and the execution of regime change. This includes training to support nations outside of the Pacific as well, such as the Israeli occupation forces.[12] These exercises train soldiers on tactics in live-fire exercises, including the sinking of ships, the landing of invasion forces and, in 2022, the mock invasion of North Korea. This was conducted by '38 surface ships, three submarines, nine national land forces, more than 30 unmanned systems, approximately 170 aircraft and over 25,000 personnel' according to a press release about RIMPAC 2022.[13] And it's all fuelled by the fuel storage facility at Red Hill, which has to date leaked over 200,000 gallons of fuel and PFAS ('forever chemicals') into the drinking water of O'ahu and poisoned over 100,000 people.[14] The interconnected nature of these issues showcases the extent to which US foreign policy relies upon the exploitation of Indigenous land in order to remain in power. This includes the US weapons industry's reliance on imperialist policy: RIMPAC concludes with a week-long weapons fair in which the United States offers fellow imperialist militaries the chance to purchase the weapons systems they spent all month showing off during the war games. While the scale and organisation of the military operation in Hawai'i may seem exhaustive and unassailable, it is matched only by the determination, organisation, and calculated resistance to it in Hawai'i that has undermined and weakened the United States time and time again.

The Hawaiian sovereignty movement has existed since the overthrow of the Hawaiian Kingdom by US Marines in 1893. Citizens of Hawai'i, of various ethnic backgrounds, rallied to fight to restore the independence of the nation. Nearly every Hawaiian alive today can trace their genealogy to a person who signed the petitions that were organised to stop the annexation of Hawai'i to the United States. The Hawaiian sovereignty movement has not forgotten its original enemy and continues to be the main force opposing the United States in Hawai'i. The anti-imperialist origins of the movement hold strong in its modern iteration, such as the occupation and rec-lamation of Kaho'olawe, where Hawaiian activists snuck onto a military controlled bombing range in secret to force an end to the bombing at the cost of the lives of two brave revolution-aries.[15] Hawaiian struggles against the military have included all age groups, often advised by the elders of the commu-nity, while the younger generations take up the fight on the frontlines. Kaho'olawe in the 1970s saw groups of organisers in their twenties helping elders off boats in order to occupy the island, while Red Hill and RIMPAC in the 2020s once again faced young and old standing together on the frontline of direct actions, demanding an end to the military abuse of our people and land. When it comes to the struggle against the Red Hill fuel storage facility and against RIMPAC, these efforts are interlinked. Both issues are struggles not just on behalf of protecting Hawai'i, but also on behalf of the global struggle against militarisation.

Where RIMPAC trains and arms the United States and other nations to go out in the world and commit crimes, from genocide to regime change to the suppression of people's movements, Red Hill fuels the weapons of war that will bomb people's homes, destabilise regions and cause mass destruc-tion. It also demonstrates how the military use of Hawai'i poses a grave danger to the people who live on these islands. When the Hawaiian movement fights to shut down military installations in Hawai'i, we fight not only for our home, our livelihoods, future generations, and our independence, but also for the independence of every other nation around the world. We fight for their sovereignty to not be invaded and attacked by the imperialist axis that the United States has con-structed. For every bomb that the US and its allies drop on Hawaiian land, another will fall on a Palestinian home, or in West Papua, or in the Philippines. Therefore it stands as the duty of the Hawaiian movement to do what it can to stop the harm being launched from our homeland against our brothers and sisters abroad. The struggle to demilitarise and de-occupy Hawai'i stands as a testament to the possibility of a world without imperialism, without the arms trade. Prior to the leak of November 2021, Hawaiian organisers had been told for decades that shutting down the Red Hill fuel storage facility was an impossible pipe dream. By March 2022, after months of mass protests, direct actions and grassroots organising, the US Navy announced it would shut down and close the Red Hill facility.[16] If it is possible for us to shutter a facility of the most powerful military on Earth, then the future free of imperialist wars of profit seems closer than ever before.

Further Reading

Beamer, Kamanamaikalani, *No Mākou Ka Mana: Liberating the Nation* (Honolulu: Kamehameha Schools Press, 2014).

Goodyear-Ka'ōpua, Noelani (ed.) *Nā Wahine Koa: Hawaiian Women for Sovereignty and Demilitarization* (Honolulu: University of Hawai'i Press, 2018).

Goodyear-Ka'ōpua, Noelani, Hussey, Ikaika and Wright, Erin Kahunawaika'ala (eds) *A Nation Rising: Hawaiian Movements for Life, Land, and Sovereignty* (Durham, NC: Duke University Press Books, 2014).

Silva, Noenoe K., *Aloha Betrayed: Native Hawaiian Resistance to American Colonialism* (Durham, NC: Duke University Press Books, 2004).

Trask, Haunani-Kay, *From a Native Daughter: Colonialism and Sovereignty in Hawaii*, 2nd edn (Honolulu: University of Hawaii Press, 1999).

Conclusion

Rhona Michie, Andrew Feinstein and Paul Rogers

In February 2022, Russian forces attempted to occupy much of Ukraine, the start of a sudden expansion of war in eastern Europe. NATO responded with immediate assistance for Ukraine, principally in the form of numerous arms supplies, a pipeline of military assistance that continued for months and then years. Russia initially used its own military resources but within a few months was sourcing specific weapons – such as armed drones, ballistic missiles and artillery munitions – from Iran, North Korea and elsewhere. Russia failed in its initial attempt to bring down the Ukraine government, even after extensive destruction of Ukrainian cities. Military spending surged around the world and the main arms manufacturers benefited greatly from the expanding markets. Many reported buoyant sales figures and stock market positions, and sales staff sought to publicise the success of their systems.

In October the following year (2023), during a surprise attack by Hamas paramilitaries from Gaza into southern Israel, 850 Israeli civilians and 350 Israeli military were killed and 200 taken hostage. The government of Benjamin Netanyahu responded with extreme force and declared that Hamas would be completely destroyed, no matter how long it might take. At the end of the first three months, the Israeli Defence Forces (IDF) had destroyed much of Gaza, including universities, colleges, schools, health centres and hospitals, and had damaged or destroyed the majority of all flats and houses. Power and freshwater were persistently restricted, as was food and fuel. The UN Relief and Works Agency (UNRWA) and the UN World Food Programme warned of the probable outbreak of famine in a matter of weeks and the World Health Organization warned of malnutrition, long-term stunting of children and outbreaks of infectious diseases.

The status of Israel crumbled across much of the world, especially the Middle East and throughout the global South, but Israel retained the support of the United States and of its junior partner, the United Kingdom. Israel's way of war, known as the Dahiya policy and rooted in a counter-insurgency strategy of collective punishment of civilians was being used to the full as it attempted to undermine support for Hamas in Gaza. Defeating the movement was proving impossible even as, by March 2024, the Palestinian death toll surpassed 32,000 and almost 75,000 more were injured. A substantial number of the deaths – over 13,000 – were children, many of them newborn or infants.[1]

There were calls for Israeli moderation, including in the United States, but these had little impact. However, Israel was massively dependent on US military assistance, primarily in the supply of bombs, missiles, drones and especially artillery shells. Without that persistent support, and backed up by the UK, Israel would have had to give up its attempts to defeat Hamas and settle for a negotiated outcome.

The supply of weapons has two major features. First, it is a matter of business and profitability. In a shareholder capitalist system, which is dominant across most of the world's arms producers, the accumulation of profit is a core function, but a secondary if important feature is the use of arms developments and sales in the pursuit of foreign policy.

New Wars, New Markets

In both Ukraine and Gaza, the early months of these wars followed a common pattern as the situations evolved rapidly, new weapons were developed and sales forces spread out to demonstrate their wares. Early examples were new types of portable anti-tank missiles provided to Ukraine by NATO allies, which proved to be effective, even against the more modern Russian tanks. The results were watched with interest across the world's arms industries, as demand for these weapons increased.

Similarly, a range of new UAVs (Unmanned Aerial Vehicles) and UCAVs (Unmanned Combat Aerial Vehicles) were available, both for surveillance and attack. Along with land- and air-based systems, international military manufacturers were particularly interested in Ukrainian domestic development of maritime UCAVs, especially as the war deteriorated into a violent stalemate, with each side looking for advantage. Ukraine used maritime UCAVs to strike at Russian warships and auxiliaries in naval bases in Crimea. Meanwhile Iran opened up a whole new field of ultra-low-cost armed drones for use against urban targets. Sold in large numbers to Russia and used with effect against cities in Ukraine, these in turn proved to stimulate the development of new generations of (much more expensive) counter-drone systems.

Given the massive support going to Ukraine from the United States and its NATO allies, world military expenditure is rising markedly and the current global total is likely to hit $2.5 trillion before the end of the decade, with at least a quarter of that coming from the sale of weapons. Sales are also rising across the Middle East following the start of the war in Gaza, with the trend likely to continue in the coming years.

A noteworthy caveat for the world's armourers comes when a much-vaunted military's claim to its own effectiveness turns out to be a myth. The start of the Israeli war in Gaza is a highly significant example. Over several decades Israel had presented itself as a remarkably successful deeply militarised state that had the means to protect itself in the face of any threat. The ever-present US support was a little reported but necessary adjunct, and a close examination of Israeli military responses to insurgencies, whether in Gaza or Lebanon, shows that the IDF performance in counter-insurgency was too often reduced to mass bombing of civilians and infrastructure. This made the emphasis on border protection even more significant: Israel could claim that its separation barriers, complex electronic arrays, anti-personnel systems and, above all, the heavily fortified border right around Gaza, showed the wider world why it was so successful in maintaining its security integrity.

That disappeared into nothing in the space of just a few minutes in the early hours of 7 October 2023 as Palestinian paramilitaries first broke through the Gaza barriers at multiple locations, simply pulling down the barriers with tractors and pouring at least two thousand paramilitaries into southern Israel. It took hastily gathered police, border guards, security and intelligence units, and regular soldiers up to 24 hours to regain control of their territory. The sheer shock of what happened immediately destroyed the image of Israeli prowess in internal security and it will take some years for its security industry to regain any kind of international reputation.

Beyond the impacts of wars on arms sales – whether in Ukraine, Gaza, Iraq, Myanmar, Sudan, the Sahel or elsewhere – the world's arms manufacturers look to new generations of weapons. Some are obvious, such as armed drones and hypersonic missiles, but others are less so. Hypersonic missiles, for example, require defensive countermeasures that operate at very high speed, and one approach in active development by China, Russia, Japan and other states is the electromagnetic rail gun (EMRG).[2] This replaces a traditional gun and its conventional propellant with an electromagnetic system capable of firing a 10 kg projectile at great speed, as much as Mach 5.5, over a range of 200 km or more. Other emergent weapons are also under development, including laser-based directed energy systems capable of intercepting hypersonic missiles. These weapons, and many others, are part of a world industry of innovation. Many stem from specific war experiences, but others come from substantial technological breakthroughs that allow for the development of weapons whose main value lies simply in being ahead of those of potential opponents.

For the most part, the arms corporations all operate within the neoliberal economic model of market fundamentalism, and work hard to avoid regulation. Arms trade agreements are, at best, weak. Meanwhile, state exporters make every effort to support their own industries. Throughout the world, embassies, high commissions and other diplomatic missions are readily available to facilitate arms sales, with a network of military attachés working hard in support of exports. Governments greatly welcome the opportunity to stage major arms 'fairs', showing off the latest equipment and making impressive facilities available to lubricate sales.

All of this is going on at a time of increased military violence, not least across eastern Europe, the Middle East and sub-Saharan Africa. It is in this challenging environment that this book seeks to remind us what a remarkable range of work is already going on to expose the system. We are not alone, and even if the book just throws more light on the possibilities for witness and positive change, it will have served a good purpose.

A Transforming World

That, though, is not all. As hinted in the introduction, the whole issue of international insecurity is itself in process of change, based on three closely related developments. One, we have dealt with at length – the military-industrial system that sustains the arms trade – but the other two integrate closely with this: the glaring challenge of climate breakdown amid the associated limits to growth, and the evolving crisis of the failing neoliberal economic system which results in the obscene accumulation of wealth.

Since 2018, the pace of climate change has accelerated alarmingly and efforts at radical decarbonisation are far too limited to halt it. The technical changes in renewable energy systems, especially the collapse in prices compared to all fossil carbon resources as well as nuclear power, are staggeringly impressive, but the fossil carbon lobby is so strong that it will simply not shift its stance. The system is intent on extracting every bit of wealth it can, for as long as it can and, even when the result is generalised climate breakdown and world-wide disasters with mass casualties, the profits will have been made. This is not a distant prospect as the timescale for effective change is at most a decade, with radical decarbonisation action essential well before 2030. If climate breakdown does happen, then military-industrial complexes will be there to protect the world's elites at the expense of the rest. The metaphorical castle gates will be closed against desperate millions of people trying to find safe space, and the neoliberal system will carry on to the end. The end result, inevitably, is an even more bitterly divided and violent world.

All the while that the process is under way, the neoliberal system itself will continue in its relentless process of diverting more and more wealth and power to the elites. The concentrations of wealth are beyond obscene in their extent. In the four years to January 2024 the world's five richest people, all men, more than doubled their wealth to $869 billion, hugely outstripping inflation, while the world's poorest 60 per cent, close to 5 billion people, lost money. Overall, the world's dollar billionaires controlled $3.3 trillion and grew their wealth by three times over the same period.[3] In short, the world's arms trade system, the subject of this book, is one part of a wider system of control. Sustained campaigning, research and action are therefore contributing not just to a less heavily militarised world, but also to the wider building of a fairer and more just world order.

Acknowledgements

With special thanks to Ismail Patel, whose input and coordination has been invaluable, and to Vijay Prashad, whose vision and guidance helped make this book a reality. We are also deeply grateful to Karen Shook and the Shadow World Investigations team for their generously given time and advice, and for rallying when the pressure was on.

Notes

Except where indicated all urls last accessed on 6 March 2024.

Introduction

1. Mwatana, *Day of Judgment*, report, 6 March 2019, accessed 16 April 2024, https://mwatana.org/en/day-of-judgement/.
2. All figures in dollars are US$.
3. Joe Roeber, 'Hard-wired for corruption', 27 August 2005, accessed 8 September 2023, https://www.prospectmagazine.co.uk/essays/56912/hard-wired-for-corruption.
4. Andrew Feinstein, *The Shadow World: Inside the Global Arms Trade* (London, UK: Penguin Books, 2011).
5. Ammerdown Group, *Rethinking Security: A Discussion Paper*, 2016, https://www.researchgate.net/publication/318129168_Rethinking_security_A_discussion_paper.
6. John Tirpak, 'Report: F-35 struggled with reliability, maintainability, availability in 2023', *Air & Space Forces Magazine*, 8 February 2024, https://www.airandspaceforces.com/f-35-reliability-maintainability-availability-2023/; Connor Echols, 'The Pentagon's $52,000 trash can', Responsible Statecraft, accessed 26 March 2024, https://responsiblestatecraft.org/2023/06/20/the-pentagons-52000-trash-can/.
7. Lucie Béraud-Sudreau et al., 'Trends in world military expenditure, 2022', SIPRI, April 2023, https://www.sipri.org/publications/2023/sipri-fact-sheets/trends-world-military-expenditure-2022.
8. Feinstein, *The Shadow World*.
9. William Hartung, 'Prophets of war: Lockheed Martin and the making of the military-industrial complex', accessed 26 March 2024, https://www.amazon.co.uk/Prophets-War-Lockheed-Military-Industrial-Complex/dp/1568586973.
10. Feinstein, *The Shadow World*.

1   *The Global Arms Trade*

1. Figures on military spending are all from Diego Lopes da Silva et al., 'Trends in world military expenditure, 2021', SIPRI, April 2022, https://www.sipri.org/sites/default/files/2022-04/fs_2204_milex_2021_0.pdf.

2. Joe Roeber, 'Parallel markets: Corruption in the international arms trade', Goodwin Paper #3, London: CAAT, 2005, accessed 16 April 2024, https://controlbae.org.uk/background/parallel_markets.pdf.

3. Figures on arms transfers are all from Pieter D. Wezemen, Justine Gadon and Siemon T. Wezeman, 'Trends in international arms transfers, 2022', SIPRI factsheet, March 2023, https://www.sipri.org/publications/2023/sipri-fact-sheets/trends-international-arms-transfers-2022.

4. Xiao Liang et al., 'The SIPRI top 100 arms-producing and military services companies, 2022', SIPRI factsheet, December 2023, https://www.sipri.org/publications/2023/sipri-fact-sheets/sipri-top-100-arms-producing-and-military-services-companies-2022.

5. Giovanna Maletta and Eric G Berman, 'The transfer of weapons to fragile states through the European Peace Facility: Export control challenges', SIPRI commentary, November 2021, https://www.sipri.org/commentary/blog/2021/transfer-weapons-fragile-states-through-european-peace-facility-export-control-challenges.

6. 'Global firearms holdings', Small Arms Survey, accessed 7 March 2024, https://www.smallarmssurvey.org/database/global-firearms-holdings.

7. Figures on small arms are all from Small Arms Survey, 'Small arms, big business: Products and producers', *Small Arms Survey 2001: Profiling the Problem* (Geneva, 2001).

8. Lucie Béraud-Sudreau et al., 'Mapping the international presence of the world's largest arms companies', SIPRI Insights on Peace and Security 2020/12 (December 2020).

9. For more detail on both examples, see Andrew Feinstein, *The Shadow World: Inside the Global Arms Trade* (London: Penguin Books, 2011).

10. Nicholas Gilby, *Deception in High Places: A History of Bribery in Britain's Arms Trade* (London: Pluto Press, 2014).

11. Perlo-Freeman, Sam, 'Business as usual: How major weapons exporters arm the world's conflicts', March 2021, https://sites.tufts.edu/wpf/files/2021/03/Business-as-Usual-final-print.pdf.

12. Lorenzo Buzzoni and Manuel Rico, 'Dockers against arms: Fighting weapons trade in Europe's ports', Investigate Europe, March 2022, https://www.investigate-europe.eu/en/posts/dockers-against-arms.

2   If You Have a Hammer …

1. For a different interpretation of these events to my own, see Arthur Kent, *Murder in Room 117: Solving the Cold Case that Led to America's Longest War* (Los Angeles: Skywriter Communications, Inc., 2021).

2. I drew from these stories when I wrote Vijay Prashad, *Washington Bullets* (New Delhi: LeftWord Books, 2020).

3. US State Department, 'Scenesetter for requested Egyptian FM Aboul Gheit meeting with the Secretary' (Wikileaks Cable: 09CAIRO231_a, February 2009), https://wikileaks.org/plusd/cables/09CAIRO231_a.html.

4. US State Department, 'General Petraeus' meeting with Saleh on security assistance, AQAP strikes' (Wikileaks: 10SANAA4_a, January 2010), https://wikileaks.org/plusd/cables/10SANAA4_a.html.

5. 'Wikileaks cable corroborates evidence of US airstrikes in Yemen', Amnesty International, 1 December 2010, https://www.amnesty.org/en/latest/press-release/2010/12/wikileaks-cable-corroborates-evidence-us-airstrikes-yemen/.

6. For an assessment of the limitations of the SIPRI data, see Gisela Cernadas and John Bellamy Foster, 'Actual U.S. military spending reached $1.537 trillion in 2022 – more than twice acknowledged level: New estimates based on U.S. National Accounts', *Monthly*

Review (blog), 1 November 2023, https://monthlyreview. org/2023/11/01/actual-u-s-military-spending-reached-1-53-trillion-in-2022-more-than-twice-acknowledged-level-new-estimates-based-on-u-s-national-accounts/. All data on military expenditure in this chapter is taken from more accurate accounting done in *Hyper-imperialism: A Dangerous Decadent New Stage*, Tricontinental: Institute for Social Research, 23 January 2024, https://thetricontinental.org/studies-on-contemporary-dilemmas-4-hyper-imperialism/.

7. United Nations Peacekeeping, 'How we are funded', accessed 28 March 2024, https://peacekeeping.un.org/en/how-we-are-funded.

8. UK House of Commons, 'The Strategic Defence Review White Paper', Research Paper 98/91, 15 October 1998, https://commonslibrary.parliament.uk/research-briefings/rp98-91/.

9. Amy Ebitz, 'The use of military diplomacy in Great Power competition', Brookings, February 2019, https://www.brookings.edu/articles/the-use-of-military-diplomacy-in-great-power-competition/.

10. For an assessment of the politics of these bases, see *Defending Our Sovereignty: US Military Bases in Africa and the Future of African Unity*, Tricontinental: Institute for Social Research, Dossier no. 42, 5 July 2021, https://thetricontinental.org/dossier-42-militarisation-africa/.

11. Anthony C.E. Quainton, 'Militarization and marginalization of American diplomacy and foreign policy', *American Diplomacy*, March 2018, https://americandiplomacy.web.unc.edu/2018/03/militarization-and-marginalization-of-american-diplomacy-and-foreign-policy; David Oakley, *Subordinating Intelligence: The DoD/CIA Post-Cold War Relationship* (Lexington, KY: University Press of Kentucky, 2019).

12. The cables have been summarised by Ben Berkowitz, 'Special report: Weapons, frozen chicken, and the art of diplomacy', *Reuters*, March 2011, https://www.reuters.com/article/uk-wiki-diplomacy-business/special-report-weapons-frozen-chicken-and-the-art-of-diplomacy-idUKTRE72332B20110304/.

13. Jeff Gerth and Tim Weiner, 'Arms makers see bonanza in selling NATO expansion', *The New York Times*, 29 June 1997, sec. World; Katharine Q. Seelye, 'Arms contractors spend to promote an expanded NATO', *The New York Times*, 30 March 1998, sec. World.

14. The figures are from *Hyper-imperialism: A Dangerous Decadent New Stage*, Tricontinental: Institute for Social Research.

15. E. Ahmet Tonak and Sungur Savran, 'The world in economic depression: A Marxist analysis of crisis', Tricontinental: Institute for Social Research, Notebook no. 4 (10 October 2023), https://thetricontinental.org/dossier-notebook-4-economic-crisis/.

16. Vijay Prashad, *The Poorer Nations: A Possible History of the Global South* (London: Verso, 2013).

17. 'Doorstep statement by NATO Secretary General Jens Stoltenberg at the start of the 2022 NATO Summit', 29 June 2022, https://www.nato.int/cps/en/natohq/opinions_197294.htm.

18. Paul Rogers, 'Putin's nuclear threat and Britain's nuclear posture – not so different?', *Declassified UK*, 14 March 2022, https://www.declassifieduk.org/putins-nuclear-threat-and-britains-nuclear-posture-not-so-different/.

19. NATO, 'London Declaration', December 2019, https://www.nato.int/cps/en/natohq/official_texts_171584.htm.

20. NATO, 'Brussels Summit Communiqué', July 2022, https://www.nato.int/cps/en/natohq/news_185000.htm.

21. NATO, '2022 Strategic Concept', June 2022, https://www.nato.int/cps/en/natohq/topics_210907.htm.

22. Gisela Grieger, 'Towards a joint Western alternative to the Belt and Road Initiative?' Briefing, Brussels: European Parliamentary Research Service, December 2021), https://www.europarl.europa.eu/thinktank/en/document/EPRS_BRI(2021)698824.

23. *Hyper-imperialism*, Tricontinental: Institute for Social Research, 2024.

24. Nan Tian and Diego Lopes da Silva, 'Military spending and Official Development Assistance in recipient states: Is there a relationship?' SIPRI Insights on Peace and Security, August 2020, https://www.sipri.org/publications/2020/sipri-insights-peace-and-security/military-spending-and-official-development-assistance-recipient-

states-there-relationship-o."plainCitation":"Nan Tian and Diego Lopes da Silva, 'Military Spending and Official Development Assistance in Recipient States: Is There a Relationship?' (SIPRI, August 2020.

25. For detailed analysis of these processes, see 'Life or debt: The stranglehold of neocolonialism and Africa's search for alternatives', Tricontinental: Institute for Social Research, 11 April 2023, https://thetricontinental.org/dossier-63-african-debt-crisis/; and 'Resource sovereignty: The agenda for Africa's exit from the state plunder', Tricontinental: Institute for Social Research, Dossier no. 16 (May 2019), https://thetricontinental.org/dossier-16-resource-sovereignty-the-agenda-for-africas-exit-from-the-state-plunder/.

26. 'Arms sales of SIPRI top 100 arms companies grow despite supply chain challenges', SIPRI, December 2022, https://www.sipri.org/media/press-release/2022/arms-sales-sipri-top-100-arms-companies-grow-despite-supply-chain-challenges.

27. Sherri Goodman, 'Kyoto Treaty doesn't compromise our national security', *Washington Times*, 18 May 1998.

28. Neta C. Crawford, 'Pentagon fuel use, climate change, and the costs of war', Costs of War Project, Watson Institute, Brown University, November 2019, https://watson.brown.edu/costsofwar/papers/ClimateChangeandCostofWar; 'Department of Defense climate risk analysis', October 2021, for the assessment of the dangers of climate change to national security.

3   *The Palestine Laboratory*

1. Sagi Cohen, 'Gaza becomes Israel's testing ground for military robots', *Haaretz*, March 2024, https://www.haaretz.com/israel-news/2024-03-03/ty-article-magazine/.premium/gaza-becomes-israels-testing-ground-for-remote-control-military-robots/0000018e-03ed-def2-a98e-cfff1e640000.

2. *Times of Israel* (*TOI*) Staff, 'IDF trials remote-controlled riot dispersal gun in Hebron', September 2022, https://www.timesofisrael.com/idf-trials-remote-controlled-riot-dispersal-gun-in-hebron/.

3. Navit Zomer, 'The Israeli inventor who turns every soldier into a sharpshooter', *Ynetnews*, December 2023, https://www.ynetnews.com/business/article/hkpuon4pp.

4. 'Israeli snipers brag about deliberately crippling Gaza protesters', *The New Arab*, March 2020, https://www.newarab.com/news/israeli-snipers-brag-about-deliberately-crippling-gaza-protesters.

5. Azad Essa, 'Learnt from Israel, Indian forces deploy drones against protesting farmers', February 2024, https://www.middleeasteye.net/news/india-haryana-protest-tactics-farmers-employed-israel-palestinians.

6. Ibid.

7. 'Israel is using the new weapons it has taken into its inventory for the first time in Gaza', Defense Here, December 2023, https://www.defensehere.com/en/israel-is-using-the-new-weapons-it-has-taken-into-its-inventory-for-the-first-time-in-gaza.

4   Militarism and the Climate Emergency

1. United Nations, 'Secretary-General calls latest IPCC climate report "Code Red for Humanity", stressing "irrefutable" evidence of human influence', August 2021, https://press.un.org/en/2021/sgsm20847.doc.htm.

2. IPCC, 'Sixth Assessment Report', 2021/22, https://www.ipcc.ch/assessment-report/ar6/.

3. Ibid.

4. Climate Analytics, 'Climate action tracker: Warming projections global update, November 2021', https://climateanalytics.org/publications/2021/glasgows-2030-credibility-gap-net-zeros-lip-service-to-climate-action/.

5. Stuart Parkinson, *The Environmental Impacts of the UK Military Sector*, SGR report, May 2020, https://www.sgr.org.uk/publications/environmental-impacts-uk-military-sector.

6. Neta Crawford, 'Pentagon fuel use, climate change, and the costs of war', Watson Institute, Brown University, November 2019, https://watson.brown.edu/costsofwar/papers/ClimateChangeandCostofWar.

7. O. Belcher et al., 'Hidden carbon costs of the "everywhere war": Logistics, geopolitical ecology, and the carbon boot-print of the US military', *Transactions of the Institute of British Geographers* 45, no. 1 (June 2019).

8. Parkinson, *The Environmental Impacts* ...; and Stuart Parkinson and Linsey Cottrell, *Under the Radar: The Carbon Footprint of Europe's Military Sectors*, SGR report, February 2021, https://www.sgr.org.uk/publications/under-radar-carbon-footprint-europe-s-military-sectors.

9. 'Climate damage caused by Russia's war in Ukraine (first and second interim assessments)', *Climate Focus*, June 2023, https://climatefocus.com/publications/climate-damage-caused-by-russias-war-in-ukraine/.

10. Stuart Parkinson and Linsey Cottrell, *Estimating the Military's Global Greenhouse Gas Emissions*, SGR, November 2022, https://www.sgr.org.uk/publications/estimating-military-s-global-greenhouse-gas-emissions.

11. Matthieu Auzanneau, *Oil Power and War: A Dark History* (Chelsea, VT: Chelsea Green Publishing Co., 2018); Neta Crawford, *The Pentagon, Climate Change, and War: Charting the Rise and Fall of U.S. Military Emissions* (Cambridge, MA: MIT Press, 2022).

12. E.g. O.B. Toon et al., 'Atmospheric effects and societal consequences of regional scale nuclear conflicts and acts of individual nuclear terrorism', *Atmospheric Chemistry and Physics* 7, no. 8 (April 2007): 1973–2002.

13. IPCC, 'Sixth Assessment Report', 2021/22.

14. Ministry of Defence, *Climate Change and Sustainability Strategic Approach*, 2021, https://www.gov.uk/government/publications/ministry-of-defence-climate-change-and-sustainability-strategic-approach.

15. RAF, 'RAF'S eco-friendly fuel takes next landmark step', July 2022, https://raf.mod.uk/news/articles/rafs-eco-friendly-fuel-takes-next-landmark-step/.

16. F. Asher, 'The mirage of zero-emissions flying'. *Responsible Science* no.4,https://www.sgr.org.uk/resources/mirage-zero-emissions-flying.

17. RAF, 'RAF'S eco-friendly fuel ...'.

18. Barbara Buchner et al., 'Global landscape of climate finance 2021', CPI, December 2021, https://www.climatepolicyinitiative.org/publication/global-landscape-of-climate-finance-2021/.

19. Diego Lopes da Silva et al., 'Trends in world military expenditure, 2021', SIPRI fact sheet, April 2022, https://www.sipri.org/sites/default/files/2022-04/fs_2204_milex_2021_0.pdf.

20. ENAAT (European Network Against the Arms Trade), 'Massive increase of military spending in EU countries', *News from the Brussels Bubble*, September 2022, https://enaat.org/wp-content/uploads/2018/03/ENAAT-NBB-2022-3_02.09.2022.pdf.

21. United Nations, 'The 17 goals', Sustainable Development, UN Department of Economic and Social Affairs, 2022, https://sdgs.un.org/goals.

22. World Health Organization, 'Global excess deaths associated with Covid-19, January 2020–December 2021', May 2022, https://www.who.int/data/stories/global-excess-deaths-associated-with-covid-19-january-2020-december-2021.

23. Matthew White, *Atrocitology: Humanity's 100 Deadliest Achievements* (London: Canongate Books, 2012).

24. World Health Organization, 'Climate change and health: Factsheet', October 2023, https://www.who.int/news-room/fact-sheets/detail/climate-change-and-health.

25. United Nations, 'What is human security?', UN Trust Fund for Human Security, 2022, https://www.un.org/humansecurity/what-is-human-security/.

26. Rethinking Security, 'Human security and the Integrated Review', Briefing, 2021, https://rethinkingsecurityorguk.files.wordpress.com/2021/04/human-security-and-the-integrated-review-april-2021.pdf.

27. For example, Ministry of Defence, 'Factsheet: National Security Risk Assessment', 2015, https://assets.publishing.service.gov.uk/government/uploads/system/uploads/attachment_data/file/62484/Factsheet2-National-Security-Risk-Assessment.pdf.

28. Paul Rogers, 'A war-promoting hydra', openDemocracy, May 2018, https://www.opendemocracy.net/en/war-promoting-hydra/.

29. Barnaby Pace, *Defence Diversification: International Learning for Trident Jobs*, Nuclear Education Trust report, June 2018, https://

nucleareducationtrust.org/wp-content/uploads/2023/03/NET-Defence-Diversification-Report.pdf.

30. Robert Pollin and Heidi Garrett-Peltier, 'The U.S. employment effects of military and domestic spending priorities: 2011 update', Political Economy Research Institute, University of Massachusetts at Amherst, 2011.

31. Pace, *Defence Diversification*, 2018.

32. Ibid.

5   *The Human Cost of the Arms Trade in Gaza*

1. Yamen Salman, 'Deir al-Balah: A massacre overlooked by history', *The New Arab*, May 2017, https://www.alaraby.co.uk/%D8%AF%D9%8A%D8%B1-%D8%A7%D9%84%D8%A8%D9%84%D8%AD-%D9%85%D8%AC%D8%B2%D8%B1%D8%A9-%D8%A3%D8%BA%D9%81%D9%84%D9%87%D8%A7-%D8%A7%D9%84%D8%AA%D8%A7%D8%B1%D9%8A%D8%AE.

2. David Rodman, 'Armored breakthrough: The 1965 American sale of tanks to Israel', *Middle East Review of International Affairs* 8, no. 2 (June 2004), https://ciaotest.cc.columbia.edu/olj/meria/meria_jun04/meria04_rod01.pdf.

3. While this story is anecdotal, other reports exist of Israeli soldiers murdering children for sport: see for example Chris Hedges, 'A Gaza diary', *Harper's Magazine*, October 2001, https://harpers.org/archive/2001/10/; Khalid Amayreh, 'Israeli soldiers "shoot boy for fun"', *Al Jazeera*, December 2004, https://www.aljazeera.com/news/2004/12/8/israeli-soldiers-shoot-boy-for-fun.

4. Emma Graham-Harrison, 'Israeli veterans recall horrors of country's victory in Six-Day War', 30 August 2015, https://www.theguardian.com/world/2015/aug/30/israel-six-day-war-film-censored-voices.

5. Yoav Gallant, October 2023, https://www.aljazeera.com/program/newsfeed/2023/10/9/israeli-defence-minister-orders-complete-siege-on-gaza.

6. Breaking the Silence is an organisation of Israeli war veterans who aim to expose the reality of life in Palestine under occupation. https://www.breakingthesilence.org.il.

7. Rebecca Stead, 'Remembering Israel's 2008 war on Gaza', *Middle East Monitor*, December 2018, https://www.middleeastmonitor.com/20181227-remembering-israels-2008-war-on-gaza/.

8. Human Rights Watch, 'Rain of fire', March 2009, https://www.hrw.org/report/2009/03/25/rain-fire/israels-unlawful-use-white-phosphorus-gaza.

9. Ibid.

10. Reporters without Borders, 'Four years of violence against Palestinian journalists covering "March of Return" protests', April 2022, https://rsf.org/en/israel-palestine-four-years-violence-against-palestinian-journalists-covering-march-return-protests; Palestinian Return Centre, 'Dozens injured in 2019's last Great March of Return protests', December 2019, https://prc.org.uk/en/news/941.

11. Frank Smyth, 'In an era of global protest, France and Israel stand out for use of dangerous ammunition', Committee to Protect Journalists, September 2020, https://cpj.org/2020/09/in-an-era-of-global-protest-france-and-israel-stand-out-for-use-of-dangerous-ammunition/.

12. James Mackenzie, 'Israeli military opens probe into reports of Oct. 7 friendly fire deaths', Reuters, February 2024, https://www.reuters.com/world/middle-east/israeli-military-opens-probe-into-reports-oct-7-friendly-fire-deaths-2024-02-06/.

6   Undermining the Chance of Peace in Yemen

1. Yemen Data Project, 'Airwar data', April 2022, https://yemendataproject.org/onewebmedia/Yemen%20Data%20Project%20Published%20Air%20raids%20database%20from%2026%20March%202015%20to%2030%20April%202022%20.csv.

2. UNOCHA, 'Yemen humanitarian needs overview 2024 (January 2024)', February 2024, https://reliefweb.int/report/yemen/yemen-humanitarian-needs-overview-2024-january-2024.

3.   Ibid.

4.   The Human Development Index (HDI): access to knowledge and a decent standard of living. Since 1990, Yemen has consistently shown low HDI value. In 2017, it ranked 178th out of 189 countries and territories. United Nations, 'Country Insights', *Human Development Reports*, accessed 26 February 2024, https://hdr.undp.org/data-center/country-insights.

5.   Stephanie Kirchgaessner, 'Saudis used "incentives and threats" to shut down UN investigation in Yemen', *The Guardian*, 1 December 2021, https://www.theguardian.com/world/2021/dec/01/saudi-arabia-yemen-un-human-rights-investigation-incentives-and-therats.

6.   UNSC, 'Security Council press statement on Yemen SC/14861', April 2022, https://press.un.org/en/2022/sc14861.doc.htm.

7.   UN News, 'UN welcomes announcement of two-month truce in Yemen', April 2022, https://news.un.org/en/story/2022/04/1115392.

8.   OSESGY, 'Update on efforts to secure a UN roadmap to end the war in Yemen', December 2023, https://osesgy.unmissions.org/update-efforts-secure-un-roadmap-end-war-yemen.

9.   OSESGY, 'Briefing by the UN Special Envoy for Yemen, Hans Grundberg, to the Security Council', February 2024, https://osesgy.unmissions.org/briefing-un-special-envoy-yemen-hans-grundberg-security-council.

10.   Hanna Taylor, David K. Bohl and Jonathan D. Moyer, *Assessing the Impact of War in Yemen: Pathways for Recovery*, UNDP, November 2021, 32, https://reliefweb.int/report/yemen/assessing-impact-war-yemen-pathways-recovery.

11.   Ibid.

12.   FAO, *Yemen: DIEM – Data in Emergencies Monitoring Brief, Round 13*, January 2024, 11, https://www.fao.org/3/cc9270en/cc9270en.pdf.

13.   UNOCHA, 'Yemen humanitarian needs overview 2024'.

14.   'Assistant Secretary-General for Humanitarian Affairs and Deputy Emergency Relief Coordinator, Ms. Joyce Msuya, Remarks to the UN Security Council on Yemen', 11 July 2022, https://reliefweb.int/report/yemen/assistant-secretary-general-humanitarian-

affairs-and-deputy-emergency-relief-coordinator-ms-joyce-msuya-remarks-un-security-council-yemen-11-july-2022.

15. UNOCHA, 'Yemen humanitarian needs overview 2024'.

16. Mwatana for Human Rights and Global Rights Compliance, *Starvation Makers*, September 2021, https://www.mwatana.org/reports-en/starvation-makers-e.

17. Yemen Data Project, 'Airwar data'.

18. Mwatana for Human Rights, 'Thousands of victims waiting for justice and redress', March 2023, https://reliefweb.int/report/yemen/thousands-victims-waiting-justice-and-redress-enar.

19. Philip Loft, *Yemen in 2023: Conflict and Status of Peace Talks*, November 2023, 28, https://researchbriefings.files.parliament.uk/documents/CBP-9327/CBP-9327.pdf.

20. Mwatana for Human Rights, University Network for Human Rights, and Pax for Peace, *Day of Judgement: The Role of the US and Europe in Civilians' Death, Destruction and Trauma in Yemen*, 2019, https://www.mwatana.org/reports-en/day-of-judgement.

21. Channel 4 Dispatches, 'Britain's hidden war', April 2019, https://www.channel4.com/press/news/britains-hidden-war-channel-4-dispatches.

22. Mwatana for Human Rights and Physicians for Human Rights, *Attacks on Healthcare in Yemen*, March 2020, https://phr.org/our-work/resources/i-ripped-the-iv-out-of-my-arm-and-started-running-attacks-on-health-care-in-yemen/.

23. Ceasefire Centre for Civilian Rights and Mwatana for Human Rights, *Undermining the Future*, August 2020, https://www.mwatana.org/reports-en/undermining-future.

24. Mwatana for Human Rights, *War of Ignorance*, December 2020, https://www.mwatana.org/reports-en/war-of-ignorance.

25. Examples from the year 2022 Mwatana for Human Rights, *Tragedy Until Further Notice*, 2023, 61, https://assets-global.website-files.com/621cfefe2b950d85b2a1e2d1/65476a3b2deb8820f6022a41_Tragedy%20until%20further%20notice.pdf.

26. Human Rights Watch, 'Yemen: Events of 2022', in *World Report 2023*, 2023, https://www.hrw.org/world-report/2023/country-chapters/yemen.

27. UNVIM reported that on average approx. 180,000 tons of fuel cargo were discharged as a monthly average in 2022. UNVIM, 'Operational analysis April 2023', April 2023, https://www.vimye.org/doc/SAMonthly/Monthly_Situation_Analysis_April2023.png.

28. In 2015 Reuters reported 'Aid and commercial assessments show Yemen needs to import over 500,000 tonnes of fuel every month'; see also Noah Browning and Jonathan Saul, 'Yemen critically short of food, fuel imports as war cuts supply lines', *Reuters*, July 2015, sec. World, https://www.reuters.com/article/idUSKCN0PI1QY/.

29. 'War in Yemen, made in Europe.', accessed 11 April 2022, https://yemen.armstradewatch.eu/naval.html.

30. Mwatana for Human Rights and Lowenstein International Human Rights Clinic, *Returned to Zero*, June 2022, https://www.mwatana.org/reports-en/zero-8.

31. Mwatana for Human Rights and Ceasefire, *The Struggle for Justice*, June 2023, https://www.mwatana.org/reports-en/the-struggle-for-justice.

32. 'Belgian arms and Yemen', *The Arms Trade Litigation Monitor*, accessed 23 February 2024, https://armstradelitigationmonitor.org/overview/belgium-yemen/.

7   The Scourge of Arms in East Africa

1. Ian Katusiime, 'Lessons from Gulu's war-scarred schools', *The Independent Uganda*, September 2017, https://www.independent.co.ug/lessons-gulus-war-scarred-schools/.

2. Roberta Russo, 'Uganda's IDP camps start to close as peace takes hold', UNHCR, September 2007, https://www.unhcr.org/uk/news/ugandas-idp-camps-start-close-peace-takes-hold.

3. ReliefWeb, 'Back to(wards) my home: Individual experiences of returning IDPs in northern Uganda', May 2008, https://reliefweb.int/report/uganda/back-towards-my-home-individual-experiences-returning-idps-northern-uganda.

4. Katusiime, 'Lessons from Gulu's war-scarred schools'.

5. Mollie Zapata, 'Enough 101: The Lord's Resistance Army in Darfur', *The Enough Project*, May 2012, https://enoughproject. org/blog/enough-101-lords-resistance-army-darfur.

6. Ian Katusiime, 'Museveni's message to South Sudan's new force', *The Independent Uganda*, September 2022, https://www.independent. co.ug/musevenis-message-to-south-sudans-new-force/.

7. IGAD is an eight-member regional bloc aimed at promoting regional cooperation and integration to achieve peace, security and prosperity. Its members are Djibouti, Eritrea, Ethiopia, Kenya, Somalia, Sudan, Uganda and South Sudan.

8. Lucy Daxbacher, speech on Kampala Declaration of 2019, IGAD, May 2022.

9. @MedAmedAbdilahi, *Twitter*, 26 March 2019, https://twitter. com/MedAmedAbdilahi/status/1110436186760318976.

10. IGAD, Revitalised Agreement on the Resolution of the Conflict in the Republic of South Sudan, September 2018, https:// docs.pca-cpa.org/2016/02/South-Sudan-Peace-Agreement-September-2018.pdf.

11. RECSA, 'Report to the UN Department of Disarmament Affairs', July 2006, https://www.un.org/events/smallarms2006/pdf/ arms060629regioncent-eng.pdf.

12. Nairobi Protocol 2004, Article 3.

13. Ian Katusiime, 'US military training: Uganda tops Africa', *The Independent Uganda*, May 2022, https://www.independent.co.ug/ uganda-and-us-military-training/.

14. UNICEF, 'Children recruited by armed forces', December 2021, https://www.unicef.org/protection/children-recruited-by-armed-forces.

15. Accord, 'Understanding the recruitment of child soldiers in Africa', August 2016, https://www.accord.org.za/conflict-trends/understanding-recruitment-child-soldiers-africa/.

16. Amnesty International, *'If You Don't Cooperate I'll Gun You Down': Conflict-related Sexual Violence and Impunity in South Sudan*, 2022, www.amnesty.org/en/documents/afr65/5569/2022/en/

17. Amnesty International, 'South Sudan: UN must renew arms embargo', May 2022, https://www.amnesty.org/en/latest/news/ 2022/05/south-sudan-un-must-renew-arms-embargo/.

18. ReliefWeb, 'World Vision warns of worsening humanitarian crisis for children and families', November 2022, https://reliefweb.int/report/democratic-republic-congo/world-vision-warns-worsening-humanitarian-crisis-children-and-families-renewed-east-democratic-republic-congo-conflict.

19. ReliefWeb, 'DRC: Children still paying highest price of conflict', November 2022, https://reliefweb.int/report/democratic-republic-congo/drc-children-still-paying-highest-price-conflict-parties-should-strengthen-engagement-un-end-and-prevent-all-grave-violations.

20. Plan International, 'How is the food crisis in South Sudan affecting girls' lives?', Plan International, 2021, https://plan-international.org/emergencies/how-food-crisis-south-sudan-affecting-girls-lives/.

21. ReliefWeb, 'Doctors of the world response to humanitarian crisis in eastern DRC', November 2022, https://reliefweb.int/report/democratic-republic-congo/doctors-world-response-humanitarian-crisis-eastern-drc.

22. Oxfam International, 'Over 20 million more people hungry in Africa's "Year of Nutrition"', February 2023, https://www.oxfam.org/en/press-releases/over-20-million-more-people-hungry-africas-year-nutrition.

23. UNICEF, 'Hunger and malnutrition being driven by climate crisis and conflict in South Sudan', November 2022, https://www.unicef.org/press-releases/hunger-and-malnutrition-being-driven-climate-crisis-and-conflict-south-sudan.

24. Fred Olouch, 'African countries defy Covid-19 challenges, increase military spending: Report', *The East African*, April 2022, https://www.theeastafrican.co.ke/tea/business/african-countries-increase-military-spending-report-3794652.

25. Otiato Guguyu, 'Uganda ups military expenditure in arms race to catch up with Kenya', *Monitor*, April 2022, https://www.monitor.co.ug/uganda/news/national/uganda-ups-military-expenditure-in-arms-race-to-catch-up-with-kenya-3794488.

26. Hereward Holland, 'Uganda helped South Sudan breach EU arms embargo', *Reuters*, November 2018, accessed 28 March 2024, https://www.reuters.com/article/idUSKCN1NY005/.

27. Judith Vorrath, 'Implementing and enforcing UN arms embargoes', Stiftung Wissenschaft und Politik, May 2020, https://www.swp-berlin.org/en/publication/implementing-and-enforcing-un-arms-embargoes.

28. Holland, 'Uganda helped South Sudan breach EU arms embargo'.

29. Conflict Armament Research, *Weapon Supplies into South Sudan's Civil War*, November 2018, 11, https://www.conflictarm.com/reports/weapon-supplies-into-south-sudans-civil-war/.

30. Quote from a personal interview with B. Arneson, conducted on 28 March 2024.

31. Nick Turse, 'Pentagon's own map of U.S. bases in Africa contradicts its claim of "light" footprint', *The Intercept*, February 2020, https://theintercept.com/2020/02/27/africa-us-military-bases-africom/.

32. Nick Turse, 'Drones and motos', *The Intercept*, April 2023, https://theintercept.com/2023/04/02/us-military-counterterrorism-niger/.

33. Ibid.

34. Mark Anderson, Khadija Sharife, and Nathalie Prevost, 'How a notorious arms dealer hijacked Niger's budget and bought weapons from Russia', *OCCRP*, August 2020, https://www.occrp.org/en/investigations/notorious-arms-dealer-hijacked-nigers-budget-and-bought-arms-from-russia.

35. Ian Katusiime, 'Uganda buys Chinese arms for war on ADF', *The Independent Uganda*, December 2021, sec. The News Today, https://www.independent.co.ug/uganda-buys-chinese-arms-for-war-on-adf/.

36. Ibid.

8   *Arms Trade in the Land of Gandhi*

1. 'Spread of 1 billion small arms, light weapons remains major threat worldwide, High Representative for Disarmament Affairs tells Security Council', UN Press Release, February 2020, https://press.un.org/en/2020/sc14098.doc.htm.

2. UN General Assembly, A/RES/50/70, January 1996.

3. Thomas Black, 'Americans have more guns than anywhere else in the world and they keep buying more', *Bloomberg.com*, May 2022, https://www.bloomberg.com/news/articles/2022-05-25/how-many-guns-in-the-us-buying-spree-bolsters-lead-as-most-armed-country.

4. Yaqut Ali, 'Uttar Pradesh, Jammu and Kashmir lead the country in gun licences', *The Wire*, July 2023, https://thewire.in/government/663162uttar-pradesh-jammu-kashmir-lead-gun-licences.

5. Aaron Karp, 'Estimating global military held firearms numbers', Small Arms Survey, June 2018, https://www.smallarmssurvey.org/sites/default/files/resources/SAS-BP-Military-Firearms-Numbers.pdf.

6. Manoj Kumar, 'India raises defence budget to $72.6 bln amid tensions with China', *Reuters*, February 2023, sec. India, https://www.reuters.com/world/india/india-raises-defence-budget-726-bln-amid-tensions-with-china-2023-02-01/.

7. '2024 India military strength', Global Fire Power, 2024, https://www.globalfirepower.com/country-military-strength-detail.php?country_id=india.

8. P.D. Wezeman et al., 'Trends in international arms transfers, 2023', SIPRI factsheet, March 2023, https://www.sipri.org/sites/default/files/2024-03/fs_2403_at_2023.pdf.

9. Huma Siddiqui, 'A nation's ascendancy: Indigenisation of defence and reforms propel India towards self-reliance', *Financial Express*, July 2023, https://www.financialexpress.com/business/defence-a-nations-ascendancy-indigenisation-of-defence-and-reforms-propel-india-towards-self-reliance-3189809/.

10. Murali Krishnan, 'How India is supporting Myanmar's military with arms', *Deutsche Welle*, May 2023, https://www.dw.com/en/how-india-is-supporting-myanmars-military-with-arms/a-65733102.

11. 'India says defence production exceeds $12 billion for first time', *Reuters*, May 2023, sec. India, https://www.reuters.com/world/india/india-says-defence-production-exceeds-12-billion-first-time-2023-05-19/.

12. Binalakshmi Nepram, 'India and the Arms Trade Treaty', Oxfam Policy & Practice, September 2006, https://policy-practice. oxfam.org/resources/india-and-the-arms-trade-treaty-114592/.

13. Utpal Parashar, 'Manipur violence: 219 killed, 10K FIRs, Rs800 cr revenue loss likely, says guv', *Hindustan Times*, February 2024, https://www.hindustantimes.com/india-news/manipur-violence-219-killed-10k-firs-rs-800-cr-revenue-loss-likely-says-guv-101709131680981.html; Anirudh Menon, 'Manipur, 10 months after: "The violence still haunts us but our family is finally moving on", says footballer Chinglensana', ESPN, March 2024, https://www.espn.co.uk/football/story/_/id/39644389/chinglensana-singh-manipur-10-months-violence-haunts-us-family-moving-on.

14. India, 'The Arms Rules, 2016', accessed 11 March 2024, http://www.thenrai.in/PDF/ed3503ce-c32d-4d97-8dfe-887ec49fd55c.pdf.

15. UN Programme of Action Implementation at National Level.

16. Nepram, 'India and the Arms Trade Treaty'.

17. Amnesty International, Oxfam, and IANSA, 'The multi-billion dollar trade that puts women in the firing line', March 2005, https://www.amnesty.org/en/wp-content/uploads/2021/09/pol300102005en.pdf.

9   *The Market of Death as Seen from Latin America*

1. Global estimates released by the UN Office on Drugs and Crime (UNODC) in 2019, compiled in 2017, https://www.unodc.org/unodc/en/data-and-analysis/global-study-on-homicide.html.

2. Public security forces in each of the federation's states.

3. Instituto de Pesquisa Econômica Aplicada (IPEA) and Fórum Brasileiro de Segurança Pública (FBSP) (eds), Atlas da violência, 2021 (Rio de Janeiro: Ipea; FBSP).

4. According to data on external trade supplied by the Economy Ministry; available at: http://comexstat.mdic.gov.br/pt/home (cited by Diego Lopes da Silva, Nan Tian and Alexandra Marksteiner, 'Trends in world military expenditure, 2020', SIPRI,

https://www.sipri.org/publications/2021/sipri-fact-sheets/trends-world-military-expenditure-2020).

5. LRCA Defense Consulting, https://www.lrcadefenseconsulting.com/2022/03/com-ebtida-de-mais-de-r-1-bilhao-taurus.html, 2022.

6. Homicide Monitor 2022, Instituto Igarapé, https://homicide.igarape.org.br/

7. IPEA and FBSP (eds), Atlas da violência, 2021.

8. Gabrielle Gorder, Chris Dalby and Parker Asmann, 'América Latina tem 76% das cidades mais violentas do mundo', openDemocracy, March 2022, https://www.opendemocracy.net/pt/america-latina-cidades-mais-violentas-mundo/.

9. IPEA and FBSP (eds), Atlas da violência, 2021.

10. Prison Studies, World Prison Brief (WPB), https://www.prisonstudies.org/ten-country-prisons-project/mudan%C3%A7as-nos-padr%C3%B5es-de-encarceramento.

11. Homicide Monitor 2022, Instituto Igarapé, https://igarape.org.br/.

12. Charles Tilly, Coerção, capital e estados europeus (São Paulo: EDUSP, 1996).

13. Rosa Luxemburg, A Acumulação de Capital, vol. II (São Paulo: Abril Cultural, 1984).

14. Ibid.

15. Alain Rouquié, O Estado Militar na América Latina, 1st edn, 1984 (Santos: Editora Alfa Omega).

16. Héctor Luis Saint-Pierre, 'Racionalidade e Estratégias', Premissas, 3 (1993): 24–51.

17. Mary Kaldor, El Arsenal Barroco (Madrid: Editora Siglo XXI de España, 1986).

18. Militarism refers to the willingness to use military force, while militarisation refers to the process of accumulating military capacities. For more, see Diego Lopes da Silva, Armas, Capital e Dependência: Um Estudo sobre a Militarização na América do Sul, PhD thesis, UNESP/UNICAMP/PUC-SP, Programa de Pós-Graduação San Tiago Dantas, 2018.

19. Kaldor, El Arsenal Barroco.

20. Keith Krause, *Arms and the State: Patterns of Military Production and Trade* (Cambridge: Cambridge University Press, 1992).

21. Ana Penido and Miguel Stedile, *Ninguém regula a América: guerras híbridas na América Latina* (São Paulo: Expressão Popular, 2021).

22. da Silva, *Armas, Capital e Dependência*.

23. Tricontinental: Institute for Social Research, *The Military's Return to Brazilian Politics*, Dossier 50, 2022, https://thetricontinental.org/wp-content/uploads/2022/03/20220311_Dossier-50_EN.pdf.

24. Alexander Wendt and Michael Barnett, 'Dependent state formation and Third World militarization', *Review of International Studies* 19 (1993): 321–347.

25. Since South America has historically had little inter-state conflict, there has been little interest among the powers to 'invite' any of its countries to become a major arms producer.

26. da Silva, *Armas, Capital e Dependência*, p. 79.

27. Frederick M. Nunn, 'Foreign influences on the South American military: Professionalization and politicization', in Patrício Silva (ed.), *The Soldier and the State in South America: Essays in Civil–Military Relations* (New York: Palgrave, 2001).

10   *A Mass Movement against Weapons and War*

1. Strategic Defence Review 1998, *Modern Forces for the Modern World*, The National Archives, https://webarchive.nationalarchives.gov.uk/ukgwa/20121018172816/http:/www.mod.uk/NR/rdonlyres/65F3D7AC-4340-4119-93A2-20825848E50E/0/sdr1998_complete.pdf.

2. Lawrence Freedman, 'Force and the international community: Blair's Chicago speech and the criteria for intervention', *International Relation* 3, no. 2 (2017): 107–124, https://www.ditchley.com/sites/default/files/2019-05/International%20Relations%20article%20on%20Chicago.pdf.

3. 'Attitudes towards Iraq and Afghanistan: British public opinion after a decade of war has implications for the viability of future missions', LSE Blog, January 2015, https://blogs.lse.ac.uk/

politicsandpolicy/british-public-opinion-after-a-decade-of-war-attitudes-to-iraq-and-afghanistan/.

4. Nicolas Watt, 'Syrian airstrikes vote: Cameron haunted by previous defeat', *The Guardian*, November 2013, https://www.theguardian.com/politics/2015/nov/03/syria-airstrikes-vote-cameron-haunted-by-memory-of-previous-defeat.

5. Martin Butcher, 'Yes, British arms are killing innocent civilians in Yemen, why is the UK Government ignoring this terrible reality?' Oxfam GB, January 2023, https://views-voices.oxfam.org.uk/2023/01/british-arms-yemen/.

6. 'BAE and Saudi Arabia', Campaign Against the Arms Trade, September 2023. https://caat.org.uk/challenges/arms-companies/bae-and-saudi-arabia/.

7. 'Chilcot report: key points from the Iraq inquiry', *The Guardian*, July 2016, https://www.theguardian.com/uk-news/2016/jul/06/iraq-inquiry-key-points-from-the-chilcot-report.

11 Direct Action against the Arms Trade

1. Rashid Khalidi, 'The Balfour Declaration from the perspective of the Palestinian people', Speech to the UN, November 2017, https://www.un.org/unispal/wp-content/uploads/2017/10/Lecture-by-Prof.-Rashid-Khalidi-100-years-since-Balfour-Decl-UN-2Nov2017.pdf.

2. Tom Bateman, 'UK apology sought for British war crimes in Palestine', *BBC News*, October 2022, sec. Middle East, https://www.bbc.com/news/world-middle-east-63145992.

3. Joseph Massad, 'Palestinians deserve reparations for Britain's colonial crimes', *Middle East Eye*, October 2021, https://www.middleeasteye.net/opinion/britain-palestine-balfour-colonial-crimes-reparations.

4. Zena Al Tahhan, 'The Balfour Declaration explained', *Al Jazeera*, October 2017, https://www.aljazeera.com/features/2018/11/2/more-than-a-century-on-the-balfour-declaration-explained.

5. Amnesty International, *Israel's Apartheid against Palestinians*, 2022, https://www.amnesty.org.uk/files/2022-01/Israel%27s%20Apartheid%20Against%20Palestinians%20Report%20-%20

244

Amnesty%27s%202022%20report.pdf?VersionId=sofIB_wt.
dMwGiAksB8nnlG_irQIqf67.

6. 'Overview', Elbit Systems, accessed 14 March 2024, http://
elbitsystems.com/about-us-introduction/.

7. 'FAQ', Elbit Systems, accessed 14 March 2024, http://elbitsystems.
com/investor-relations/faq/.

8. 'Elbit Systems' Hermes 900 UAV', Israel Defense, February
2015, https://www.israeldefense.co.il/en/content/elbit-systems
%E2%80%99-hermes-900-uav-headed-fifth-country.

9. War on Want, 'Killer drones', December 2013, https://waronwant.
org/sites/default/files/Killer%20Drones,%20War%20on%20
Want.pdf.

10. 'Elbit Systems Ltd', AFSC Investigate, accessed 14 March 2024,
https://investigate.afsc.org/company/elbit-systems.

11. 'Hermes™ 450', Elbit Systems, accessed 14 March 2024, http://
elbitsystems.com/product/hermes-450/.

12. 'Tactical unmanned air systems for the international market',
U-TacS, accessed 14 March 2024, https://u-tacs.co.uk/.

13. Adam Forrest, 'British Army drone to fly over English Channel to
monitor migrant boats', *The Independent*, August 2020, sec. News,
https://www.independent.co.uk/news/uk/home-news/british-
army-channel-crossings-migrants-drone-monitor-a9696956.html.

14. UNICEF, 'State of Palestine year end situation report', February 2022,
https://www.unicef.org/mena/reports/unicef-state-palestine-
year-end-situation-report.

15. 'Elbit Systems', Who Profits, accessed 14 March 2024, https://
whoprofits.org/company/elbit-systems/.

16. David Graeber on Anarchism, Capitalism, Direct Action and
the Internet, 2006, https://www.youtube.com/watch?v=F4tRT
8b5txQ.

17. The Raytheon 9 is a group of direct activists who took action
against a Raytheon factory in Derry, Northern Ireland, in 2006.
The jury on their trial accepted their argument that the Israeli
Defence Forces were guilty of war crimes in Lebanon and thus
cleared them of the charges of criminal damage.

18. Palestine Action, 'Palestine Action permanently shut Elbit down
in Tamworth', March 2024, https://www.palestineaction.org/
tamworth-shutdown/.

19. 'Elbit Systems reorganizes UK activities', Elbit Systems, January 2022, https://elbitsystems.com/pr-new/elbit-systems-reorganizes-uk-activities/.
20. Palestine Action, 'Israeli Weapons Maker Shuts London HQ Following Sustained Protest', *Mondoweiss*, June 2022, https://mondoweiss.net/2022/06/israeli-weapons-maker-shuts-london-hq-following-sustained-protest/.

12 Workers against the Arms Trade

1. Rory Carroll, 'Dozens killed after Israeli airstrikes on Gaza refugee camp', *The Guardian*, October 2023, https://www.theguardian.com/world/2023/oct/31/dozens-killed-after-israeli-airstrikes-on-gaza-refugee-camp.
2. António Guterres, 'Secretary-General's statement – on the situation in Gaza', United Nations, October 2023, https://www.un.org/sg/en/content/sg/statement/2023-10-31/secretary-general's-statement-the-situation-gaza.
3. UN Office for the Coordination of Humanitarian Affairs (OCHA), 'Hostilities in the Gaza Strip and Israel | Flash Update #25', OCHA website, October 2023, https://www.ochaopt.org/content/hostilities-gaza-strip-and-israel-flash-update-25.
4. Reuters, 'Belgian unions refuse handling arms shipments for Israel-Hamas conflict', Reuters, October 2023, https://www.reuters.com/world/europe/belgian-unions-refuse-handling-arms-shipments-israel-hamas-conflict-2023-10-31/.
5. Middle East Research and Information Project (MERIP), 'Palestinian trade unions call for an end to arming Israel', October 2023, https://merip.org/2023/10/palestinian-trade-unions-call-for-an-end-to-arming-israel/.
6. *El Periodico*, 'Los estibadores de puerto de Barcelona "no permitirán la actividad" de los barcos de armas', November 2023, https://www.elperiodico.com/es/internacional/20231106/estibadores-puerto-barcelona-barcos-armas-palestina-israel-gaza-ucrania-rusia-94275197.
7. Unione Sindacale di Base (USB), 'Appello congiunto dei sindacati dei trasporti Grecia-Italia-Turchia: STOP al massacro in

Palestina! STOP al trasporto di morte!', USB website, November 2023, https://www.usb.it/leggi-notizia/appello-congiunto-dei-sindacati-dei-trasporti-grecia-italia-turchia-stop-al-massacro-in-palestina-stop-al-trasporto-di-morte-1651.html.

8. Peoples Dispatch, 'Palestine solidarity activists stage strategic shut downs in Italy', November 2023, https://peoplesdispatch.org/2023/11/10/palestine-solidarity-activists-stage-strategic-shut-downs-in-italy/.

9. Lucas Cumiskey, 'Hundreds of trade unionists blockade BAE Systems factory in Israel-Gaza protest', *Independent*, November 2023, https://www.independent.co.uk/business/hundreds-of-trade-unionists-blockade-bae-systems-factory-in-israelgaza-protest-b2445173.html.

10. Simon Zinnstein, 'Greek railroad workers block delivery of U.S. tanks to Ukraine', Left Voice, April 2022, https://www.leftvoice.org/greek-railroad-workers-block-delivery-of-u-s-tanks-to-ukraine/.

11. Pisa Today, 'Guerra Ucraina: 'Dall'aeroporto di Pisa armi "mascherate" da aiuti umanitari', March 2022, https://www.pisatoday.it/cronaca/partenza-armi-aeroporto-pisa-guerra-ucraina.html.

12. Lorenzo Buzzoni and Manuel Rico, 'Dockers against arms: Fighting weapons trade in Europe's ports', Investigate Europe, March 2022, https://www.investigate-europe.eu/posts/dockers-against-arms.

13. Stockholm International Peace Research Institute (SIPRI), *SIPRI Yearbook 2023*, 2023, https://www.sipri.org/sites/default/files/2023-06/yb23_summary_en_0.pdf.

14. Disclose, 'The itinerary of a secret shipments', 15 April 2019, https://made-in-france.disclose.ngo/en/chapter/the-route-of-a-secret-shipment.

15. Benoit Tessier and John Irish, 'Rights groups try to block Saudi vessel loading French arms', Reuters, May 2019, https://www.reuters.com/article/idUSKCN1SF1EX/.

16. The Left in the European Parliament, 'Civil harbours & airports – No arms for war and oppression', June 2022, https://left.eu/events/civil-harbours-airports-no-arms-for-war-and-oppression/.

17. Marco Preve, 'Papa Francesco ai portuali che fermarono le navi delle armi: "Bravi! Basta ipocrisia"', *La Repubblica*, November 2019, https://genova.repubblica.it/cronaca/2019/11/28/news/papa_francesco_ai_portuali_che_fermarono_le_navi_delle_armi_bravi_basta_ipocrisia_-242088651/.

18. Buzzoni and Rico, 'Dockers against arms …'.

19. Italian Law 185/90, 'New provisions on controlling the export, import and transit on military goods', https://www.esteri.it/mae/resource/doc/2017/06/legge_09_07_1990_n185.pdf.

20. Shipping Italy, 'Un altro pieno di armi su una nave Bahri in porto a Genova', November 2022, https://www.shippingitaly.it/2022/11/06/un-altro-pieno-di-armi-sulla-nave-bahri-in-porto-a-genova-foto/.

21. Pietro Barabino, 'Portuali e sindacalisti contro il traffico di armi, a Bruxelles l'assemblea internazionale: "Serve rete europea, politica schiacciata da industria bellica"', *Il Fatto Quotidiano*, June 2022, https://www.ilfattoquotidiano.it/2022/06/23/portuali-e-sindacalisti-contro-il-traffico-di-armi-a-bruxelles-lassemblea-internazionale-serve-rete-europea-politica-schiacciata-da-industria-bellica/6637207/.

22. International Middle East Media Center (IMEMC), 'Union workers refuse to load weapons to Israel', March 2024, https://imemc.org/article/union-workers-refuse-to-load-weapons-to-israel/.

23. International Court of Justice (ICJ), 'Order of 26 January 2024', January 2024, https://www.icj-cij.org/node/203447.

24. Office of the UN High Commissioner for Human Rights (OHCHR), 'Arms exports to Israel must stop immediately: UN experts', OHCHR website, February 2024, https://www.ohchr.org/en/press-releases/2024/02/arms-exports-israel-must-stop-immediately-un-experts.

25. UN, 'The Arms Trade Treaty', https://www.thearmstradetreaty.org/hyper-images/file/TheArmsTradeTreaty1/TheArmsTradeTreaty.pdf.

26. European Union (EU), European Common Position on Arms Export, https://eur-lex.europa.eu/LexUriServ/LexUriServ.do?uri=OJ:L:2008:335:0099:0103:EN:PDF.

27. Simone Wisotzki and Max Mutschler, 'No Common Position! European arms export control in crisis', *Zeitschrift für Friedens- und Konflforschung* 10 (2021): 273–293.

28. Hannah Neumann, 'Arms export: Implementation of Common Position 2008/944/CFSP (debate)', European Parliament website, September 2020, https://www.europarl.europa.eu/doceo/document/CRE-9-2020-09-14-ITM-024_EN.html.

29. The Greens/EFA, 'Frequently asked questions on EU arms exports', The Greens/EFA website, October 2021, https://www.greens-efa.eu/en/article/policypaper/frequently-asked-questions-on-eu-arms-exports.

30. Ryan Gilbey, 'On yer way, Pinochet!', *The Guardian*, November 2018, https://www.theguardian.com/film/2018/nov/01/on-your-way-pinochet-factory-workers-fought-fascism-from-glasgow-chile-coup-nae-pasaran.

13 Student Campaigns against the Arms Trade

1. Laura McCann, Norman Hutchison and Alastair Adair, 'Calibration of stakeholder influence in the UK higher education sector', *Studies in Higher Education* 47, no. 7 (April 2021), https://doi.org/10.1080/03075079.2021.1916908.

2. Kenneth Heineman, 'Protests at the University of California, Berkeley', Bill of Rights Institute, https://billofrightsinstitute.org/essays/protests-at-the-university-of-california-berkeley.

3. Kenneth Heineman, 'Students and the anti-war movement', Bill of Rights Institute, https://billofrightsinstitute.org/essays/students-and-the-anti-war-movement.

4. 'Mexico's 1968 massacre: What really happened?' NPR, All Things Considered, December 2008, https://www.npr.org/templates/story/story.php?storyId=97546687.

5. Connor Woodman, *The Repression of Student Movements in the UK* (London: Pluto Press, 2017) https://www.plutobooks.com/blog/repression-student-movements-uk/.

6. 'The rise of student movements', in *Brazil: Five Centuries of Change*, Brown University, https://library.brown.edu/create/fivecenturiesofchange/chapters/chapter-7/student-movement/.

7. Amanda Waterhouse, '"La esperanza de America Latina": The ongoing student revolution in Columbia', in *Age of Revolutions*, October 2020, https://ageofrevolutions.com/2020/10/26/la-esperanza-de-america-latina-the-ongoing-student-revolution-in-colombia/.

8. Jane Powell, 'Greenham Common Women's Peace Camp changed the world – and my life', Open Democracy, November 2021, https://www.opendemocracy.net/en/opendemocracyuk/greenham-common-womens-peace-camp-changed-the-world-and-my-life/.

9. 'What forms of peace activism took place in the UK?', London School of Economics, 2020, https://www.lse.ac.uk/ideas/projects/peace-security/cnd-archives/peace-activism-uk-1980s.

10. Ian Harris and Charles Howlett, 'Educating for peace and justice in America's nuclear age', Catalyst: A Social Justice Forum, December 2021, https://core.ac.uk/download/pdf/268736345.pdf.

11. Andrew Anda Wöndu, 'Discourse on decolonizing the education system in South Sudan', CoAct, https://coactproject.eu/news/discourse-on-decolonizing-the-education-system-in-south-sudan/.

12. Suren Pillay, 'Decolonizing the university', Africa is a Country, April 2015, https://africasacountry.com/2015/06/decolonizing-the-university/.

13. Ngakiya Camara and Kya Chen, 'Students are pushing US colleges to sever ties with military-industrial complex', Truthout, November 2021, https://truthout.org/articles/students-are-pushing-us-colleges-to-sever-ties-with-military-industrial-complex/.

14. Alexander MacDougall, 'Student group demands UMass cut ties with Raytheon', *Daily Hampshire Gazette*, November 2022, https://www.gazettenet.com/UMass-students-protest-against-Raytheon-48831420.

15. 'Demilitarise education: Get weapons companies out of schools', Wage Peace Disrupt War, https://www.wagepeaceau.org/noplaceinschools1/.

16. Kai-Uwe Dosch, Sarah Roßa and Lena Sachs, 'Resisting the militarisation of education', War Resisters' International, July

2013, https://wri-irg.org/en/story/2013/resisting-militarisation-education?language=en.

17. Enric Prat Carvajal, 'The peace movement and anti-militarism in Spain: 2003–2008', Materials of Peace and Human Rights, 7, March 2009, https://www.gencat.cat/governacio/pub/sum/dgrip/MPDH_7_eng.pdf.

18. Sarah Freeman-Woolpert, 'How grassroots activists made peace with North Korea possible', Waging Nonviolence, September 2018, https://wagingnonviolence.org/2018/09/grassroots-activists-peace-movement-north-korea/.

19. See Chapter 6.

20. Discussed in more detail in Chapter 14.

21. 'Blocking and exposing the arms fair in 2017', Stop the Arms Fair, September 2018, https://stopthearmsfair.org.uk/blocking-and-exposing-the-arms-fair-in-2017/.

22. 'Victory for disarm UCL', CAAT Blog, December 2008, https://caat.org.uk/news/victory-for-disarm-ucl/.

23. 'Lobby to end UCL's relationship with arms companies', Students' Union UCL, October 2021, https://studentsunionucl.org/policy/up2101/lobby-to-end-ucls-relationship-with-arms-companies.

24. 'UCL links with arms companies', dED Database, FOI Request by Gordon-Polomski, May 2021, https://ded1.co/data/foi/12.

25. 'University College London', People and Planet University League, 2023, https://peopleandplanet.org/university-league/2023/u1250/university-college-london.

26. Mike Allwright, 'Southampton students call for ethical investment', CAAT Unis, October 2015, https://caatunis.net/southampton-students-call-for-ethical-investment/.

27. Joe Creffield, Murray Jones and Jake Tacchi, 'UK universities funded £190 million from major arms manufacturers since 2013', Action on Armed Violence, August 2021, https://aoav.org.uk/2021/uk-universities-funded-190-million-from-major-arms-manufacturers-since-2013/.

28. Okopi Ajonye, 'Weaponising universities: Research collaborations between UK universities and the military industrial complex', CAAT and Demilitarise Education, February 2024, https://caat.org.uk/

publications/weaponising-universities-research-collaborations-between-uk-universities-and-the-military-industrial-complex/.

29. Megan Slack, 'Leeds Uni denies it ended investment in companies because of ties to Israeli military', *The Leeds Tab*, November 2018, https://thetab.com/uk/leeds/2018/11/11/leeds-become-first-uni-to-end-investments-in-companies-supplying-equipment-to-israeli-military-45279.

30. Yousef Abdul-Fattah and Evie Russell-Cohen, 'VICTORY!! Leeds University divests from companies complicit in occupation & arms trade', CAAT Unis, November 2018, https://caatunis.net/leeds-university-divests-from-companies-complicit-in-occupation-arms-trade/.

31. 'Palestine Solidarity Campaign defeats UK government over pensions divestment', Palestine Solidarity Campaign, April 2020, https://www.palestinecampaign.org/palestine-solidarity-campaign-defeats-uk-government-over-pensions-divestment/.

32. See: Demilitarise UoN (Nottingham), Sheffield Action Group, Warwick Action Group, Demilitarise Cambridge, Demilitarise Lancaster, Bristol Action Group, Action Against Oxford War Crimes, Disarm UCL, Demilitarise King's (King's College London), Demilitarise SOAS (University of London) and Glasgow Against Arms & Fossil Fuels.

33. 'Universities committed to pursuing fossil fuel divestment', People and Planet, December 2022, https://peopleandplanet.org/fossil-free-victories.

34. 'Universities committed to fossil free careers', People and Planet, December 2022, https://peopleandplanet.org/fossil-free-careers/victories.

35. 'The Demilitarise Education Treaty', October 2023, https://ded1.co/how-we-do-it/treaty.

14 Strategic Litigation against the Global Arms Trade

1. UN Working Group on Business and Human Rights, Responsible business conduct in the arms sector, Information Note, 5, 8, https://www.ohchr.org/sites/default/files/2022-08/BHR-Arms-sector-info-note.pdf.

2. *CAAT v Secretary of State*, High Court judgment, Case No. CO/3579/2020, June 2023, para. 144; Katie Fallon, 'UK arms sales to Saudi Arabia: Making (non)sense of the judgement', CAAT, July 2023, https://caat.org.uk/news/uk-arms-sales-to-saudi-arabia-making-nonsense-of-the-judgment/.

3. Valentina Azarova, Roy Isbister and Carlo Mazzoleni, 'Domestic accountability and arms transfers: Law, policy and practice', 2021, https://www.saferworld.org.uk/resources/publications/1366.

4. ECCHR, 'Italy fails victims of war crimes in Yemen despite proof of violation of Arms Trade Treaty', March 2023, https://www.ecchr.eu/en/press-release/italy-fails-victims-of-war-crimes-in-yemen/.

5. ECCHR et al., 'Made in Europe, bombed in Yemen: How the ICC could tackle the responsibility of arms exporters and government officials', https://www.ecchr.eu/fileadmin/Fallbeschreibungen/CaseReport_ECCHR_Mwatana_Amnesty_CAAT_Delas_Rete.pdf.

6. UN Working Group on Business and Human Rights, 'Responsible business conduct in the arms sector', https://www.ohchr.org/sites/default/files/2022-08/BHR-Arms-sector-info-note.pdf.

7. See, on ambiguities of the definition of overriding risk: 'Saferworld, Key issues for ATT implementation: Preventing and combating diversion', Briefing No. 2, February 2015, https://www.saferworld.org.uk/resources/publications/885-key-issues-for-att-implementation-preventing-and-combating-diversion. Brian Wood and Clare de Silva, 'Article 7 Export and Export Control', in Brian Wood and Clare de Silva (eds), *Weapons and International Law: The Arms Trade Treaty* (Brussels: Intersentia, 2015), p. 130 onwards.

8. Saferworld, Emergent Justice Collective and the International Commission of Jurists, Arms Trade Litigation Monitor, https://armstradelitigationmonitor.org/. See also, Emergent Justice Collective, Arms Trade Litigation Monitor: Resisting the Arms Trade, Reviving Antimilitarist Movements, https://emergentjusticecollective.org/Arms-Trade-Litigation-Monitor.

9. See also generally Anna Stavrianakis, 'Missing the target: NGOs, global civil society and the arms trade', *Journal of International Relations and Development* 15, no. 2 (2012).

10. See e.g. the Court for Intergenerational Climate Crimes, 'Framer Framed', exhibition and public hearings, https://framerframed. nl/en/exposities/court-for-intergenerational-climate-crimes/. A similar initiative is in the making for the global arms trade.

15   Lynchpin of the Pacific: Ending the Militarisation of Hawai'i

1. A popular nineteenth-century US doctrine that represented the idea that the settler-colonial population of the United States would spread across North America. The resulting genocide of Native Americans and invasion of Mexico were justified by rhetoric around American exceptionalism and 'civilisation'.

2. Schofield to Sherman (telegram), April 1873.

3. Department of Defense, 'About United States Indo-Pacific Command', 2023, www.pacom.mil/About-USINDOPACOM/.

4. Kyle Kajihiro, 'Nation under the gun: Militarism and resistance in Hawai'i', *Cultural Survival Quarterly* 24, no. 1 (2000): 28–33.

5. Edward H. Ayau, *Reprint: Testimony of Edward Halealoha Ayau Before the Senate Select Committee on Indian Affairs: Subject: The Restoration of Hawaiian Sovereignty and Land*, 14 American Indian Law Review 14, no. 2 (1989): 353–357.

6. Harold L. Beck et al., 'Fallout deposition in the Marshall Islands from Bikini and Enewetak nuclear weapons tests', *Health Physics* 99, no. 2 (2010): 124–142, doi:10.1097/HP.0b013e3181bbbfbd.

7. Bengt Danielsson, 'Under a cloud of secrecy: The French nuclear tests in the southeastern Pacific', *Ambio* 13, no. 5/6 (1984), accessed 14 March 2024, http://www.jstor.org/stable/4313070.

8. Alvin L. Young and Kristian L. Young, *Investigations into Sites where Agent Orange Exposure to Vietnam-era Veterans has been Alleged*, Agent Orange Investigative Report no. 8 (2013).

9. Kalamaoka'aina Niheu et al., 'The impact of the military presence in Hawai'i on the health of Na Kanaka Maoli', *Pacific Health Dialog* 14, no. 1 (2007).

10. Earthjustice, 'US Navy ship sinking exercise resumes', Sept. 2012, earthjustice.org/press/2012/u-s-navy-ship-sinking-exercise-resumes-healthy-ocean-first-casualty.

11. Christina Jedra, 'Marine Corps discharged high levels of fecal bacteria into Kailua Bay', *Honolulu Civil Beat*, February 2022, www.civilbeat.org/2022/02/marine-corps-discharged-high-levels-of-fecal-bacteria-into-kailua-bay/.

12. Amnesty International, *Israel's Apartheid against Palestinians*, February 2022, www.amnesty.org/en/documents/mde15/5141/2022/en/.

13. Department of Defense, 'RIMPAC 2022 concludes', August 2022, https://www.navy.mil/Press-Office/News-Stories/Article/3118649/rimpac-2022-concludes/.

14. Sierra Club Hawai'i, 'Red Hill water security', 2021, sierraclubhawaii.org/redhill.

15. Rodney Morales (ed.), *HoʻiHoʻi Hou, a Tribute to George Helm & Kimo Mitchell*. Special issue of *Bamboo Ridge* (Hawaiʻi writers' quarterly) 22 (1984).

16. US EPA, REG 09, 'Defueling plan and closure of the Red Hill bulk fuel storage facility', 29 August 2022, www.epa.gov/red-hill/defueling-plan-and-closure-red-hill-bulk-fuel-storage-facility.

Conclusion

1. Imogen Foulkes, 'UN rights expert accuses Israel of acts of genocide', *BBC News*, accessed 2 April 2024, https://www.bbc.co.uk/news/world-middle-east-68667556; Sarah Ferguson, 'More than 13,000 children reported dead in Gaza', UNICEF USA, accessed 2 April 2024, https://www.unicefusa.org/stories/more-13000-children-reported-dead-gaza-famine-nears.

2. Naval News, 'Japan makes maritime history', *Navy Recognition*, October 2023, https://navyrecognition.com/index.php/naval-news/naval-news-archive/2023/october/13688-japan-makes-maritime-history-with-first-successful-sea-based-electromagnetic-railgun-test.html.

3. Oxfam, 'Wealth of five richest men doubles since 2020', January 2024, https://www.oxfam.org.uk/mc/hffm8s/.

Glossary

Al-Qaeda: An Islamist militant organisation. Originating from networks fighting the Soviet Union occupation of Afghanistan in the 1980s, it later carried out the September 11, 2001 attacks on the New York World Trade Center, and became a focus of the US 'War on Terror'.

Ansar Allah: see 'Houthis'.

Arab Spring: A series of anti-government uprisings in Arab countries beginning in 2010–11. Uprisings were often violently repressed. Multiple large-scale armed conflicts followed, including the Syrian civil war.

arms conversion: The process of transitioning from arms production to civilian production.

Arms Trade Treaty (ATT): A multilateral treaty regulating the international trade in conventional weapons that entered into force in December 2014. See Chapter 14 for a detailed discussion of the process of forming the ATT as well as its strengths and weaknesses.

'Axis of Evil': A term introduced in US president George W. Bush's January 2002 State of the Union Address used to describe foreign governments that had allegedly sponsored terrorism and sought weapons of mass destruction, originally including Iran, Iraq, and North Korea. Used to rally support for the 'War on Terror', the term was later applied to others as well.

BAE Systems: British multinational arms company, sixth largest arms company in the world and largest in Europe.

Balfour Declaration: A 1917 letter from Britain's then foreign secretary Arthur Balfour declaring Britain's aim to establish a 'national home for the Jewish people' in Palestine. It is often seen as one of the key catalysts of the Nakba.

Boeing: US-American multinational aerospace company, fourth largest arms-producing company in the world. Boeing's production includes civilian and military aircraft.

BRICS: An intergovernmental organisation of key rising economies founded in 2009. Although BRICS is an acronym for early members Brazil, Russia, India, China, South Africa, today's members also include Egypt, Ethiopia, Iran, and the United Arab Emirates, with an invitation to Saudi Arabia pending as of mid-March 2024.

Cold War: The Cold War was a period of geopolitical tension between the United States and the Soviet Union and their allies between 1947 and 1991. It involved, among other things, a nuclear arms race, conventional military deployments, propaganda campaigns, and proxy wars.

Condor: Brazilian manufacturer of non-lethal weapons products such as rubber bullets, tear-gas grenades, disabling electroshock devices, and pyrotechnics for signalling and rescue.

COP: Abbreviation for 'Conferences of Parties', the mostly annual supreme decision-making forum of the United Nations Framework Convention on Climate Change, which entered into force in 1994.

Court of Justice of the European Union: Judicial branch of the European Union composed of the Court of Justice and the General Court overseeing the uniform application and interpretation of European Union law.

Defence and Security Equipment International (DSEI): A bi-annual arms fair held in London.

defence diversification (see arms conversion)

Elbit Systems: Israel-based international arms company, a primary provider of land-based equipment and unmanned aerial vehicles (drones) to the Israeli military.

European Convention on Human Rights: A treaty established to protect human rights and fundamental freedoms in Europe, enforced by the European Court of Human Rights.

European Court of Human Rights: A judicial body tasked with ensuring compliance with the European Convention on Human Rights and adjudicating cases involving violations of human rights within Europe.

European Union (EU): A political and economic union of 27 European countries, facilitating cooperation in various domains such as trade, law, and governance.

G20: An international forum comprising 19 major economies and the European Union, aimed at addressing global economic challenges and promoting financial stability and sustainable development.

G7: A group of seven major advanced economies, including Canada, France, Germany, Italy, Japan, the United Kingdom, and the United States, conducting discussions on economic policies and global issues.

General Dynamics: US arms company, it is the world's fifth largest arms company and known for large weapons systems such as jets, vehicles and submarines.

Geneva Conventions: A set of international treaties established to protect victims of armed conflict, outline rules regarding the treatment of individuals during wartime and provide a framework for humanitarian aid organisations' activities in conflict zones. The first convention was agreed in 1864, with updated versions from 1949 as well as subsequent additional protocols in place today.

Geneva Protocol (1925): The Geneva Protocol of 1925 is an international treaty prohibiting the use of chemical and biological weapons in warfare. It was signed as a result of growing concerns about the devastating effects of these weapons on both combatants and civilians. The protocol aimed to prevent the use of such weapons and promote disarmament efforts.

Hague Conventions: A series of treaties and declarations negotiated at international peace conferences at The Hague in 1899 and 1907. The conventions were key to the formalisation of rules of conduct in warfare under international law; they also established the Permanent Court of Arbitration to resolve disputes between nations.

Halliburton: A US multinational engineering and construction company. It is the second-largest oil-services company, and provides construction and other services to the US military.

Houthis: Originally a political and religious rebel group from northern Yemen, the Ansar Allah 'Houthis' took control of the Yemeni capital Sana'a in 2014, following a series of smaller wars in Saada, Al-Jawf, and Amran, north of Sana'a, in alliance with deposed president Ali Abdullah Saleh. This led to the eruption of the internationalised civil war in Yemen. The Houthis are a party to this conflict and, today, the de facto authority in much of the country. The group is accused of receiving military, technical, and political support from the Iranian government.

Inter-American Development Bank: A financial institution supporting economic and social development in Latin America and the Caribbean through loans, grants, and technical assistance.

International Court of Justice (ICJ): The International Court of Justice is the principal judicial organ of the United Nations, headquartered in The Hague, Netherlands. It settles legal disputes between states and provides advisory opinions on legal questions referred by UN organs and specialised agencies.

International Criminal Court (ICC): The International Criminal Court is a permanent international tribunal established to prosecute individuals for the most serious crimes of international concern, such as genocide, crimes against humanity, war crimes, and the crime of aggression.

International Human Rights Law (IHRL): Legal norms and principles governing the rights and freedoms of individuals, enshrined in international treaties, customary law, and conventions.

International Humanitarian Law (IHL): Legal rules and principles regulating the conduct of armed conflict, aiming to protect civilians, prisoners of war, and other non-combatants, and limit the effects of warfare on vulnerable populations.

Intifada: Arabic term for 'uprising' denoting Palestinian popular uprisings against Israeli occupation. It is often used to describe the periods between December 1987 and September 1993 (the first Intifada) and September 2000 to approx. late 2005 (the second Intifada).

ISIS: Abbreviation for the Islamic State of Iraq and Syria, a militant extremist group that has perpetrated widespread violence in the Middle East and beyond, including the 2014 genocide of the Yazidi people, with the aim of establishing a caliphate.

Israel Aerospace Industries: A major Israeli arms company specialising in the development and production of military and civilian aircraft, missiles, and space systems.

League of Nations: Intergovernmental organisation founded after the First World War with the aim of promoting peace, security, and cooperation among nations through diplomacy. It was ultimately unable to prevent the outbreak of the Second World War and ceased operations in 1946.

Lockheed Martin: US arms company, and the largest arms-producing company in the world. Its wide range of production includes fighter jets such as the F-16 and F-35, as well as the submarine-launched Trident missile, the main element in the strategic nuclear force of the USA and the UK.

Lord's Resistance Army (LRA): militant group operating primarily in Uganda and neighbouring countries, known for its brutal tactics including abduction, forced recruitment of child soldiers, and widespread violence against civilians. Led by Joseph Kony, the LRA has been accused of numerous human rights abuses and war crimes.

Military-industrial complex: A term which refers to the symbiotic relationship and intertwined interests between the military establishment, arms companies, and government policymakers, often leading to the promotion of military expenditure and influence over national security policies.

Nakba: Arabic term meaning 'catastrophe', commonly used to refer to the displacement and expulsion of hundreds of thousands of Palestinians from their homes and land during the establishment of the state of Israel in 1948.

Nexter: French arms company specialising in the production of land defence systems, including armoured vehicles, artillery systems, and ammunition.

North Atlantic Treaty Organisation (NATO): a military alliance established in 1949 among North American and European countries.

Northrop Grumman: US arms company, third largest arms-producing company in the world. Production includes fighter jets, unmanned systems, missile defence systems, and military communications.

Nuclear Non-Proliferation Treaty (1968): An international treaty aimed at preventing the spread of nuclear weapons and promoting disarmament among signatory countries while facilitating the peaceful use of nuclear energy.

Organisation for Economic Co-operation and Development (OECD): An intergovernmental organisation with 38 member countries, founded in 1961 to stimulate economic progress and world trade.

Organisation for Joint Armament Cooperation: International organisation that facilitates collaborative arms procurement projects among European countries.

Palestinian Authority: Governing body of the Palestinian autonomous regions of the West Bank and formerly the Gaza Strip. Established in 1994 as part of the Oslo Accords peace agreement between Israel and the Palestine Liberation Organization.

Paris Agreement: International treaty negotiated within the United Nations Framework Convention on Climate Change, aiming to limit global warming to well below 2 degrees Celsius above pre-industrial levels, with efforts to limit it to 1.5 degrees Celsius.

Pentagon: The headquarters of the United States Department of Defense, serving as the centre for military planning, operations, and administration.

Presidential Leadership Council: Executive body of Yemen's internationally recognised government, established in April 2022 when President Abdrabbuh Mansur Hadi stepped down and handed over power to the eight-member council.

Quadrilateral Security Dialogue ('Quad'): A strategic forum comprising the United States, Japan, India, and Australia aimed at enhancing regional security cooperation and addressing shared challenges in the Indo-Pacific region.

Raytheon: US arms company, second largest arms-producing company in the world. Production includes missiles, missile defence systems, radar systems, and aircraft components.

Red Hill Storage Facility: Storage complex for jet fuel and marine diesel fuel located on the island of Oahu, Hawaii, operated by the United States Navy to support military operations in the Pacific region. The US Department of Defense committed to the closure of the facility in 2022.

Rheinmetall: German arms company, producing armoured vehicles, artillery systems, ammunition, and more.

Rim of the Pacific (RIMPAC): The world's largest international maritime warfare exercise, conducted biennially in the waters around the Hawaiian Islands, involving military forces from multiple countries.

Riyadh Agreement: Peace deal signed in 2019 between the Yemeni government and the Southern Transitional Council (STC) aimed at resolving power struggles in southern Yemen and stabilising the region.

Rolls Royce: British arms company, specialising in engines. Arms comprise one third of its total sales.

RWM Italia: Italian subsidiary of German arms company Rheinmetall. Its core business is the manufacture of ammunition, bombs and missiles.

Saudi/UAE-led Coalition: A coalition, originally made up of member states of the Gulf Cooperation Council (GCC), that is conducting a joint campaign of economic isolation and air strikes against the Ansar Allah insurgents. The coalition initially involved Saudi Arabia, the United Arab Emirates, Sudan, Bahrain, Kuwait, Qatar (2015–17), Egypt, Jordan, Morocco (2015–19), and Senegal. Saudi Arabia and, most significantly, the UAE have also supported local Yemeni militias financially and with arms. It has been alleged that the UAE hired foreign contractors/mercenaries to operate within Yemen. The coalition has received operational support from Western countries, notably the United States and the United Kingdom.

Smart Shooter: Israeli arms company specialising in optics for small arms.

Shoah: a Hebrew term meaning 'catastrophe' used to refer to the Holocaust, the genocide of approximately 6 million Jews by Nazi Germany during the Second World War.

SIPRI: Stockholm International Peace Research Institute, an independent international institute dedicated to research into conflict, armaments, arms control and disarmament. Their databases are regarded as the authoritative resource for government-supplied data on arms imports and exports.

Six-Day War: A conflict that took place in 1967 between Israel and neighbouring Arab countries, including Egypt, Jordan, and Syria; Israel captured the West Bank, East Jerusalem and the Gaza Strip. Thousands of Palestinians were prevented from returning to their homes in the newly occupied territories and numerous villages and camps were destroyed.

Small Arms and Light Weapons (SALW): This refers to firearms and other weapons that are easy to carry, and operate with a limited crew, typically including handguns, rifles, and light machine guns.

Southern Transitional Council: A political organisation based in southern Yemen. It was formed in May 2017 with the aim of advocating for the secession of southern Yemen from the Republic of Yemen.

Sudan People's Liberation Army: A military organisation formed in 1983, initially to fight for the independence of South Sudan from Sudan. They now serve as the army of South Sudan under the name of the South Sudan People's Defence Forces.

Taliban: A fundamentalist Islamist militant group that emerged in Afghanistan in the 1990s and ruled most of Afghanistan from 1996 until 2001, being ousted by the US intervention. They eventually returned to power in Afghanistan in August 2021 as the US-led forces withdrew from the country.

Taurus: Brazilian firearms manufacturer known for producing a wide range of handguns and long guns for civilian, law enforcement, and military markets worldwide.

Teknel: Italian company specialising in energy generators with both civilian and military applications.

Trade Union Congress: A national federation of trade unions that collectively represent most unionised workers in England and Wales. There are 48 affiliated unions with a total of about 5.5 million members.

Treaty of Versailles: Peace treaty signed in 1919 that formally ended the first World War and imposed harsh penalties and territorial changes on Germany, setting the stage for economic hardships and contributing to the conditions that led to the Second World War.

UN Relief and Works Agency: UN agency established in 1949 to provide assistance and protection to Palestinian refugees who were displaced during the 1948 Arab-Israeli conflict and their descendants.

United Nations (UN): International organisation founded in 1945 with the aim of promoting peace, security, cooperation, and diplomacy among its member states.

United Nations Security Council: The principal organ of the UN responsible for maintaining international peace and security, composed of fifteen member states, including five permanent members with veto power.

Universal Declaration of Human Rights: Document adopted by the United Nations General Assembly in 1948, outlining fundamental human rights and freedoms to be universally protected and respected.

US AFRICOM: A combatant command of the United States Armed Forces responsible for coordinating military operations and engagements on the African continent.

War crimes: Serious violations of the laws and customs of war, encompassing acts such as targeting civilians, torture, and the use of prohibited weapons.

War on Terror: A global military and political campaign initiated by the United States following the September 11, 2001 attacks, with said aims of combating terrorist organisations and reducing the threat of terrorism worldwide.

Warsaw Pact: A political and military alliance formed in 1955 by the Soviet Union and several Eastern European countries in response to the establishment of NATO, aimed at mutual defence and cooperation among communist states in Europe during the Cold War. It was dissolved in July 1991.

WikiLeaks: A multi-jurisdictional public service designed to publish sensitive materials, including documents that have exposed human rights violations of many governments and officials, and to protect the whistleblowers, journalists and activists who sourced them.

World Health Organization: A specialised agency of the United Nations responsible for international public health.

Contributors

Jeremy Corbyn MP, founder and director of PJP (Peace & Justice Project), is a twice elected leader of the UK Labour Party from 2015 to 2020. He has served as a Member of British Parliament in Islington North for 40 years and is a Parliamentary Member of the Council of Europe. His expansive and lifelong campaigning for peace, justice and human rights has taken him across the world, advocating in senior roles for the Campaign for Nuclear Disarmament, the Palestinian Solidarity Committee, Stop the War, the UN Human Rights Council in New York (review of the Geneva Convention), nuclear non-proliferation, trade unions, employment rights, Indigenous rights and many social movements. Corbyn has twice been awarded prizes for promoting peace, including the Seán MacBride Peace Prize for his sustained and powerful political work for disarmament and peace. He founded the Peace & Justice Project in 2020.

Andrew Feinstein is the executive director of Shadow World Investigations. Andrew resigned as an African National Congress (ANC) Member of Parliament in South Africa in 2001, in protest at the government's refusal to investigate corruption in a $10 billion arms deal. His first book, *After the Party*, reveals the impact of this deal. He also wrote the critically acclaimed book *The Shadow World: Inside the Global Arms Trade*, and worked on an award-winning feature documentary, *Shadow World*. Andrew appears regularly in a range of global media, has contributed chapters on arms trade issues for a number of volumes, and was named among the 100 most influential people in the world working in armed violence reduction by Action on Armed Violence. He serves on the advisory boards of the Platform to Protect Whistleblowers in Africa, Lighthouse Reports, Declassified UK, and Demilitarise Education.

Paul Rogers (PhD) is Emeritus Professor of Peace Studies at Bradford University and international security adviser to Open Democracy. After lecturing at Imperial College and working in East Africa in crop research, he taught Environmental Science for eight years before moving to Bradford University in 1979. He works primarily on the changing causes of international conflict, including environmental and economic factors as well as political violence. He has lectured regularly at the UK's senior defence colleges, including the Royal College of Defence Studies, for over forty years, and has written or edited thirty books. A fourth edition of his book, *Losing Control: Global Security in the 21st Century*, was published by Pluto Press in 2021 and he is currently working on a new book, to be published in November 2024, called *The Insecurity Trap: A Short Guide to Transformation*.

Rhona Michie is the director of projects and planning at Shadow World Investigations and a co-founder and coordinator of the Corruption Tracker. She previously coordinated a free legal advice clinic in Islington. She has published works on corruption in the arms trade and open source investigations, and was listed as an Emerging Expert by the Forum on the Arms Trade in 2022. She is a member of the Steering Committee of Campaign Against the Arms Trade.

Tabitha Agaba is a researcher and an advocate whose work focuses on transnational organised crime, illicit financial flows and corruption. In an era where globalisation is the norm, its challenges are alive too, ranging from human trafficking, arms smuggling and wildlife crime to counterfeit medical supplies. Tabitha interrogates the interconnection with the role of corruption in enabling these vices. This she has done through her work at the Initiative against Illicit Finance and Transparency Advocacy. Tabitha is an experienced media researcher as well as a published researcher on issues of transnational organised crime. She recently published a paper with the Committee on Fiscal Studies titled 'Transnational organized crime and its impact on the tax base'. She has previously worked with the Nile Post as a researcher as well as the NBS investigations desk.

Ahmed Alnaouq is a former Palestinian diplomat who served in the Palestinian Mission to the UK. He is the co-founder of We Are Not Numbers, which empowers Palestinian youth to share their stories globally. With a Chevening Scholarship, he earned a Master's in International Journalism at Leeds University. As an advocacy officer for the Euro-Mediterranean Human Rights Monitor, he raised awareness on human rights issues. His work has been featured in the *Washington Post*, the *New Arab*, and *Gulf News*. A sought-after commentator, he has appeared on Sky News, the BBC, and MSNBC, offering nuanced perspectives on the Palestinian struggle.

Valentina Azarova (PhD) is a researcher and practitioner centring movement law/yering, transformative justice and abolition feminism as responses to international and interpersonal violences. They have practised with social movements on anti-militarism, conflict transformation, community accountability and no-borders, and migration justice and decolonial reparations, and have lived and taught in universities in Palestine, Lebanon and Turkey. Their research interests include Palestine in/and international law, the violence of/in international law, and the role of legal mobilisation in social justice struggles. They are co-founder and member of the de:border // migration justice collective, and of the Emergent Justice Collective, and a member of the Feminist Autonomous Centre for research, where they co-convene the research area: Intersectionality, Abolition, and Transformative Justice.

Lorenzo Buzzoni is an investigative journalist and documentary filmmaker based in Italy. After obtaining an Master's in Philosophy at the University of Pisa, he completed a two-year Master's in Reporting in Turin. Since 2021, he has been part of Investigate Europe (IE), an awarded cross-border cooperative of journalists from 12 European countries. He has worked on health, military, environmental and financial investigations, such as the one concerning the French care home giant Orpea, nominated in 2022 at the Daphne Caruana Galizia Price for Journalism. Lorenzo has also been published in several newspapers, including *Il Fatto Quotidiano* (Italy), *Mediapart* (France), *Tagesspiegel* (Germany), *Infolibre* (Spain), and *EuObserver* (Belgium), as well as in TV investigative programmes with RTP (Portugal) and ORF (Austria).

Demilitarise Education (dED_UCATION/dED) is a community and guide for modern-day peacemakers, working to see universities break ties with the global arms trade and become champions for peace. dED uses research, media and community to untangle, expose and end university partnerships with the military and defence sector, and see them focus their efforts on peace development. Further, dED works to build the most extensive database on university partnerships with the global arms trade, and to build an innovative movement to break these ties.

Lindsey German is a long-time socialist and campaigner. She went on her first demonstration against the all-white South African rugby tour in 1969. She helped form the Stop the War Coalition in 2001 and is its convenor. She has organised hundreds of protests and activities against war, imperialism and oppression. Her publications include several books on women and a jointly authored *People's History of London*.

Kawena'ulaokalā Kapahua is a community organiser rooted in the Hawaiian independence movement and union organising. Kapahua actively engages in anti-imperialist struggles in Hawai'i, including combating the Red Hill fuel storage facility and opposing the Rim of the Pacific war games. With years of militant organising against Pacific imperialism, he advocates for expanding the struggle against endless war and exploitation. As a PhD student in Political Science at the University of Hawai'i, Kapahua promotes awareness of the Pacific's revolutionary history, reigniting interest and pride in the revolutionary tradition of Pasifika organisers and movements. As a member of the historic Hui Aloha 'Āina, Kapahua is part of a long-standing Hawaiian liberation organisation dedicated to ending militarism in the Pacific and advocating for a free and independent Oceania.

Ian Katusiime is a Ugandan journalist, researcher, governance consultant and foreign policy analyst. He is the author of 'Foreign policy by troop deployment', an article on how Uganda conducts its foreign policy in the East, Central and Horn of Africa regions published by Friedrich Ebert Stiftung. He has also written an article on the troop drawdown in the African Union Transition Mission in Somalia (ATMIS) published by Konrad Adenauer Stiftung (KAS) Regional Programme Security Dialogue for East Africa. Ian is the founding editor of *Leo Africa Review*, where he is a contributor, and a senior reporter at *The Independent*, where he covers politics, security and foreign affairs.

Antony Loewenstein is an independent journalist, bestselling author, filmmaker, and co-founder of Declassified Australia. He has written for *The Guardian*, *The New York Times*, *The New York Review of Books*, and many others. His latest book is the global bestseller *The Palestine Laboratory: How Israel Exports the Technology of Occupation Around the World*, which won the 2023 Walkley Book Award, the Australian Pulitzer. His other books include *Pills, Powder and Smoke, Disaster Capitalism* and *My Israel Question*. His documentary films include *Disaster Capitalism*, and the Al Jazeera English films, *West Africa's Opioid Crisis* and *Under the Cover of Covid*. He was based in East Jerusalem from 2016 to 2020.

Mwatana for Human Rights (Mwatana) is an independent Yemeni organisation that works to achieve a society in which everyone is guaranteed justice and access to their rights. Founded in 2007, gaining a permit to practice its work in 2013, Mwatana documents violations committed by parties to the conflict in Yemen, and publishes the results of its investigations. Mwatana also provides legal support and advice to victims of arbitrary detention and enforced disappearance, in addition to advocating and campaigning with decision makers at the international level. The organisation also works to ensure accountability of violators, justice for victims, and capacity building for human rights campaigners. Mwatana has received many awards and honours, including the Baldwin Award, the Roger N. Baldwin Medal of Liberty, and the 10th International Hrant Dink Award. In 2021, Mwatana for Human Rights and Campaign Against Arms Trade (CAAT) were nominated for the Nobel Peace Prize.

Binalakshmi Nepram is an Indigenous peacebuilder and scholar, fellow at the Asia Centre at Harvard, spearheading the women-led peace and disarmament movement. She is an author and editor of five books, including *Where Are Our Women in Decision Making on UNSCR 1325* and *India and the Arms Trade Treaty*. Bina co-founded India's first civil society organisation for conventional disarmament issues, Control Arms Foundation of India, as well as the Manipur Women Gun Survivor Network and the Global Alliance of Indigenous Peoples, Gender Justice and Peace. Bina has received the Seán MacBride Peace Prize, the CNN IBN Real Heroes Award, and the Anna Politkovskaya Award. Action on Armed Violence listed Bina as one of the '100 most important people in the world working on Armed Violence Reduction'. She sits on the board of the International Peace Bureau and is senior adviser on Indigenous Issues at USIP (United States Institute of Peace).

Palestine Action is a direct action network of groups and individuals that began in England and Wales, and has since expanded to Scotland, the US, Italy, France, Belgium and the Netherlands. They were formed with the mandate of taking action against the UK sites of Israeli arms manufacturer Elbit Systems and other companies complicit in Israeli apartheid, disrupting their operations and calling for all such sites to be shut down. Their aim is to dismantle British complicity with Israeli apartheid.

Stuart Parkinson (PhD) is executive director of Scientists for Global Responsibility (SGR), a UK-based membership organisation promoting science and technology that contribute to peace, social justice, and environmental sustainability. During his more than twenty years in this role, he has authored/ co-authored numerous reports and articles on issues including science and security, climate change science and policy, and energy technology and policy. A particular focus in recent years has been military carbon emissions. Prior to SGR, he worked in roles in academia, industry, and environmental campaigning. He holds a PhD in climate change science, and has also been an expert reviewer for the Intergovernmental Panel on Climate Change.

Ana Penido (PhD) is a Brazilian political scientist, with a Master's in Strategic Studies and a PhD in International Relations. She is currently a FAPESP postdoctoral fellow in Political Science at Unicamp. She is a researcher at Tricontinental: Institute for Social Research and the International Defense and Security Study Group (GEDES). She studies topics of strategy, defence and armed forces, particularly military education in Latin America. She is a popular educator of Brazilian social movements, and co-author of the book *Ninguém Regula a América*, published by Editora Expressão Popular (2021).

Vijay Prashad (PhD) is an Indian historian and journalist. Prashad is the author of forty books, including *Washington Bullets*, *Red Star Over the Third World*, *The Darker Nations: A People's History of the Third World* and *The Poorer Nations: A Possible History of the Global South*. His latest book *The Withdrawal: Iraq, Libya, Afghanistan, and the Fragility of U.S. Power* (2022) was written with Noam Chomsky. He is executive director of Tricontinental: Institute for Social Research, and chief correspondent for *Globetrotter*. He is also the chief editor of LeftWord Books (New Delhi) and a senior non-resident fellow at Chongyang Institute for Financial Studies, Renmin University of China. He has appeared in two films – *Shadow World* (2016) and *Two Meetings* (2017).

CONTRIBUTORS

Anna Stavrianakis (PhD) is Professor of International Relations at the University of Sussex and Director of Research and Strategy at Shadow World Investigations in London. She researches and teaches on the international arms trade, militarism and global (in)securities. She works with activists, NGOs, journalists, parliamentarians and lawyers on issues of UK, EU and international arms export controls and efforts to rein in the arms trade. Her first book, Taking Aim at the Arms Trade: NGOs, Global Civil Society and the World Military Order analysed the ways that NGOs work for tighter controls on the arms trade. She writes regularly for print media and can be found on X at @StavrianakisA

Carmen Wilson is the director of operations for Demilitarise Education (dED_UCATION/dED), a self-proclaimed professional hippie challenging militarism in higher education and a passionate advocate for peace, youth work, critical discourse and education. Originally from New Mexico, USA, she is a world citizen, the daughter of US veterans, and raised in East Asia for 14 years. She has a BS in Media Management and an MA in Globalisation & International Development Studies, having completed her Master's dissertation on the importance of freedom of the press and information for democratic accountability. She is also on the steering board for the UK network for the Global Campaign on Military Spending (GCOMS).

Peace &Justice Project

Monstrous Anger of the Guns is brought to you by the Peace & Justice Project ('the Project'). Founded by Jeremy Corbyn in 2021, we bring people together in Britain and across the world to work for social and economic justice, peace and human rights. Our organisation is a home for those who were inspired by the hopeful politics and vision of the future that animated the UK Labour Party during the 2015–20 period, which reached a membership of 600,000 people when Jeremy Corbyn served as party leader.

The Project decided to produce this important book to shine a light on an industry that ruins lives and breeds insecurity while enriching a tiny few. We view efforts to reduce conflict and tensions around the world as being at the heart of a politics for peace and justice.

We live in dangerous times, but also times of hope. The old certainties that insisted that workers, women and the global South be held down are melting away. Into that gap could step the liberating hope of the many, or the violent repression brought by the few.

The first quarter of this century has been filled with wars, environmental crises, refugees and shattered hopes. The second quarter could be even more violent.

Now, as a genocide unfolds in Palestine, Yemen is bombed, the decades-long conflict in the Democratic Republic of Congo rages on amidst phenomenal mineral riches and Sudan's civil war spreads across the country, lubricated with arms from abroad, we need – more than ever – to understand how the arms trade works. We at the Project hope that this book gives you the knowledge and tools:

- To raise awareness about the danger of the arms industry and the consequences of weapons in the world because in the end it will destroy humanity;
- To push for the development of sustainable green industries which benefit human life and the environment;
- To help to change the narrative pushed by the mainstream media and governments around the world;
- To demand that governments stop increasing defence spending, which in the UK is planned to rise from 2 per cent to 2.5 per cent of the gross domestic product (GDP), and instead invest in public services that benefit and protect the many;
- And, finally, to campaign internationally for a future where everyone can live collectively in a world of peace, equality and justice.

Laura Alvarez
International Coordinator
Peace & Justice Project
https://thecorbynproject.com

Index

Thanks to our Patreon subscriber:

Ciaran Kane

Who has shown generosity and
comradeship in support of our publishing.